# FANÁTICOS, EXILES, AND SPIES

*Connecting the Greater West Series*

# FANÁTICOS EXILES, and SPIES

## REVOLUTIONARY FAILURES ON THE US-MEXICO BORDER, 1923–1930

JULIAN F. DODSON

Texas A&M University Press
College Station

First edition

This paper meets the requirements of ANSI/NISO Z39.48-1992 (Permanence of Paper).
Binding materials have been chosen for durability.
Manufactured in the United States of America

Library of Congress Cataloging-in-Publication Data

Names: Dodson, Julian F., author.
Title: Fanáticos, exiles, and spies: revolutionary failures on the US-Mexico border, 1923–1930 / Julian F. Dodson.
Description: First edition. | College Station, [Texas]: Texas A&M University Press, [2019] | Series: Connecting the greater west series | Includes bibliographical references and index.
Identifiers: LCCN 2018045355 (print) | LCCN 2018051156 (ebook) | ISBN 9781623497576 (ebook) | ISBN 9781623497538 | ISBN 9781623497538 (cloth: alk. paper)
Subjects: LCSH: Mexican-American Border Region—History—20th century. | Insurgency—Mexican-American Border Region—History—20th century. | Exiles—Mexico. | Catholic Church—Mexico—Influence. | Espionage—Mexican-American Border Region—History—20th century. | Intelligence service—Mexico—History—20th century. | Mexico. Departmento Confidential—History. | Mexico—Politics and government—1910–1946.
Classification: LCC F1234 (ebook) | LCC F1234 .D7385 2019 (print) | DDC 972/.1—dc23
LC record available at https://lccn.loc.gov/2018045355

*To Becky, Rory, and Riley*

# CONTENTS

# ACKNOWLEDGMENTS

In almost every sense, the net product of scholarly research and writing is the result of a community effort, and I am deeply indebted to my extended academic community for their love, support, and critique in helping me bring this book to fruition. I would like to thank the generous support of the Latin American and Iberian Institute (LAII) at the University of New Mexico for the financial assistance required to carry out the in-country research of this project. The LAII's Field Research Grant allowed me to spend a total of six months over three summers for predissertation research, and the focus of the present project has been improved greatly as a result. The LAII also awarded a PhD Dissertation Fellowship for the writing and revising of the dissertation. The history department at the University of New Mexico provided generous financial support for further research in the form of the Dorothy Woodward Memorial PhD Fellowship for the 2011–12 academic year. The in-country research performed during that period has been invaluable to the completion of the early stages of this work. To say how grateful I am to have enjoyed such caring mentorship on this long journey could scarcely begin to express my thanks to my friend and mentor Linda Hall for her support throughout the process and her perpetually open door and generous nature. This book could not have been completed without the support and advice of Elizabeth Hutchison, Sam Truett, Judy Bieber, and Jürgen Buchenau. Thank you all for your support.

I am eternally grateful to the staff of the Fideicomiso Archivos Plutarco Elías Calles y Fernando Torreblanca (FAPECFT). Amalia Torreblanca and Norma Mereles have always made me feel welcome and helped me find exactly what I needed to complete my work. To Guadalupe Bracho Loaeza, Edgar Medina Luna, and the entire staff of archivists at the FAPECFT, I owe a sincere debt of gratitude for all of their assistance and wonderful conversations during the course of my research. I would like to thank Dr. Ignacio Almada Bay at El Colegio de Sonora for advising me to have a look at the collection of the Dirreción General de Investigaciones Sociales at the Archivo General de la Nación, the documentary collection that yielded the bulk of the archival material for this project. I would also like to thank the staff at the Archivo General de la Nación in Mexico City; the Centro de Estudios de Historia de México, Grupo CARSO; and the Archivo Histórico Genaro Estrada at the Secretaría de Relaciones Exteriores for all of their kind help in locating the collections I needed to complete my research. Thanks go to my wife, best friend, and colleague, Becky Ellis, for her patience with the writing process and her critique of various portions of this book. The project is certainly better for her critique and advice. Likewise, I owe a debt of gratitude to Jordan Biro, Bryan Turo, Brandon Morgan, Shawn Austin, Chris Steinke, Colin Snider, and Scott Crago as well as my colleagues in the Department of History at Washington State University, Jesse Spohnholz, Lawrence Hatter, Sean Wempe, and Clif Stratton, for reading various portions of this work and offering their valuable time and feedback.

# FANÁTICOS, EXILES, AND SPIES

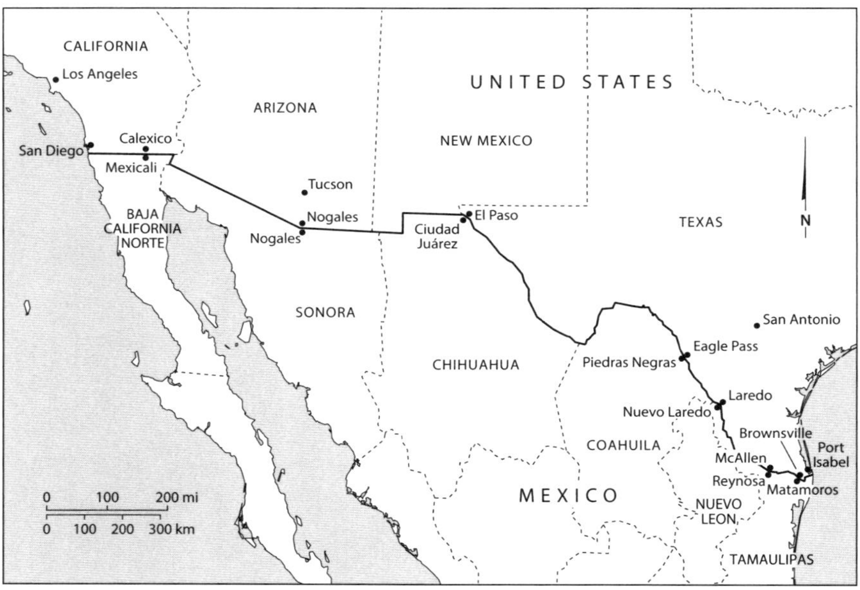


*Map of US-Mexico borderlands*

# INTRODUCTION

On the evening of Tuesday, 7 December 1926, Estanislao Mazuka stood in the San Antonio home of Gen. César López de Lara, the famed tamaulipeño general, then working in exile for the delahuertista faction. It was a dreary, cloudy evening. It had been raining intermittently since Monday, and more rain was forecast throughout the night.[1] The occasion was Mazuka's promotion to the rank of colonel in the rebel army under the command of Gens. César López de Lara and Pablo Gonzáles. Gonzáles, like López de Lara, had run afoul of the Sonoran victors of the revolution during the 1920 interim presidency of Adolfo de la Huerta. Also present were two other generals, Vidal Silva and Alfredo Cisneros, as well as other lower-ranking military leaders. General López de Lara was cordial but inquisitive. He asked Mazuka if he had ever been in the military, and Mazuka explained that he had fought with Francisco "Pancho" Villa, the leader of the northern conventionalist faction during the revolution, but that since the Convention of Aguascalientes, he had retired to private life. The general then turned to Mazuka, placed his right hand on his shoulder, and stated proudly that "experienced elements like yourself are what we need . . . we don't want innocents in our ranks . . . from now on, you will be named Colonel and under the immediate command of General Cisneros." He then told him to go with General Cisneros and await orders in Uvalde, Texas, and to continue producing propaganda for recruitment. As Colonel Mazuka and Cisneros left the meeting and stepped out into the damp and chilled evening air, Cisneros informed him of a larger plan to seize the border city of Nuevo Laredo from their base in Uvalde.

Gen. Pablo Gonzáles was slated to be at the head of the invasion, and the bishop of San Antonio, Arthur J. Drossaerts, had offered to donate $20,000 through a priest in Castroville, Texas, to help fund the expedition.[2]

López de Lara and Cisneros were unaware that Estanislao Mazuka was one of many deep-cover operatives that the Mexican Departamento Confidencial (Confidential Department) utilized in the 1920s to infiltrate some of the most notorious counterrevolutionary groups in exile in the United States. The work was dangerous, as Mazuka himself explained to one of his only contacts in the Mexican government, Consul Emiliano Támez: "I beg you to inform our Government of the role that I am playing so that I will not be confused with the rest [of the lopezlaristas] and put my life at risk. I was able to observe that these men do not distrust each other . . . and they are all armed and have a bandit's instincts . . . all they talk about is blowing up trains and stealing money."[3] There were never any arrests in this case, the plot to seize Nuevo Laredo never materialized, and the voice of Estanislao Mazuka fell silent in the historical record after December 1926. While there are no clear answers regarding what might have happened to the agent, one can assume that his cover had been blown and he ceased to be an effective source of information. Perhaps he was being used in an elaborate counterespionage operation intended to disseminate false or misleading information among the agents of the Mexican government.[4] Worse still, perhaps he lost his life at the hands of the group of "bandits" he had infiltrated.

*Fanáticos, Exiles, and Spies: Revolutionary Failures on the US-Mexico Border, 1923–1930* tells the story of the postrevolutionary Mexican government's attempts to protect its northern border from various plots hatched among Mexican exile groups in the United States. These plots, designed by those I call the "losers of the revolution," were meant to overthrow the government of Pres. Plutarco Elías Calles (1924–28). This borderland battle was fought in the field of espionage between the undercover agents of the Confidential Department and groups of political exiles temporarily residing in cities such as Los Angeles, Tucson, San Antonio, and Brownsville—among them already seasoned spies who had provided their services to previous Mexican regimes. In successive waves, political and military exiles from the period of the Mexican Revolution (1910–20) sought refuge in urban centers along the international boundary.

The 1920s witnessed the de la Huerta Rebellion of 1923 and the Cristero Rebellion, the bloody religious conflict that dominated the final three years of the decade. These were accompanied by smaller rebellions along the border that were funded by politically connected exiles. Previous scholarship on the immediate postrevolutionary period has tended to treat these various rebellions as isolated episodes of violence, sharing only the decade of revolutionary state reconstruction in which they occurred in common. One of the overarching goals of this book is to demonstrate that the continued violent popular and military uprisings of the 1920s in Mexico were not episodic or isolated; they were nothing less than an extension of the violence and fratricidal warfare that so distinctly marked the preceding decade of the revolution. Moreover, these rebellions were intimately entwined with exile movements that traversed the border between the United States and Mexico. Throughout the decade, these exile movements sought to arrest the revolutionary process in Mexico by any means necessary.

In recent years, various scholarly works have placed much emphasis on the border as a space beyond the reach of either nation-state, whose agents pretended to maintain control in the region. In these narratives, the relationship between the agents of the US government and Mexican communities on both sides of the border is one of inequality in agency and capacity.[5] This study recognizes the importance of these works in understanding those relationships but presents a case in which those interactions were inverted, highlighting the borderland space as a level playing field on which agents on both sides of the border expressed and exercised distinct but analogous notions of authority. My research details the Mexican government's attempts to utilize, at times in very creative and extralegal ways, the law enforcement and surveillance apparatuses of the United States along the border to ensure that exile plots would not cross into Mexico, neutralizing the various threats to the Calles government. Agents of the Mexican Confidential Department operated in a borderlands world of diffuse local authority, and these conditions allowed them to meddle in local politics, to play on local political conflicts, and to make alliances accordingly to achieve their goals. This is a borderlands story that places Mexican agents in an active rather than a passive role. The nodes of power and authority along the border in the 1920s were myriad and complex, relying on a diverse interplay between Mexican political agents and borderlands agents in the United States.

While the governments that pretended to patrol and protect the border respected the significance of the political boundary, exiles in the 1920s were restrained by no such concern with regard to jurisdictional regulations or restrictions. The transnational and, in many cases, supranational, cultural, political, social, and economic networks in which they operated served them extremely well despite the political boundary. In taking up temporary residence in El Paso, San Antonio, Tucson, or Los Angeles, exiles took full advantage of these locations of refuge consisting of like-minded communities and groupings—exile, refugee, or otherwise émigré networks. The border as a dividing line between understood legal jurisdictions was important to these exile groups. When they fled across the border, they understood that they were moving outside the reach of the Calles government and its agents. These exiles would have understood their temporary state as part of a longer tradition of political exile dating to the national period in Latin America, in which political battles between liberals and conservatives often resulted in exile for the political opposition.[6] My research contributes to this larger body of scholarship on political exile by pointing out that where the interaction among the nation, borders, and exiles is concerned, there is more continuity than rupture between the nineteenth and the early twentieth centuries.

The popular and military rebellions that marked the 1920s produced some of the most active exile groups in the United States, including large numbers of militant Catholics who settled in El Paso, San Antonio, and Los Angeles. The religious conflict in Mexico at the time, La Cristiada, generated three years of social, military, and political instability, and many of the most dangerous exiles were determined to take advantage of the chaos.

These movements were nurtured by groupings of exiles along the border, Anglo arms smugglers, North American Catholics, Mexican migrant populations, and established Mexican American communities with familial, economic, and political ties on both sides of the border. Mexican exiles operated in communication networks that sustained their efforts in the United States because they transcended the political, administrative, and commercial boundary that divides the two nations. These communities made use of the still-fluid nature of the international boundary to transport arms, ammunition, and capital to support the Cristero cause. They did so at a moment when the border between the two nations was being transformed into the hardened political boundary we know today—but not yet complete in that transition.

With regard to race and the racialization of migrant workers in the US South and Southwest, Kelly Lytle Hernández has argued that the racial dimensions of gatekeeping along the US-Mexico border came about in the era of the Great Depression. In the 1930s, immigration law enforcement, in the hands of the newly created US Border Patrol, increasingly targeted Mexican immigrant workers, as Mae Ngai has asserted elsewhere, as the "iconic illegal aliens."[7] Examining contraband trade along the border, George T. Díaz argues that the border was always a space across which citizens of both nations flouted customs regulations that were increasingly applied by both the US and Mexican governments in the early decades of the twentieth century. In this sense, Díaz places the closing of the border in the realm of trade regulations in the 1910s.[8] By the 1930s, cross-border plots hatched by Mexican exiles in the United States came to an end, and the political boundary between the United States and Mexico became, as Rachel St. John has argued, a line demarcating Mexicans from Americans rather than a simple political boundary.[9] Following the failure of the last military rebellion of the decade, the rebellion of Gen. José Gonzálo Escobar, Mexican exiles ceased to understand the borderlands as a safe haven in which they could hatch their various plots for rebellion. No longer would the tradition of revolution from the border, sustained by the likes of Porfirio Díaz, Catarino Garza, Ricardo and Enrique Flores Magón,

Francisco I. Madero, and so many other exiles from the late nineteenth and early twentieth centuries, serve Mexicans hoping to force political change in their home country. This book both complements and complicates the work of previous scholars by examining a distinct facet of the relationship between Mexico and the United States along the border in a relatively understudied period of borderlands history. I argue that by the end of the 1920s, the continuation of the violence of the Mexican Revolution, the "religious question," and the activities of the revolution's losers in exile along the border led to a further tightening of the border that made impossible further military incursions against the Mexican government from the United States. Mexican and US government concerns about exile plots, the still-local nature of authority along the border, and recurring political and social instability in Mexico led to a reinforcement of the border by the end of the 1920s that would make rebellion from the borderlands a losing proposition for Mexican political and religious dissidents.

## THE (POST)REVOLUTIONARY CONTEXT

Suffice it to say that postrevisionist scholarship has thoroughly challenged the revisionist take on the Mexican Revolution as interrupted, stilted, and hijacked by a burgeoning Mexican bourgeoisie. The flurry of microhistories and local histories that emerged between the late 1970s and the 1990s have given us a more complete understanding of the scope of the many revolutions that took place between 1910 and 1940. Clearly, the revolution was a mix of the orthodox and revisionist understandings of the conflict and is complicated still by the existence of the popular and military rebellions that appeared and disappeared until the end of the 1920s. The revolution was popular in nature from the very beginning, and the upheaval instilled in the minds of those who fought in the armies, or otherwise felt the weight of the revolutionary violence, that the constitution ratified in 1917 held within it a set of rights accessible to all Mexicans. While scholars have debated the origins, presidencies, and ultimate motivations of the Sonorans after 1920, most agree that the policies they enacted—secular public education, land reform, anticlericalism, and labor reforms—were intended to bring to bear some of the most important ideals contained in the Constitution of 1917. It was also clear that those very reforms would be contested by large sectors of the population—the clergy, *hacendados* (large landowners), and domestic and foreign capital—and that those sectors of society would attempt to change the course of the revolution to fit the vision of postrevolutionary reconstruction they imagined. The postrevisionist scholarship on the negotiated nature of rule in postrevolutionary Mexico is incredibly rich and has given us a more nuanced understanding of the complexity of the reconstruction of the Mexican state in the near absence of a centralized government.[10] As Jennie Purnell has noted, the postrevisionists have shown that there were many revolutions, and as such, there were many counterrevolutions as well.[11] In many cases, local-level contestations over the implementation of policy became part of the process by which policy on the national and local levels was established. Local political bosses jockeyed for power, and their struggles became the heart of community conflicts over land and religious liberty, among other things.

This book seeks to understand the counterrevolutions that marked the 1920s and the way in which they spilled over the border. At stake in the discussion of the negotiation of rule and the contestation of power during the revolution is precisely the condition in which the revolutionary state found itself in the 1920s. Mexico was still a conglomeration of regional and local power centers that had not been brought under any sort of state centralization. The new revolutionary government was weak and embattled on a number of different fronts—the most important for this study are revolutionary anticlericalism and the problem of the military, particularly on the northern border. Calles, despite his dreams of state centralization, could not seem to rein in rebellious governors, congressmen, and generals, and the additional strain of the Cristero Rebellion of 1926 threatened to weaken his already tenuous grip on the revolutionary state. Álvaro Obregón and Calles laid the foundations for a stable state, one that would allow for the more radical presidency of Lázaro Cárdenas, but they did so at great cost. By the end of the 1920s, Calles had proven adept at quelling the threats posed to the state and established the stability that allowed for the institutionalization of the revolution. It is important to emphasize that the establishment of this stability was always contingent on the Calles administration's capacity to manage the crises of the 1920s.

The narratives of the de la Huerta Rebellion and the Cristero Rebellion have been told by a handful of scholars in both US and Mexican academies.[12] Both conflicts have served as illustrations of the prolongation of the struggle for supremacy among the remaining strains of revolutionary thought in the years following Obregón's ascent to power. Both the de la Huerta and the Cristero rebellions were driven by a host of factors, political and social, that brought into sharp relief the vulnerability of the postrevolutionary state and its tenuous grip on national power. The de la Huerta Rebellion laid bare the deficiencies in the national military, with its bloated, inefficient, unpredictable, and untrustworthy officer corps, which in many instances enjoyed more local political influence than governors and other municipal administrators. The Cristero Rebellion illustrated that the strain of revolutionary anticlericalism that had been present since the early days of the revolution—and found its permanent embodiment in the Constitution of 1917—had run afoul of such significant portions of the population as to lead to an extension of the bloody civil war that had only just subsided with the ouster of First Chief Venustiano Carranza.[13] The political conflict that Calles had hoped to keep between his administration and the ecclesiastical hierarchy spilled over into the popular realm when, in the summer of 1926, the archbishop of Mexico, José Mora y del Río, initiated a nationwide cessation of all religious services and the closure of churches. In response, the Liga Nacional Defensora de la Libertad Religiosa (LNDLR), the political Catholic organization centered in Mexico City that directed the armed rebellion in the countryside, established a Catholic National Guard to support disparate bands of the faithful already in arms in the center-west region of the republic. The ideological battle between the church and the state became a full-blown popular rebellion.

While the de la Huerta and the Cristero rebellions cast a long shadow over the 1920s, they cannot be viewed as separate from the complex of issues that gave rise to the smaller, but no less significant, military uprisings of the latter years of the decade. The military uprising led by Gens. Francisco Serrano and Arnulfo Gómez in October 1927 and the rebellion of Gen. José Gonzálo Escobar in March 1929 must be seen as fundamentally linked with and dependent upon the forces that drove the Cristero Rebellion from the US side of the border. Political tensions over the presidential election of 1928 and the already fractured loyalties between the obregonista and callista contingents in the ranks of the military would come to a head when the candidacies of Gómez and Serrano were denounced by Obregón as divisive and detrimental to the good of the nation. In order to ensure that Gómez and Serrano would not threaten Obregón's candidacy, Calles ordered their arrest, at which point Gómez and Serrano announced the uprising.[14]

Just as accusations of presidential imposition had raised the specter of rebellion against Venustiano Carranza in 1920 and against Obregón in 1923, the opposition to Obregón's second presidential bid believed that military rebellion was the only way to avoid yet another imposition. The choice of Emilio Portes Gil to succeed Calles as interim president in 1929 would drive the wedge further between the obregonistas and callistas, leading to the Escobar Rebellion, a military uprising of border generals that actively sought support among the Catholic and ex-military contingent in the United States. It is also worthy of note that the military uprisings of the latter half of the decade were decidedly Norteño in their demographic makeup. Moreover, the rebellions that were caused by and exacerbated the political rifts between the obregonistas and the callistas were headed by military leaders who believed that they had been passed over for the presidential seat and that their rebellions would be sure to earn them that which they most deserved. Thus it is impossible to ignore the connections between the political and military discontent over a national reconstruction project that had been directed almost entirely by the Sonorans and that, by the middle of the decade, showed no signs of abating. The rebellions of Generals Gómez, Serrano, and Escobar are constituent parts of the larger contestation of state reconstruction directed by the victors of the revolution.

## THE STATE, SOVEREIGNTY, AND EXILES

James C. Scott has noted that there are moments of discontinuity between the fall of one regime and the consolidation of a new regime in which the state is weak and unable to implement policy at the local and regional levels. As Scott asserts, "Between the moment when a previous regime disintegrates and the moment when a new regime is firmly in place lies a political terrain that has rarely been examined closely. . . . For many citizens and communities . . . it *may* represent a remarkable period without taxes and state surveillance, a period when perceived injustices can be reversed; in short, a respite of autonomy."[15] When the Mexican Revolution ousted the aging dictator Porfirio Díaz, it left in its wake the political terrain that Scott describes. In the process, it opened the door to a host of alternate and competing visions of the course that the Mexican nation would take. The competition among these alternate visions manifested in mass violence for nearly a decade, plunging the republic into a bloody war among revolutionary factions. Despite cessation of the violence of the revolution in 1920, popular groups continued to battle with the state over the modernizing project it hoped to implement.

This study treats the idea of the state as a set of institutions and ideas that sometimes overlap, sometimes contradict each other, and in many cases are founded upon somewhat confused conceptualizations of the implementation of national policy. When we think of agents of the state, we imagine armored police officers, soldiers, public school administrators, national health and welfare officers, customs and immigration agents, and other assorted bureaucrats. In the best of cases, some sort of central federal administration drove the mission and purpose of these arms of the state. Although they rarely operate toward the same ends, they all exist for the same purpose—namely, the exercise of state sovereignty—ostensibly within the territorial limits of the nation. I utilize this understanding of the state as a starting point for an assessment of the Mexican state in the 1920s, a crucial decade of reconstruction and a period when many of the elements of the state were being reanimated and reconfigured to fit the needs of the postrevolutionary Mexican nation. In this sense, several of the elements that might constitute the model state, such as public schools and national programs of health and hygiene, were in the early stages of implementation in many regions of the republic, while others, such as the military and policing bodies, were still terribly unreliable. By referring to the postrevolutionary state as weak and contested, I do not mean to suggest that there was no state apparatus of which to speak—simply to posit that in the case of postrevolutionary Mexico, it is very difficult to speak of a functioning state driven by a unified central government.[16]

Scholars have noted that apart from the successes and failures of these institutions in various regions of the republic, they seem to have had a coherence of purpose that was quite distinct from the actual material resources and political exigencies faced by the postrevolutionary government.[17] Most important for this study is the assertion that while the postrevolutionary state was weak, and the central government perhaps even weaker, the attempt to mold minds and shape consciousness among what was considered an uneducated, unwashed, and superstitious Mexican populace was well defined if, at times, poorly implemented. This study, unlike the above-mentioned body of scholarship, seeks to understand how the Calles regime was able to control its exiles abroad and protect itself from a nearly constant barrage of external threats utilizing an already taxed state infrastructure. The Mexican state was overextended and weak, and it was struggling simply to defend its sovereignty within its established boundaries. The war among the revolutionary factions prior to the rebellion of Agua Prieta evidenced that ultimate sovereignty was literally up for grabs, but it was especially contested after 1924. Sovereignty, understood as the right to rule within the bounds of national territory, was assessed by the opposition in terms of legitimacy, and the Calles government was never considered legitimate among the military, political, and religious leaders in the opposition. Calles's constitutional right to rule, then, was under a state of constant contestation throughout the 1920s.

The notion of state sovereignty and its exercise has been addressed by a number of political and social theorists, philosophers, and cultural critics.[18] The consensus regarding the capacity of states to express their particular power is that states are generally bound by what has been termed "territorial" sovereignty, meaning that political authority is bounded within well-delineated territorial limits. "Modern definitions of territorial sovereignty," Peter Sahlins tells us, "focus on political boundaries as the point at which a state's territorial competence finds its ultimate expression. States are defined by their exclusive jurisdiction over a delimited territory; and the boundaries of territorial competence define the sovereignty of a state."[19] The exercise of sovereignty, however, can also be subject to strange and unpredictable permutations, especially at the fringes of territorial limits—in other words, along borders and within borderlands.

Borderlands have the capacity to confound the application of territorial sovereignty in cases in which the bounds of the nation-state are poorly defined, poorly defended, or understood by local populations as entirely insignificant. Sahlins illustrates this concept in the case of the development of the border between France and Spain in the seventeenth century, which formed as a result of "the complex interplay of two notions of boundary—zonal and linear—and two ideas of sovereignty—jurisdictional and territorial."[20] In the case of the boundary between the US and Mexico in the 1920s, there was already a hardening of the boundary that turned the region or zone between the two nations into a border—a line demarcating the territorial limits for each nation. In relations between Mexico and the United States from the late nineteenth century on, there was never a lack of understanding that the border signified the bounds of territorial sovereignty, but attempts to push those limits were rife throughout the period and into the early twentieth century. The most obvious, but certainly not the only, example of such pushing of the limits of territorial sovereignty is represented in the case of the "Punitive Expedition" led by Gen. John "Blackjack" Pershing in pursuit of Pancho Villa following his 1916 raid on the border town of Columbus, New Mexico.

In the 1920s, the operation of agents of the Calles government as spies in the United States suggests that the Mexican government was attempting to extend its authority over its citizens in exile. Neither the United States nor Mexico consciously considered its jurisdiction to traverse the border into the territory of the other nation. However, in many cases, it was understood that the Mexican government could extend its jurisdiction over its citizens who were suspected of being engaged in seditious activities. It was for this reason that the Confidential Department placed its agents in the United States to keep watch on the enemies of the Calles regime abroad. Confidential agents were prohibited from taking legal actions against their fellow citizens in exile. Their surveillance of these exiles, however, suggests that the Mexican government's understanding of its capacity to maintain surveillance of its citizens outside of its territorial boundaries was based on an understanding of sovereignty that naturally overstepped the realm of the territorial and into the jurisdictional.[21] Confidential agents generally respected their subordinate role in the policing of the exile cohort in the United States. However, they often attempted to assert dominion over enemies of the Mexican government in exile, either openly and directly through the US Department of Justice or through extralegal means such as backroom agreements with friendly US immigration inspectors and elected officials along the border.

The notion of "effective" sovereignty helps conceptualize the particular approach that the Mexican government took with regard to its exiles in the United States.[22] Political geographer John Agnew has questioned the narrowly defined terms of the study of sovereignty and its overreliance on the state's territorial authority, arguing that the "dominant approach continues to privilege the state as the singular font of authority even when a state's sovereignty may be decried as hypocrisy and seen as divisible or issue-specific rather than 'real' or absolute."[23] We must consider a multiplicity of expressions of sovereignty in cases in which the states under examination cannot be considered to exert the sort of central territorial authority normally associated with the traditional notion of state sovereignty. This perspective is essential to understanding the ways in which the Mexican government, at the helm of a weak and contested revolutionary state, exercised sovereignty over its citizens in exile in the United States.

The assumption that state sovereignty and state territoriality have been and remain interdependent has led to the notion that sovereignty is simply a tool by which states enforce internal order and protect against external threats. "Implicit in all claims about state sovereignty as the quintessential form taken by political authority," Agnew notes, "are associated claims about distinguishing a strictly bounded territory from an external world and thus fixing the territorial scope of sovereignty."[24] The concept of effective sovereignty, which Agnew has applied largely to imperialist modes of rule, is understood as a projected sovereignty that spans beyond the territorial limits of the nation. It can also be applied to great effect in the specific case of the Mexican state and its exiles abroad in the 1920s. The concept of effective sovereignty is salient to understanding how the Mexican government operated in the United States in the 1920s to protect itself against its dangerous exiles. The Mexican government would have considered it a right to maintain dominion over its dangerous citizens in exile. However, consular officials and confidential agents had no right to operate as law enforcement agents for the Mexican government in US national territory. The sovereignty that they hoped to exercise then, can be termed jurisdictional, but it was never complete simply because of the restraints imposed upon the agents of the Mexican government by international treaties and laws.

Throughout this study, I have chosen to use the word *exile* to identify the individuals and groups operating in the United States to topple the Calles regime. I have chosen to refer to them as exiles instead of refugees, immigrants, or ex-patriots. The study of exiles and political refugees in the history of twentieth-century Latin America has been shaped by the legacy of the Cold War and the United States' campaign to stop the spread of communism in its hemisphere—a campaign that gave rise to some of the most socially and politically repressive regimes of the century. Political exiles most often studied are those who have sought refuge from dictatorial right-wing governments. The literature on exile in the twentieth century has taken as its premise a dichotomy in which exiles are inherently progressive and the regimes from which they seek asylum are inherently repressive and undemocratic—certainly the case not only in Latin America but also on a global scale in the context of the Cold War. Postrevolutionary Mexico presents an example in which the opposite was true.

The individuals that this study treats were, in the case of foreign-born members of the clergy and some militant priests, forcibly ejected from their homeland for their opposition to the constitutionally established government or, in the case of political and military leaders of the opposition, disembarked voluntarily because political trends in Mexico did not agree with their political or moral proclivities. Those individuals who left of their own volition were following a long tradition of exile based on the understanding that plots against the government in Mexico City could be much more easily hatched in the relative safety provided by the borderlands between the United States and Mexico. They were confident that they would find waiting on the other side of the international line communities of Mexican immigrants, devout Catholics, political sympathizers, as well as familial connections established over centuries of migration across the border. Moreover, they knew that they could rely on those communities for assistance in their transborder plots to topple the Calles regime. Those plots involved military planning and recruitment, financial planning, and the establishment of networks with like-minded groups within the exile community for very specific political and military ends. The Catholics, delahuertistas, felicistas, carrancistas, porfiristas, and other affiliated groups were utilizing the border environment as a means to foment political instability. They gathered armies, drafted manifestos denouncing the Calles government, and armed citizens for military engagements against the federal government from within and without Mexican national territory. Moreover, the heads of these military engagements were commissioned officers, generals, and other high-ranking members of the Mexican military. They were considered traitors by the revolutionary government in Mexico. At no point during their exile did they made attempts at resettlement in the United States because they maintained hope that their efforts would ultimately bear fruit and allow for their return to Mexico. Thus Victoria Lerner has quite rightly pointed out that all the political and military exiles from the revolution, "men with power—lesser or greater—that had to go into exile defeated by other political forces that retained greater political power," held many of these characteristics in common.[25] They were unsuccessful in their grabs for power while inside Mexico and were forced into exile for their transgressions.

They always held faith, however, that with the right combination of money, support from political elements within the US government and business communities, and dire social and economic conditions in Mexico, they would be able to vanquish the ruling administration that held them in their miserable state of affairs and return to their homes. It is for these reasons that I have elected to refer to them exclusively as exiles.

The Mexican Revolution, over the course of the first two decades of the twentieth century, produced an overwhelming number of exiles. Those who found their way to the border as a result of the de la Huerta Rebellion or the Cristero Rebellion two years later were certainly not the first of the revolution's exile population. The successive waves of exiles came in several distinct periods that corresponded with major shifts in the political landscape of the revolution. The exiles that these specific periods produced had varied goals and missions during their tenure in the United States. Far from the counterrevolutionary activities of the felicistas and the Cristero supporters and representatives, the revolution's early exiles carried with them the literature and ideologies of revolution. The Flores Magón brothers, operating first from San Antonio and then from St. Louis, Missouri, published their revolutionary anarchist periodical *Regeneración*. Francisco I. Madero drafted his revolutionary proclamation, the Plan de San Luis Potosí, from San Antonio, Texas. Even before the strikes at Cananea, Sonora, and the Rio Blanco textile mill, a journalist named Catarino Garza made what were some of the first political challenges to Porfirio Díaz's regime from the Texas-Mexico border in September 1891.[26] After the maderista revolution of 1910–13 and the huertista period of 1913–14, the composition of the revolution's political exiles shifted. Villistas joined the ranks of porfiristas and huertistas, and after the assassination of First Chief Venustiano Carranza in the wake of the rebellion of Agua Prieta, carrancistas joined the list of the revolution's losers in exile. When the last of the most recalcitrant military generals in the country were defeated in the final months of the de la Huerta Rebellion, revolutionary generals like Enrique Estrada joined their old foes in exile along the border.[27]

As distinct as the individual experiences in the revolution and regardless of how divisive the politics over which many of these exiles fought during the years of revolutionary violence were, they all had one important thing in common: they had all emerged on the losing side of the revolution. As Lerner has noted regarding alliances, there were various couplings within this community that would have only occurred in exile. She posits, "The exiles that arrived between 1920 and 1940 were united with those who had been forced to leave between 1910 and 1920, and had not been able to return." In 1921, for example, carrancistas joined with old porfiristas, huertistas, and felicistas.[28] The list of the "losers of the revolution" becomes quite extensive, adding newly arrived delahuertistas and estradistas after 1923 and a wave of Catholic exiles after 1926. Apart from the specific personalities involved, felicistas, carrancistas, and villistas would never have been able to reconcile their factional hostilities while still residing in Mexican national territory. Those bonds forged in exile, however, were that which made them all the more threatening. In Mexico, they were defeated—the vanquished. But in places like El Paso, Deming, New Orleans, Brownsville, San Antonio, and Los Angeles, their conspiracies breathed new life into a new exile cohort.

It was within these exile communities that Cristero supporters, dissident prelates, and Mexico City's Catholic elite sought solace and support, and the location of temporary settlement was everything. Many of the Cristero leaders and supporters went to places where they would find large Mexican immigrant populations. El Paso and San Antonio were special places in this regard. The choice of location also had much to do with exiles' familiarity with the host regions. In other words, exiles tended to gravitate toward areas that they had previously visited or in which they could count on familial relations. For example, exiles fleeing from Sonora might settle in Arizona or California. Indeed, Adolfo de la Huerta operated out of Tucson and made regular visits to associates in San Diego and Los Angeles, where he later settled. Exiles from Chihuahua and the oil-producing regions on the Gulf of Mexico tended to head for South Texas and New Mexico. The delahuertistas under the command of Gen. César López de Lara, from Tamaulipas, set up operations in the area around Brownsville.[29] Catholic exiles tended to settle in El Paso or San Antonio, two cities that had traditionally been home to larger faith-based communities and where many among the lay Catholic elite had visited, shopped, and vacationed.[30]

There are many political and state actors, on both sides of the border, that make appearances throughout this rather complicated border story. Federal judges, district attorneys, Bureau of Investigation agents, border district sheriffs and deputies, immigration agents, US congressmen, and Mexican consular officers—not to mention the exiles and the confidential agents who pursued them—all interacted in various ways with the exile populations examined here. However, the newly created Border Patrol is a very small part of this narrative. My intention is not to ignore or dismiss the historical significance of the development of the Border Patrol after its establishment in May 1925. The reason that it is deemphasized in this work is that the subjects of my study were not "illegal" immigrants. It was never the exiles such as Enrique Estrada, Adolfo de la Huerta, Félix Díaz, or any of the prelates or elite Catholic activists who made their way across the border with whom the Border Patrol was concerned. These individuals were not among the illegal border crossers that the immigration quotas attached to the Immigration Act of 1924 were intended to curb. On the one hand, the exiles in this study crossed the border with ease, through main ports of entry, passports and bags in hand. They were not among the throngs of migrant workers and other border crossers who, at the height of the revolutionary violence in Mexico, were subjected to bathing, delousing, and branding with indelible ink prior to entry in the United States.[31] As such, many of my subjects simply were outside of the Border Patrol's jurisdiction. Moreover, the main points of contact for Mexican confidential agents were the Department of Justice and, in cases in which they sought speedy deportation of suspects, the Department of Labor, but they rarely utilized the resources of the Border Patrol. Only in the case of the arrest of Enrique Estrada's army in Southern California in the summer of 1926 did the Confidential Department consult Border Patrol agents. Because the Border Patrol's mandate did not include law enforcement capacities, it had no authority to make arrests or serve warrants or to investigate potential violations of US neutrality laws. As such, Mexican consular officers and confidential agents had no reason to communicate the results of their own investigations to the Border Patrol. Unlike Bureau of Investigation agents, the Border Patrol had no authority to act on their intelligence.[32]

## BORDERLANDS CONSIDERED

Michiel Baud and Willem Van Schendel have posited quite rightly that despite the precautions that states take to define and defend their borders, people will always transgress those borders whenever it suits them. "National borders," they proclaim, "are political constructs, imagined projections of territorial power. . . . No matter how clearly borders are drawn on official maps, how many customs officials are appointed, or how many watch towers are built, people will ignore borders whenever it suits them."[33] The most tangible expression of a national boundary, thus, exists primarily in the minds of policy makers and cartographers. They delineate the boundaries of the nation and of sovereignty, but on the ground, those boundaries become much more of a fiction than a reality. In terms of borders and states, the authors note the importance of the cartographic fascination of the nineteenth-century state as the foundation of the demarcation of modern national boundaries. This was certainly the case with the regime of Porfirio Díaz.[34] However, of signal importance for the present study is the notion that, after the demarcation of those territorial limits, the maintenance and protection of borders continues to correspond to the strength and control that those very same states project along the border. In the case in which local authority persists despite incursions of central authority along the border, the capacity for any state to maintain control of that boundary region is compromised. The degree to which authority in such spaces is limited defines the behaviors of local elites and the ways in which they choose to interact with the boundary line. As Baud and Schendel put it, "State employees stationed in the borderland and their superiors in the provincial or state capitals could develop very different perspectives on their mission in the borderland. Customs officials might become involved in smuggling, school teachers might resist assimilatory language policy, and security forces might refuse to risk their lives against well-armed separatists."[35] Specifically in the case in which the presence of the state along the border is weak, the delineated border becomes a farce for many who would attempt to engage in any number of nefarious or subversive activities. The border at this point fades from that strictly regimented line in the imaginations of state actors and into the realm of a sometimes negotiated, sometimes ignored line.

For the Mexican state, border security was a constituent part of the larger process of reconstruction and centralization. State centralization, a process that Obregón began but was continued under Calles, was already a major part of the reconstruction project. Border crossings and political instability along the border, such as that generated by the rebellions of the 1920s and the cross-border networks that supported them, hindered the process of state reconstruction because they drew resources and capital away from the necessary reforms that the revolution promised to deliver. As scholars of the period of administration under President Calles have noted, his first two years were marked by a rapid implementation of land reform, educational reforms, and budgetary innovations that allowed the government to begin repayment on its foreign debt. The Cristero Rebellion and the military conflicts that erupted in the intervening years forced Calles to roll back some of those reforms and postpone others until stability could be restored. For this reason, many scholars of the period have characterized Calles's rule as authoritarian and repressive.[36]

State reconstruction, a process that once complete would allow for the populist reforms of Lázaro Cárdenas, has been obscured by the perceived repressive nature of the Calles administration's approach to popular and military discontent. However, Mexican consuls and the agents of the Confidential Department in the United States were able to secure the border until the major threats to the state, both internal and external, were neutralized. Centralization and the neutralization of those threats allowed the process of state reconstruction to move forward, but as this book posits, the border was not completely secured against exile military threats until the end of the 1920s. We generally assume that the United States projected a stronger force along the border than its weaker southern neighbor. In the case of border violence and intrigue in the 1920s, however, the United States and Mexico were quite equally matched in their lack of control over the movement of contraband and people across the border.

This book also hints at a larger story. In addition to violence, lack of control, and instability along the US-Mexico border, much of what is discussed here deals with more dangerous cross-border networks. In part, this is a border story, in that much of the activity takes place in that space between the two nations. It is also a story about the relationship between the weak post-revolutionary Mexican state and its exiles in the United States, exiles who had a particular understanding of the revolutionary process that clashed with the vision of the state builders of the 1920s. Exiles' cross-border networks highlight both the boundary that separated them and also the frequent insignificance and malleability of that boundary in the larger systems of communication they utilized in their conspiracies. That physical boundary did very little to sever the familial, military, political, and religious ties that exiles relied upon for support. In this sense, the networks that my research discusses were, at times, of far greater concern than the smuggling routes and other weaknesses in the borderlands.

Also important to consider in assessing border security and the strength of the state is the relationship between central authority and what Baud and Schendel call "borderland elites." The failure to incorporate borderland elites into the state could be catastrophic for the maintenance of order along the border.[37] In the case of the US-Mexico border during the most intense revolutionary violence following the fall of Porfirio Díaz, borderland elites could be identified as prelates, municipal authorities, governors, and military generals with questionable allegiances. In the wake of the de la Huerta Rebellion, the border became a meeting place, as I call it—a place of refuge and regeneration where those excluded from state power and who saw their local influence threatened went to carry out their plans to destabilize the Calles regime.

In response, Calles attempted to tighten his military grip on the borderlands and sent secret agents to the region to keep watch on his enemies.

In these endeavors, the results were a mixed bag. Calles could never ensure the loyalty of the military leaders along the border, as the example of the Escobar Rebellion demonstrates. However, Calles was quite successful in that very few of the plots devised by the exile community came to fruition. It was not so much that Obregón and Calles failed to incorporate the generals along the border into the state. Obregón had given them nearly everything they wanted, and while they enjoyed almost limitless local authority, the one thing that Obregón was not willing to offer them was a seat at the presidential table. That would be reserved for Calles. The failure of Calles to integrate these border generals into the state was due to their own intransigence and their perception that they had been passed over as presidential hopefuls for a man they believed to be less qualified for the position. This conglomeration of interests on the border, along with the weakened condition of the Mexican state, resulted in chronic instability and the prolongation of the violence of the revolution for the entirety of the 1920s.

A confluence of events put an end to the endemic violence along the border after 1929. US-Mexico borderlands scholars have pointed to the ultimate solidification of the international boundary as a key turning point in international relations between the two countries.[38] While the stiffening of security along the border is significant, it does not completely explain the end of counterrevolutionary hostilities on both sides of the border after 1929. It must also be said that the counterrevolutionaries in exile were ultimately deprived of a key source of popular motivation for rebellion when the Emilio Portes Gil administration, with the support of Amb. Dwight Morrow, settled the church-state conflict in the summer of 1929. Moreover, the failure of the Escobar Rebellion removed the military connections that the exiles maintained along the border. After the end of the Cristero Rebellion and the Escobar Rebellion, upon which many had pinned their remaining hopes, there was scant possibility for a resurrection of their counterrevolutionary designs. Finally, Calles, the figure who had been the object of so much of their disdain, had relinquished his presidential power to Emilio Portes Gil. While most agreed that Calles was still *el jefe máximo*, Portes Gil undertook the task that Calles could not: negotiations with the Mexican clergy. In essence, Calles, Portes Gil, and Morrow deflated the balloon of counterrevolution. As such, the 1930s stood relatively absent of the border conflict that had characterized the previous two decades.

## THE METHODOLOGY OF RESEARCHING ESPIONAGE

It is no surprise that the literature dealing with the Mexican Revolution and cross-border espionage is quite thin. Not until recently have scholars taken up the challenge posed by Michael C. Meyer, Charles Harris III, and Louis R. Sadler to dive into the scattered and cryptic documentation associated with state surveillance and espionage in the revolutionary period.[39] These scholars have done so with aplomb and have produced a number of works that have enhanced our understanding of the ways in which the Mexican security services, in various forms between the late days of Porfirio Díaz's regime to the mid-twentieth century, have operated to quell internal dissent and protect the Mexican state from external threats.[40]

As exciting as stories of undercover agents, sting operations, and counterrevolutionary plots along the border can be, the methodological underpinnings of the research required to put together such stories, and to do it well, is quite complex. The present project has been enhanced greatly by the well-organized and recently opened collection of the Dirección General de Investigaciones Políticas y Sociales at the Archivo General de la Nación in Mexico City. The collection contains a treasure trove of documentation on secret investigations in Mexico and the United States from 1920 to the 1980s. As complete as the collection is, it is still quite tedious to sift through the minutia of the numerous memoranda and orders from the Ministry of the Interior to consular officials in the United States, the sometimes unfounded rumors that were a staple component of much of the news released in the Spanish-language presses in the United States, and daily investigative reports from confidential agents on the border. However, it is from these minutiae that the most important aspects of this story have emerged.

As chapter 1 demonstrates, the Confidential Department was not the only intelligence-gathering unit working clandestinely along the border. The exiles working to topple the Calles government had at their disposal a wealth of military and intelligence-gathering resources, many of whom had gained their experience working to protect previous regimes under Venustiano Carranza, Victoriano Huerta, and Porfirio Díaz. The nature of their clandestine and criminal activities in the United States makes them nearly invisible in the documentary record, especially when they were particularly good at their jobs. I have compiled documentary evidence from a number of sources that include the records of the Department of State and the Department of Justice; the Mexican Departamento Confidencial and the Secretaría de Relaciones Exteriores; news reports from Spanish-language presses in the United States that were supportive of the Mexican exile community, such as the San Antonio daily *La Prensa* and the Los Angeles–based *La Opinión*; as well as the memoirs of Adolfo de la Huerta and the documentary collection of Félix Díaz's personal papers at the Centro de Estudios de la Historia Mexicana, Grupo CARSO.

Within these collections can be found fragments of stories about spies, gunrunners, smugglers, and the Knights of Columbus. Putting the slivers together to tell a coherent story about the broader field of espionage in the 1920s has been much more difficult. Confidential agents may have conveyed a wealth of intelligence in their daily reports, but their information was only as good as their confidential informants, some of whom, as we will see, had less than clearly discernable allegiances. Confidential agents were often given incomplete, misleading, or outright false information, and the agents themselves realized quite quickly when they had been double-crossed and amended their reports. I have had to be very patient with their documents and careful not to accept the intelligence that they provided to their superiors at face value. At times, we find that agents of the Confidential Department subcontracted undercover operatives to infiltrate exile cohorts, who were only identifiable by the agents who had contracted their labor. The cases in which their identities are revealed to the historian are rare and leave one only to assume that there were many more who will remain hidden in the documents, referred to only as enemies of the Mexican government in exile.[41]

It is at least as difficult to pull apart the threads of intrigue for the researcher of espionage as it was for the confidential agents to make sense of the intelligence that they were gathering and passing on to Mexico City, border consulates, and the Department of Justice. I have utilized documentary collections from law enforcement agencies on both sides of the border to piece together a narrative of their operations during the period under examination, and I have utilized an even more fragmented record produced by the exiles themselves, such as the memoirs of Adolfo de la Huerta and his documentary collection housed at the Fideicomiso Archivos Plutarco Elías Calles y Fernando Torreblanca in Mexico City, the papers of Félix Díaz, and the statements made by various exiles who had been arrested and detained as a result of their activities in the United States. These latter sources have helped me verify certain details left incomplete in the broader espionage narrative.

Even with the best triangulation of historical sources, this study still maintains silences regarding key aspects of the activities of exiles and the confidential agents who pursued them in the 1920s. There remain lines of inquiry that agents began about which findings were never reported and instances in which agents' informants became so unreliable that their information had to be discarded. Their trajectories disappear from the record. There are still other instances in which informants seemed to be working as double agents, but their exact roles cannot be elucidated because their behavior became too unpredictable and their presence in the documentary record too fuzzy. I have done everything possible to interrogate the sources from which I draw my analysis and construct my narrative, understanding that the fundamental nature of international espionage demanded secrecy, misinformation, and subterfuge, all of which greatly complicate the historian's work even in the best of conditions.

## ORGANIZATION

Chapter 1 examines the prehistory of espionage and the Mexican Revolution, comparing the Confidential Department to its late nineteenth and early twentieth-century predecessors. Professionalization was the key to establishing the most effective security services possible and the feature that most distinguished the Confidential Department of the mid-1920s from those secret service organizations that came before it. Professionalization of the Mexican intelligence services was one of the keys to directing an efficient and, for the most part, incorruptible espionage service, loyal not to any specific administration but to the Mexican state. This chapter seeks to outline the early development of the Confidential Department's operations, from its mission to spy on potential opposition to the Calles government in the wake of the de la Huerta Rebellion to international espionage against those same enemies in exile. This chapter demonstrates the fact that the 1920s are important because there were real attempts on *both* sides of the border to bring this region under control. The Department of Justice, Department of Labor, Confidential Department, consular officials, and to a much lesser degree, the Border Patrol were all working to secure the border against contraband—material and human—and external threats to the Mexican state. At times, they worked in concert. At other times, their work was highly contentious, fraught with jurisdictional misunderstandings and outrageously high expectations for dealing with the enemy. Chapter 1 details the conflicts between Mexican secret agents and their American counterparts as well as the implications of international espionage along the border and the diplomacy of border security in the early 1920s. This chapter also illustrates the vast resources and capacity possessed by the exiles for the art of counterespionage. Many of the exile groups operating along the border utilized their own information networks to obtain intelligence about the identities of confidential agents and their operations and to stay a few steps ahead of the Confidential Department. Their counterespionage networks saved them from arrest on more than one occasion and sometimes confounded the efforts of even the best and brightest Mexican secret agents.

Chapter 2 examines the early years of exile organizing through the example of Adolfo de la Huerta. In exile, de la Huerta became much more of a determined political actor than in his previous experience with rebellion in 1923 and made effective use of networks, political and commercial, that he had already established in his former career as governor of the state of Sonora, provisional president of Mexico, and secretary of the treasury under Obregón. Through his efforts, he was able to establish himself as a formidable opponent of the Calles regime and maintain an extensive communication network of spies, agents, and arms smugglers well before any of the other dissident groups were able to do so. At the conclusion of the de la Huerta Rebellion, don Adolfo found himself in a new political environment in the United States, and he took his mission to topple the Calles regime as a personal crusade. The political and business connections that he had already cultivated in the United States would serve him well as he moved in a world of high finance, industry, and politics. He enjoyed a certain advantage over other Mexican exiles. While military men such as Gen. Enrique Estrada and Félix Díaz, as well as those who would rebel later in the decade, had the brawn and the connections in Mexico, they were largely shut out from the circles of political power and finance in the United States that were open to de la Huerta. De la Huerta also utilized the relationship with the Yaquis that he fostered during the period of his governorship of his home state of Sonora to take strategic advantage of the Yaqui Uprising of 1926–27. This chapter posits that Adolfo de la Huerta, carried away by the military rebellion that took his name, took full control of his own operations in exile as a man possessed of a singular desire to overthrow the Calles regime by any means possible.

Chapter 3 serves as a case study of what counterrevolutionary exiles could accomplish when they took full advantage of the resources available to them, both in the United States and in Mexico. The coordinated efforts of Gen. Enrique Estrada to lead a rebellion across the border into Baja California was the first example of an attempt to utilize the forward political momentum of the Cristero Rebellion in Mexico. Thus this chapter highlights the multifaceted and complex nature of alliances among the diverse exile community in the United States. It was a network of exiles both new and old, hardware store owners (early twentieth-century small-arms dealers), and political Catholics in Mexico City that made Estrada's expedition possible. It was, however, the weaknesses of these same alliances and various networks that ultimately doomed the expedition to failure. As impressive as the effort was, its importance is that it represented one of the strongest and best-organized expeditions to take advantage of Catholic connections, financial and political, in Mexico, even before many of those involved in the plot ended up in exile. Estrada's failed rebellion on the California-Mexico border resulted in not only the arrest and highly publicized trial of Estrada and a large portion of his expeditionary force but also the imprisonment and subsequent exile of many of the more aggressive elite political Catholics that the LNDLR, the national organization driving the popular rebellion in the countryside, had to offer. While the expedition failed, it ultimately resulted in the arrival of many more of the Cristero Rebellion's exiles to San Antonio and El Paso, who would then lend support to other counterrevolutionary plots and intrigues throughout the remainder of the decade. The failure of Estrada's rebellion thus marked a turning point in the fortunes of many of Mexico's enemies in the United States and began a new period of counterrevolutionary activity focused principally on the Catholic contingent in exile. Prior to the summer of 1926, law enforcement agencies in the United States, consular officials, and the agents of the Confidential Department had approached the prevention of counterrevolutionary plots with a certain confidence that exiles such as de la Huerta, Estrada, Díaz, and López de Lara lacked the resources necessary to constitute a legitimate threat. The Cristero Rebellion forced a reassessment of those beliefs and concentrated the Mexican government's focus on the activities of Catholics in exile.

Chapter 4 examines the efforts of the Catholic elite in exile and the expansion of the conspiratorial networks discussed in chapter 3. While the efforts of counterrevolutionary exiles after the de la Huerta Rebellion had been to supply their own supporters with money, guns, and ammunition for the purpose of waging war against the Mexican government from without, the Cristero Rebellion afforded counterrevolutionary plots a new opportunity. The Cristero Rebellion was generating instability from within, and exiles hoping to capitalize on the potential success of the Catholic rebellion redoubled their efforts to get as much armament as they could, within the bounds of their limited resources, to the Cristeros. The initiation of the Cristero Rebellion rejuvenated an already quite vigorous Catholic support movement in the United States that sought to affect policy in Washington favorable to the church in Mexico. It also brought out the darker, more clandestine side of Catholic activism. While key leaders within the American episcopate busied themselves raising funds and publishing and distributing propaganda, their supporters in the Knights of Columbus were involved in complex international arms-smuggling rings intended to ship armaments from Canada into ports all along the western coast of Mexico, the heartland of the Cristero Rebellion.

The Cristero Rebellion complicated border security for both the United States and Mexico in a way that had not been seen since the de la Huerta Rebellion. The capacity of distinct exile groups to make amicable alliances increased when the Cristero Rebellion began in the summer of 1926. This chapter details a few of the most important and illustrates a shift in the exile community's approach to cross-border rebellion. The new approach involved utilizing the political momentum of the Catholic contingent in exile and their capacity to influence the opinion and loyalties of military leaders already feeling the sting of callista manipulations of national military structures. The seeds of the Escobar Rebellion of March 1929 were planted well before the assassinations of Gens. Arnulfo Gómez and Francisco Serrano in 1928, and it was Catholic leaders in exile and their supporters who planted those seeds, in large part. The Catholic contingent in San Antonio and El Paso had quite a lot of influence on military leaders, such as Gen. Francisco Manzo in Sonora and ex-general Marcelo Caraveo in Chihuahua. As early as 1927, Caraveo, ex-chief of military operations and then gubernatorial candidate for Chihuahua, was in communication with some of the important Catholic dissidents in El Paso—namely, Luz de Perches, the mother of the former private secretary to Archbishop José Mora y del Rio. The ex-chief of police in Mexico City and longtime Calles confidant Roberto Cruz was also involved in backdoor dealings with General Manzo, *jefe militar* in Sonora. Although these military leaders may not have agreed with the Cristero position, they could all agree that Calles's intransigence with regard to the religious question was threatening to destroy the nation. A number of factors contributed to this disgust: a continuation of military reorganization, the assassination of Generals Gómez and Serrano, and the fact that the Cristero Rebellion had gone on far longer than it should have.

Chapter 5 discusses the convergence of the Cristero and Escobar rebellions and the connivance between the counterrevolutionary exile cohort in the United States and military leaders who maintained virtually complete control of the border at the end of the 1920s. Even into the late 1920s there were serious deficiencies in the professionalization of the officer corps, and it is clear that their fidelity was never sufficiently guaranteed. Despite the victory over the delahuertistas, there were other officers who expressed their loyalty but contented themselves with watching and waiting to see if Obregón and Calles would be capable of holding on to national power. Moreover, the reorganization and professionalization of the military that Calles had been undertaking along with Secretary of War Joaquín Amaro ruffled the feathers of some of the more powerful generals in the northern states. In the case of other military conflicts in the course of the revolution, the generals who rebelled against the state were almost always driven by personal ambition and a desire to defend against any encroachment upon their own local power. The same was true for the Escobar Rebellion of March 1929. This chapter illustrates that since 1924, Calles never had complete control over the military or the governors in the border regions. The case of the Escobar Rebellion illustrates that the governors, military leaders, and political machines along the border in Mexico fiercely resisted the centralizing efforts of the Calles regime. That the northern states remained independent and had connections to the Catholic contingent in exile made those military commands prime targets for the Catholics, delahuertistas, and felicistas in their plots to overthrow the Mexican government.

Twenty-five years ago, Michael C. Meyer pointed out that the revolution along the border in the 1910–20 period was at its core a clandestine revolution. "The revolutionaries," Meyer noted, "understandably sought to hide their motives, conceal their fundraising activities, misrepresent their alliances, and disguise their contemplated military operations not only from their enemies but from federal, state, and local officials on both sides of the border."[42] The following is the story of the clandestine counterrevolutions of the 1920s and the attempts of the fledgling Mexican state to combat that counterrevolution from beyond its territorial limits. In the same way that the followers of Catarino Garza in the late nineteenth century and the floresmagonistas and maderistas in the early twentieth century concealed their activities and relied upon the support of local borderlands populations to carry out their revolutionary designs, the losers of the revolution utilized similar networks. It was their hope that they might be able to direct the course of the revolution in accordance with their vision of social and political reform and to perhaps undo portions of the change that the revolution had already accomplished.

# ONE

# THE CONFIDENTIAL DEPARTMENT

## ORGANIZATION AND PROFESSIONALIZATION

Between the late porfiriato—the long presidency of Porfirio Díaz—and the revolution, Mexican governments always utilized some form of cross-border espionage to keep tabs on their enemies abroad.[1] The need for cross-border spy networks was great because the border had been the source of periodic conspiracies since at least 1875, when Porfirio Díaz himself, from Brownsville, Texas, waged the rebellion that brought him to power.[2] Until 1916, the intelligence service remained under the control of the Mexican consular system. It had been part of the consular system since Díaz's minister of foreign relations, Enrique Creel, established his International Detective Agency in 1900.[3] Despite the efforts of US law enforcement agencies that closely cooperated with Díaz's consuls to neutralize the threats from anarchists, floresmagonistas, and maderistas at the turn of the twentieth century, all these groups enjoyed a certain amount of support from individuals or groups on the US side of the border. A number of elected officials and law enforcement agents maintained ties and interests in the course of Mexican politics and had no scruples when it came to giving their favored faction a bit of an advantage over others. Local law enforcement officials on the border in Texas—rangers, marshals, sheriffs, district attorneys—had a long history of intervening in border affairs that preceded the period under examination here. This was certainly the case with John A. Valls, a familiar personage in the 1920s in Webb County, Texas. As the district attorney for Laredo, Valls was a fierce supporter of Madero and prosecuted quite viciously the participants in the reyista conspiracy of 1911. He consistently favored Madero's supporters in exile in Texas. He was later an antiobregonista and a rabid anticallista and actively worked against the agents of the Confidential Department as well as Mexican consular officers associated with the Calles government.[4] These local actors intervened in ways that confounded and frustrated the efforts of state agents—confidential agents, consular officials, and ambassadors—in their quest to defend the nation against external threats from those feared by the porfiristas at the turn of the twentieth century to the callistas in the 1920s.

The history of local intervention in border affairs reinforces the notion that the border between the United States and Mexico was, for the most part, out of reach of either state. In this sense, the United States government, at least where rogue border agents were concerned, was equally disadvantaged along the international boundary. This is not to suggest that the United States' state apparatus was as weak and contested as that of its southern neighbor; I mean simply to posit that the border in the 1920s and the specific conditions generated by the Mexican Revolution and the alliances it engendered on either side of the line presented a specific set of difficult problems for both the United States and Mexico. At stake for the Mexican government was the issue of reconstruction. The porous nature of the border and the strength and intensity of the work of exile groups in the United States meant that until those external threats were neutralized, there would be serious hurdles to overcome in the process of state reconstruction. More than the external exile threat, the revolution had produced such deep political fissures among the various factions that had battled with each other in the previous years of civil war that discerning political foe from friend was nearly impossible for the Sonoran victors. Therefore, dealing with political dissent at home was also at the top of the list of the Calles administration. Securing the border against the exile threat would be one of the principal objectives of the Mexican government if state reconstruction were to proceed.

Examining the development of the surveillance arm of the Mexican state and its interactions with confidential agents' law enforcement counterparts on the US side of the border demonstrates the very real necessity for *both* states to bring this region under control in the 1920s. A close look at the case of the early phases of professionalization of the Mexican Confidential Department and its activities in the United States also highlights the haphazard approach to law enforcement and intelligence gathering along the border. The agents of the Confidential Department certainly lacked the years of experience that various US border agents had. However, those US border agents operated under their own set of ambitions, motivations, local political allegiances, and most important, prejudices against Mexicans. However tenuous, the 1920s represent the starting point of a reevaluation of state control of the border.

## SPIES AND ESPIONAGE IN THE DAYS OF DON PORFIRIO DÍAZ

In the days of Porfirio Díaz, prior to the revolution, Mexican consulates in the United States served mainly as commercial agents. It was their job to ensure that trade and commerce continued unabated between Mexican and US capitalists and to provide assistance to Mexican citizens temporarily residing in the United States. With the initiation of hostilities between Díaz and his ever-increasing opposition in the late nineteenth and early twentieth centuries, consular officials began to serve an additional role—that of state intelligence officer. To protect the ailing dictatorship from its enemies across the border, Díaz's consuls assisted with investigations and worked closely with US law enforcement agencies. Mexican consuls served as intelligence officers through the Madero and Carranza periods and, in many cases, acted as independent investigative units, hiring their own detective agencies.[5] With the introduction of the Mexican Secret Service in 1918 and, later, the Confidential Department, the role of the consuls reverted to their original charges to a certain degree, but they still operated as cooperative intelligence-gathering units. Individual secret agents, however, shouldered the majority of the investigative responsibilities. The means by which the Díaz regime was able to neutralize the opposition plotting in exile was via the consuls, who were to provide as much evidence as possible to appropriate law enforcement agencies of violations of the US neutrality laws.

Section 5286 of the US neutrality laws of 1873 defined a violation as initiating or providing or preparing the means for any military expedition or enterprise against a state with which the United States was at peace.[6] However, the interpretation of terms such as *military expedition*, *setting foot*, and *preparing means* would change depending on the US State Department's opinion of the rebels under consideration. In terms of prosecution, attorneys had the most success in prosecuting cases that could be clearly identified as hostile expeditions—namely, those that had a military structure with an armed rank and file and the undeniable purpose of attacking other military personnel. The law, however, also allowed for a very broad set of interpretations. According to the letter of the law, the perpetrators need not wear uniforms or even be trained soldiers. It was not even necessary for them to carry arms to be in violation of the neutrality laws—only to have arms waiting for them at a future time and place. Nor did the individuals involved need to be in contact with each other prior to the expedition. In most cases, just the fact that those involved in the planning took part in the minutiae of the design was enough evidence to prove guilt.[7] This understanding of the spirit of the law was, in the 1910s, strictly enforced as interpreted, especially when it came to prosecuting alleged anarchists. In the case of the floresmagonistas, properly prosecuting overt violations was the ultimate goal in the first decade of the twentieth century, due in part to a climate of rabid antianarchism in the United States. This antianarchism was the long-term result of a high tide of eastern European immigration but was readily applied to all anarchists, regardless of national origin. The Flores Magón brothers became favorite targets of the Departments of Justice and State.

Enforcement of the neutrality laws was never simply about adhering to established policy emanating from Washington, DC. It also had much to do with issues such as international relations, legal precedent, and most important, the attitudes of federal and nonfederal local officials along the border with regard to the prosecuted. With prior hard-line enforcement in the case of the floresmagonistas and, after 1909, the support of the Bureau of Investigation and improved communication between the border and Washington, scholars have suggested that the neutrality laws were enforced more effectively in the 1910s and beyond.[8] Certainly the elements for improved enforcement existed after 1909, but they did not always translate to improved results in intelligence gathering, arrests, and convictions. At any point in the process, the opinions and actions of various agents, customs, immigration officers, and local and state authorities could affect the ultimate outcome of the prosecution of an alleged violation. The aforementioned case of DA John Valls is instructive. His support of Madero against Bernardo Reyes in 1911 had, in part, to do with the fact that the opposition to Madero in South Texas that supported Reyes consisted of two of Valls's most bitter political enemies, Gov. Oscar B. Colquitt and Amador Sánchez, the sheriff of Webb County.[9] Valls's approach to dealing with the reyista conspirators and his actions against them were affected by his own perception of the rebels and their associations with his enemies.

On the federal level, the attitude of the Department of State would change as often as regimes changed in Mexico throughout the revolution. The US government's position with regard to arms shipments to Mexican rebels shifted when the State Department came to understand that Madero was not the radical anarchist that the floresmagonistas were considered to be but was rather moderate in his revolutionary thinking. The US State Department noted that the arms trading taking place among the maderistas could not be considered constitutive of neutrality law violations because it was commercial in nature and thus legal.[10]

It is clear that the stigma of anarchism hindered floresmagonista activities in the United States while maderista arms shipments were allowed to take place unimpeded by US authorities. US federal policy bent the rules on neutrality when it suited the ends of the administration in power. When anarchists challenged the porfirian regime, the policing and judicial machinery in the United States was used to neutralize them. When the moderate revolutionary, Madero, challenged don Porfirio, Secretary of State Philander C. Knox redefined the parameters of neutrality to excuse arms purchases and shipments to Mexico. When later the reyistas challenged the legitimacy of the Madero government, Bureau of Investigation agents quickly infiltrated the conspirators' ranks in San Antonio and prevented a counterrevolution.[11] Again in 1915, under Woodrow Wilson, government agents cracked down on the enemies of Carranza in the United States—huertistas, orozquistas, and others—because the Wilson administration favored the constitutionalist faction.

While scholars have quite rightly noted that the attitude of the US State Department had some bearing upon the success or failure of revolutionary movements in Mexico, the implementation of federal policy on the local level also affected how the enemies of the Mexican government organized their activities in the United States. For example, while the US government was interested in protecting the Calles administration, it was beset with a number of problems that complicated Washington's support for the regime. The religious conflict and the level of polarization it caused, in the realms of both federal policy and public opinion, made support for the Calles administration an unpopular proposition. Moreover, their own political allegiances, notions of racial superiority, and moral proclivities affected and complicated state and local officials' treatment of border vice. These local actors often contradicted federal policy with regard to the Calles administration. Agents of the Bureau of Investigation certainly made arrests and successfully tried individuals and groups when the evidence was sufficient. Collecting that evidence, however, was often problematic when exiles were operating with official support on the state and local levels.

Just as in the early days of the revolution, the enemies of First Chief Venustiano Carranza continued to plot and scheme in the United States and received, much as they had in the past, financial assistance from powerful people in the country—political officials, capitalists, and religious leaders. The ability of Gen. Francisco "Pancho" Villa, for example, to obtain funding from willing financial backers, and later by extortion, all along the border was legendary. Moreover, the forces opposing Carranza, both in Mexico and in the United States, were quite powerful, Villa not the least among them. Nevertheless, by 1914, Carranza had been able to take full control of consular offices in the United States and began assembling the Mexican Secret Service that would most closely resemble the Departamento Confidencial of the 1920s.[12] The process of professionalization and reorganization of the Mexican security services started under Carranza. The Mexican Secret Service was not a temporary measure designed simply to defend Carranza's regime solely in the moment; rather, it served as a relatively well-designed institution meant to serve future regimes. Carranza actively sought to improve and professionalize the service in the short tenure of the constitutionalist government. What was established as the Servicio Confidencial in 1918 became the Confidential Department, officially, in 1924. It is important to note, however, that the department and intelligence gathering in general would still not reach a high point of professionalization until the mid-twentieth century.[13] After the rebellion of Agua Prieta, which brought a victorious Álvaro Obregón to the presidency, the new head of state relieved many of the old carrancista agents and replaced them with loyal operatives intended to perform similar duties to those of their predecessors.[14]

## THE CONFIDENTIAL DEPARTMENT: PROFESSIONALIZATION, THEORY, AND PRAXIS

It was apparent that the structure that had supported the work of agents in Carranza's Secret Service was not sufficient to deal with the new external threats faced by the Calles government. Training and professionalization of new and old agents was the subject of heated debates within the leadership of the Confidential Department in its early stages of reorganization. In March 1925, the highest-ranking agents in the Confidential Department hosted a series of discussions regarding the proper training of new recruits. Prominent in these discussions was Agent Francisco Delgado, who by May of that year would replace Col. Martín Barcenas as the head of the department. Delgado came from a well-to-do Jalisciense family, was well educated, and prior to the revolution, was a lawyer in Guadalajara. His approach to intelligence gathering relied heavily on a firm understanding of how politics were defined and understood, and he drew heavily from the Enlightenment political thinkers for his own understanding of politics.[15] The problem with Mexico, in Delgado's estimation, was that the political landscape was understood as a battlefield on which generals and other powerful and ambitious men could potentially make their fortunes. Delgado was very much a political idealist, but when it came to understanding the postrevolutionary situation, he was a realist. "Unfortunately," Delgado posited, "we understand politics as a rebellion of parties, the divergence of opinions, the clash of opposing interests . . . and ambition to power."[16]

Delgado understood that it was the responsibility of governments to defend the rights of its citizenry and that the only way to maintain harmony between governments and the governed was to respect that responsibility. It followed that the only way to achieve this goal was to generate unity among distinct political parties and avoid the major conflicts that had, in the past, led to civil wars. In many ways, Delgado was a perfect spokesperson for callista state centralization. If the nation's rulers maintained harmony among them and managed to project that unity onto the people, it could "be said that their political situation [was] good."[17] On the other hand, of course, if a government disregarded its responsibility to the governed, order might dissolve into chaos, and rebellions could crop up. Such maladies could invite foreign intervention. For Delgado, it was absolutely necessary that agents employed by the Confidential Department be well versed in government matters, as well as the roots of the political conflicts they were charged with investigating, in order to keep them loyal to the ideal of the Mexican state as the ultimate arbiter of political conflict.

In addition to political theory, new recruits to the department received very practical training. Agent Gaspar Trouselle placed this practical knowledge on high because, as he put it, there were no universities that could teach the art of covert investigations, and there were no schools to instruct agents in the art of governance that Delgado had discussed. Trouselle pointed to major deficiencies in the Confidential Department's structure, such as the lack of a systematized method of gathering and processing intelligence as well as the lack of instructional materials upon which to found a common investigative methodology. The state of the Mexican intelligence service was such that the Confidential Department had no other recourse but to "sharpen our rickety intelligence, seeking the means to become artists" in political intrigue.[18] In addition to a working understanding of politics, there was also certain behavior expected of a confidential agent that went along with the practical experience Trouselle discussed. According to Agent Carlos Flores, the qualities that a confidential agent should possess were "absolute discretion, ample social relations, solid instruction on diverse materials, [and] complete loyalty to the government."[19] In short, a confidential agent was someone who possessed the complete trust of the government "and to whom a delicate mission could be entrusted with confidence that he will know how to carry it out."[20] He was to possess a certain sophistication; should be well aware of the history and geography of Mexico, electoral laws, and the 1917 Constitution; and was expected to pay attention to all of the memos emanating from the Ministry of the Interior as well as the general state of the country. The confidential agent should be aware of revolutionary tendencies by region in Mexico—which state legislatures had implemented reforms, which had not, who presented obstacles to reform, what regions were particularly dangerous, and what legal means existed to remove said obstacles. Not surprisingly, Flores pointed out that the most fundamental obligation of the agent was discretion and secrecy. It was considered disgraceful and dangerous for an agent to present his identification for personal gain or to brag about his job. The badge was only to be used as identification to obtain police assistance or the help of other functionaries—"never to inspire fear, nor to open a line of credit in a store, nor to obtain any kind of credit without proper payment."[21] If we are to take these as general guidelines for agent recruitment, it is safe to assume that potential recruits were not plucked from the streets at random. The department would be very careful in the selection process. The agents they chose would have to be urbane; at least moderately educated or capable of learning about Mexican politics, history, geography, and general social conditions; and preferably possessing of a certain revolutionary pedigree (obregonista or callista).

The fact that these issues were points of such extensive discussion reinforces the notion that the intelligence services in Mexico were woefully inadequate to meet the challenge presented by the exiles already at work in the United States. It also evidenced the necessity for a more professionalized intelligence-gathering service than had existed prior to the mid-1920s. The agents present in these discussions realized that without the proper training—in some cases, training that even they had not formally received—the Confidential Department's capacity to investigate the threats that faced the Mexican government would continue to be hindered by shoddy investigative techniques. Without proper professionalization, the Confidential Department could expect apathetic or, worse, personally ambitious undercover agents with questionable loyalties and a profound lack of understanding regarding the motivations and political antecedents of the very groups that they were charged with investigating. Moreover, the ideas presented in these discussions suggest that the goals for the new Confidential Department were well defined by a leadership that would foster a brand of agent in its own image. Francisco Delgado had proven his mettle as a junior-ranked agent prior to the de la Huerta Rebellion and as a senior officer throughout the period directly following the rebellion, in which confidential agents spent most of their time carrying out investigations on political dissidents and supporters of various dissenting factions in Mexico. He was known to have had a very good working relationship with all of his subordinates and approached his charge in the Confidential Department with a singular confidence and determination. As the head of that department from May 1925 until 1930, he consistently fought for increased amounts of administrative funding from the Ministry of the Interior and to ensure that his agents in the field were well paid, especially when it came to travel compensation.

In the early 1920s, there was little centralization in the gathering or processing of intelligence, and few methods by which information received from agents in the field could be sorted and verified. The Confidential Department, in the years directly following the de la Huerta Rebellion, was charged with the purpose of domestic intelligence gathering. This meant that confidential agents spent much of their time maintaining surveillance on congressmen and senators with questionable allegiance to the government. There were only fifteen agents in 1925, and they were all engaged in domestic intelligence gathering operations.[22] Their reports focused primarily on the activities of potential opposition candidates, potential sedition, weapons and ammunition caches, and activities of foreign dignitaries and whether said activities were denigrating to the Mexican government. The agents involved in these investigations were charged with the task as a direct result of the political conflicts that gave rise to the de la Huerta Rebellion. It is reasonable to argue that all these investigations were ordered by the Ministry of the Interior as a means to prevent subsequent rebellions that might also have been led by disgruntled political or military figures.

It was the failure of the de la Huerta Rebellion that necessitated the extension of the Confidential Department beyond the border and into the United States. Between 1920 and 1925, the Ministry of the Interior and the Confidential Department gave little thought to exiles in the United States until many of the delahuertistas were forced to flee across the border. Prior to the de la Huerta Rebellion, the only potential rivals to the reins of power residing in the United States were the felicistas and a smattering of disgruntled carrancistas. The felicistas were never considered a viable threat until after 1926, and only in association with the Catholic exile contingent. The carrancistas were so few in number as to constitute a minimal challenge to Obregón. The only constitutionalist revolutionary of note left in exile and who still had some military ties in Mexico was ex-general Candido Aguilar, and he was never considered a threat, as even he stayed clear of the felicistas and delahuertistas.[23] It is important to note that there were already a limited number of confidential agents stationed along the border before the de la Huerta Rebellion. In 1924, there was a flourishing of counterrevolutionary activities and a corresponding necessity to put more agents on the border and, a year later, to extend them into the United States. The Mexican state was expanding its intelligence services, both inside and outside Mexico, but it still seemed quite weak, overextended, and paranoid.

Delgado, in December of 1925, now at the helm of the department, identified the border as the greatest source of support for rebellious exiles. "Emboldened by the mood of opposition . . . in the United States to the immigration and petroleum laws," Delgado noted, "the enemies of the Mexican government that have taken refuge there have deployed activities . . . to bring to our country a new rebellion."[24] The individuals cited as the main organizers of this effort were Jorge Prieto Laurens and Francisco Coss, delahuertistas who had recently arrived in exile. Delgado proposed an extension of the Confidential Department to the border and beyond—a "special service . . . that would be established on the border, in connection with Immigration Inspectors [and] Military Chiefs, only for the period in which this state of affairs endures."[25] He argued for the establishment of a core of twenty agents, well paid and provided for, who would specialize in covert operations and infiltrations of exile groups. Immigration inspectors' and consular representatives' cover could be too easily compromised. The agents chosen for this task were all to be located on the Mexican side of the border initially, with the greatest concentrations in Tamaulipas, Chihuahua, and Coahuila.[26] Delgado received authorization for only nine of the proposed twenty agents to be paid at the rate of $10 pesos per day. Each agent received one pistol valued at $70 pesos each, and the Ministry of the Interior estimated the operating expense for 1926, the first year of operations, at $3,330 pesos, a mere $1,665 US in the currency of the day.[27]

## BUREAUCRATIC AND ADMINISTRATIVE MALADIES

Despite the urgent need for the reinforcement of the Confidential Department's surveillance apparatus across the border, there were interdepartmental conflicts over the use of government funds to invest in the work of agents in the field. On 3 February 1926, just a few days after Delgado received notice that his confidential border operation had been approved, the Department of the

Treasury suspended his office's access to the paymaster's office. The record does not provide a reason for the suspension, but funds from the treasury had been used routinely to pay travel and housing expenses for confidential agents in the field operating in Mexico. As Delgado explained to his superiors in the Ministry of the Interior, it had been the Confidential Department's policy to dip into these funds occasionally to pay travel expenses for agents since December of the previous year.[28] As a result of the suspension, Delgado's agents had been left in the field with no money to pay their expenses, and as such, they might be forced to open up lines of credit with those from whom they had procured housing or services, not only leaving them in precarious positions, but violating one of the key mandates regarding confidential agent comportment in the field—namely, to avoid using their position to open credit or demand services. He urged the chief clerk of the Interior to develop procedures for procuring these funds in light of the financial difficulties that some agents were experiencing. While Delgado won the immediate administrative battle, his office would be under similar scrutiny for the remainder of the decade, and he would be forced to justify all expenditures made by his agents in the field.

The general suspension of funds for agents' travel expenses in this case may have been ill advised, but in other situations, superiors had more reasonable justifications for docking individual agents' pay. In some cases, agents operating in the United States simply did not perform their duties according to the standards set forth by the Confidential Department or appeared to be regularly shirking their duties. In a memo from the secretary of the Interior to Francisco Delgado, it was explained that a number of confidential agents had been neglecting their duties, claiming temporary illness. The consulate, in these cases, dispatched a medical professional to the agents' places of residence, only to find them absent. The agents claimed that they had gone out to seek medical attention for themselves and that was why they had not been home when the doctor called. The argument for not paying these agents was simple: because they had not been on the job, the Treasury Department would not authorize payment for work not done. If, in the future, the report of the doctor did not match what the employee had previously stated, "said absence will be considered unjustified," and the equivalent of one day's wages would be deducted from the agent's pay.[29] Aside from these legitimate complaints of misconduct among confidential agents, Delgado certainly had well-founded notions of what constituted proper treatment of his agents. Inadequate pay could lead to shoddy investigative techniques and could leave agents open to bribery and other forms of graft in the field. These sorts of issues could severely compromise the effectiveness of intelligence gathering, putting the Mexican government at risk. Delgado was not alone in his concerns. Agent Trouselle warned against the very same scenario in pointing out that the enemy had already taken advantage of the most economically vulnerable segments of the immigrant community in the United States. Trouselle's argument was that the agents in the field should be well paid, lest they fall to the aforementioned temptations.

By the end of 1926, the pecuniary condition of confidential agents had not improved. Agent Trouselle lamented that the enemies of the Mexican government were utilizing the poorest sectors of society, in both Mexico and the United States, to move arms and ammunition into Mexico. Counterrevolutionary exiles recruited the economically vulnerable and gave them a little bit of money—in some cases, a semisteady pay—and for this reason, the smuggling of contraband materials was nearly impossible to combat. This complaint was common among confidential agents, but Trouselle made a more potent argument, tying it to the issue of proper payment of agents in the field.

For Trouselle, the problem was not that the exiles in the United States presented any real threat. Rather, he pointed out that the practice of recruiting the poorest of the poor among the immigrant community in the United States for arms smuggling activities ultimately put the lives of Mexican nationals in danger, impeded the reconstruction of the Mexican state, and could potentially disrupt international relations should the situation be allowed to get out of hand. The problem was that the arms, after crossing the border, were placed in the hands of "bandits, that at the least, can create for the government problems of moral order, economic and international problems, such as an increase in government expenditures and a decrease in sources of revenue, [and] to provoke disputes with other countries due to the destruction to foreign property." He argued that these "bandits" had the capacity to damage business relations, resulting in capital flight and "leaving [Mexico] with only hunger and misery for [its] citizens and desperation in their homes."[30] It was necessary, according to Trouselle, to avoid this national failure, to augment the existing forces of agents with undercover operatives to infiltrate exile groups and report on their activities. However, in order to carry out these undercover operations with efficiency, the pay that the agents earned would have to be much higher to guarantee that they could travel to any destination without worrying about the cost. Low rates of pay had been a constant point of contention for confidential agents, and Trouselle drove the point home: in order to protect the Mexican government from its enemies, that same government must pay its agents adequately. The pay that was provided for agents to protect the Mexican government from its enemies was "not even sufficient for [the agent's] own maintenance and much less now that Mexican silver is valued here at $0.35 in gold and everyday life is valued on the basis of dollars, it is materially impossible to survive, much less divert any of it to make emergency expenditures that present themselves at every turn and that are necessary to be able to discover the maneuvers of the enemy."[31] Agents simply could not be expected to keep up with the enemies of the nation, a task that required a substantial amount of travel and hotel stays, on the pay established by the Ministry of the Interior.

Although there are no hints in the documentary record regarding wage increases or changes in agents' pay scales throughout the decade, general complaints in connection to problems with insufficient pay for field agents seem to decline after 1926. This suggests that Delgado was able to convince the Ministry of the Interior either that the heightened threat posed by the influx of Cristeros to border cities was great enough to warrant a higher expense allowance for his agents or that wages, paid in pesos or dollars, rose to a rate commensurate with duties performed. What is clear is that the ranking agents in the department were convinced that reluctance to pay them a sustainable wage compromised not only their capacity to gather quality intelligence but possibly their ultimate loyalties to the Mexican government.

## INTERAGENCY AND JURISDICTIONAL DISPUTES

In addition to interdepartmental and administrative conflicts over pay and the exact role that agents were to play at their border posts, the agents of the Mexican government also clashed with US federal and local law enforcement officials. Consular officials and secret agents often expected a more proactive stance from US law enforcement agents than the bounds of US law would allow. In particular, consuls operating in regions of high counterrevolutionary exile activity, such as Tucson, Laredo, El Paso, and San Antonio, often complained that they could not always count on the cooperation of agents of the Department of Justice, even in the face of what they considered incontrovertible proof of their subjects' culpability in violations of the US neutrality laws. These alleged violations often resulted from the suspect's attendance at a meeting that had been called by high-profile political exiles or military leaders. In many cases, the intelligence that consuls presented to Bureau of Investigation agents had come to them third hand—from confidential agents who had themselves received the information from informants of questionable integrity. It was the expectation of these consular officials and, at times, confidential agents, that the proof they had provided to the bureau was sufficient to make an arrest, or at least to divert manpower toward surveillance of a particular individual or group of individuals.

In response to a State Department inquiry into allegations that bureau agents were ignoring obvious signs of neutrality law violations, special agent in charge at the San Antonio bureau office, Gus T. Jones, complained that very few of such "violations" were worth the effort to attempt verification. Jones was less than impressed by constant reports of revolutionary activities, specifically in the areas around Brownsville and Laredo. South Texas was the zone of operations for the delahuertista general Cesar López de Lara. The Confidential Department's most trusted and capable agent in San Antonio,

Fernando de la Garza, was convinced that López de Lara's crew was hiding large stashes of weapons just across the border in Nuevo Laredo, Tamaulipas. Jones assumed that de la Garza and other confidential agents simply lacked the capacity to carry on proper intelligence-gathering operations, generally lacked key evidence, or were following leads provided by consular agents who had less intelligence experience than the same confidential agents. For Jones, the Mexican consular officials at Brownsville and Laredo were "unduly alarmed based on exaggerated reports they receive daily from Secret Service Agents of the Mexican Government who are operating on this side of the border and, who, in order to stay on the payroll, must always have something to report."[32]

While there had been an increase in the population of Mexican dissidents in the San Antonio district, as many had been recently deported from Mexico by the Calles government, Jones had no evidence that they were involved in activities that would constitute violations of neutrality laws. On the other hand, there were middling revolutionaries and smugglers who had family just on the Mexican side of the border in Tamaulipas who would shelter them. Jones pointed out the absurdity of his position on the border by claiming that at the first chance that these revolutionaries had to announce their revolution, agents on the Mexican side of the border transferred the information to Mexico City, then to the consuls on the border, and eventually to the State Department in the form of complaints to the effect that the US authorities were lax in their duties or willfully allowing revolutionary groups free access to the border for the purposes of overthrowing the Mexican government. The fact that the Mexican authorities were jumping at even the slightest provocation from their own exiles was not the concern of the bureau, according to Jones. His seeming apathy was the direct result of the constant barrage of claims of seditious activities of Mexican exiles accompanied by very little of the sort of evidence that the bureau needed to make arrests. Moreover, Jones never attributed a desire for regime change to the various "revolutionists" with whom he came into contact in South Texas. Rebel groups came and went, and while they would inevitably get across the border, taking a certain amount of arms with them, they were incredibly difficult to prosecute, and their primary motivation could always be reduced to personal gain. "While of course they are revolutionists in the sense that they would line up with most any leader who happened to hoist the revolutionary flag in any section of Mexico," Jones clarified, "the primary purpose in their crossing is for personal gain and not that they hope to overthrow the established government."[33]

Clearly, Jones misjudged, or perhaps deliberately misinterpreted, the motivations of many exiles who actually *did* hope for the end of the Calles regime and who worked toward that end, but his statements speak to a broader frustration stemming from the impossible nature of the international boundary. The issue of manpower on the border also hindered Jones's efforts to follow up on all the reports of alleged threats coming from Mexican officials. According to Jones, there were hundreds of miles along the border in his district where smugglers and rebels could cross practically undetected. "As you know," Jones asserted, "we do not in any way undertake to patrol the 500 miles of border in this district with the seven investigators assigned to this office." Bureau agents had to rely on the cooperation of customs officers and local law enforcement agents to intercept potential revolutionary bands before they crossed the border.[34] Jones went on to point out that it was incredibly easy to pass contraband materials into Mexico because the checks on crates crossing the border involved merely checking the manifest, not matching the manifest with the contents. According to Jones, there simply were not enough agents available to check every container.[35]

No matter the urgency that Mexican consular officials attached to rebel activities, bureau agents had to be very selective about what they chose to investigate. Moreover, the complaints of consular officials were often unfounded or founded on the flimsiest of evidence. Time and time again, bureau agents insisted on more concrete proof in order to make an arrest. Anything less would have constituted a waste of time. In one case, the Mexican consul general in San Antonio, Alejandro P. Carrillo, informed Jones that there was a plan afoot among rebels to make a crossing into Mexico between Hidalgo and Zapata, Texas, an area, according to Jones, separated by approximately 125 miles. However, Carrillo neglected to tell Jones at what point between Hidalgo and Zapata these rebels might have been located. Jones continued, "He [Carrillo] then stated to me that he thought that I should use my force of Agents to round up these alleged revolutionists and to tell them 'if they did not quit holding meetings and plotting against and threatening the established government, I would place them all in jail.' I advised the Consul General that we would collect and submit to the United States Attorney all evidence possible concerning any violations of the Neutrality law for such action as he [the attorney general] deemed appropriate."[36]

Consular officials and confidential agents, in their turn, complained to their superiors in the Ministry of the Interior that US officials were not providing them the level of support they needed to carry out their charges in the United States. In many cases, local law enforcement—sheriffs, deputies, and judges—in border districts were accused of outright collusion with exile rebel groups, especially when it came to the Catholic contingent in exile. In one case, Consul A. P. Carrillo reported that a seditious meeting had been held at the local lodge of the Knights of Columbus in San Antonio and that in attendance were Octavio Hinojosa and Modesto García Cavazos, known Catholic agitators with felicista inclinations. However, the local authorities could not be alerted to these activities because they were also known to be members of the Knights of Columbus.[37] It was later ascertained that two of the individuals present at the meeting were Lucio Guerra, a deputy sheriff for Roma County, Texas, as well as one Doctor Valdez from Saenz, Texas. According to the report, the local authorities had been overlooking the activities of the good doctor, who had been, for some time, practicing medicine without a license.[38]

In a much later case, Consul Enrique Santibáñez, Carrillo's replacement in the consulate in San Antonio in 1928, had an epic struggle with a Spanish priest, Camilo Torrente, who reserved a public auditorium for the production of a Catholic play titled "Los martires de León" ("The Martyrs of León") in April 1929, just as the Escobar Rebellion was raging across the border in Chihuahua and Sonora. Without reading the script, or having seen the play, Santibáñez assumed that its content was injurious to the Mexican government and, as such, quite erroneously considered the production of the play tantamount to a violation of neutrality laws. The consul took up a protest with the mayor of San Antonio, C. M. Chambers, stating that the play was "an insult to the Constitutional Government of my country; probably you do not know that, but it would be looked upon with much disgust by Mr. Portes Gil, President of Mexico, should this play take place."[39]

As the city's municipal auditorium had been reserved for the play, Santibáñez argued that the mayor had a duty to revoke Torrente's permit. Chambers's secretary promptly replied to the consul, stating unequivocally that city hall could not go around canceling permits held by people against whom the consul held a personal grudge.[40] Of course, the appropriate action for Santibáñez was to write to the Mexican ambassador in Washington and make the argument that the bishop of San Antonio, Arthur J. Drossaerts; Torrente; and Chambers were in league together. "The resistance to cancelling the permit held by the Spanish priest Torrente, to present in the [Municipal] Auditorium, the play titled 'Los Martires de León,'" Santibáñez railed, "is owed to, in my opinion, political agreements."[41] Upon further investigation, Santibáñez found that Torrente had paid $300 to reserve the auditorium, which contradicted his original assumption that the bishop of San Antonio and the mayor were conspiring against his efforts. Further, the play, although inflammatory by the consul's standards, made no reference to any specific presidential administration in Mexico and was, in the end, no matter of concern for the US authorities.[42] While Santibáñez eventually dropped the issue, these cases illustrate that the agents of the Mexican state stationed in the United States did not always enjoy a perfect working relationship with local officials in their districts. If consuls and confidential agents could, with any regularity, count on support from US federal agents, they often ran up against subterfuge, if not outright collusion, among local officials and Mexican exiles. Some members of the exile cohort had prior experience in the espionage business. Some of them, like Andrés García, gained their experience through their work under the previous porfirista, huertista, and carrancista regimes.

## ESPIONAGE AND COUNTERESPIONAGE: SPY VERSUS SPY

Andrés García served as Carranza's consular official in El Paso from 1914 until 1920. He placed his stamp on any number of espionage operations and was active well before the creation of Carranza's Secret Service.[43] The list of Consul García's accomplishments during his tenure was quite impressive. He took up his duties as consul in El Paso on 16 November 1914 and succeeded in building a propaganda and intelligence network, spending large sums of money to buy the loyalty of as many Spanish-language presses as he could. He also built an intelligence-gathering network that included consular employees, undercover operatives, and agents in both the United States and Mexico. The undercover contacts that García used in his intelligence-gathering networks were informal, consisting of average civilians in the hospitality industry such as hotel clerks, bartenders, and in many cases, prostitutes.[44]

When the Carranza government fell to the obregonistas at the conclusion of the rebellion of Agua Prieta in 1920, Obregón purged many of the carrancista consuls, replacing them with agents he considered trustworthy. García was one who was replaced. Consul García had acquired all the intelligence sources that he needed to do the work of any confidential agent tasked with exile surveillance in the United States in the 1920s during his tenure as Mexican consul in El Paso under Carranza. His command of the techniques of espionage and the contacts he had fostered made him an excellent practitioner of counterespionage operations in the service of the delahuertistas.[45] One of the more difficult tasks for the researcher working on cross-border espionage is actually finding the agents of counterespionage in the documents. Men like Andrés García made sure that their work was anonymous. Thus scholars seeking to understand spy networks must look for spies where they are less than obvious or in the frustrations and failings of their pursuers.

In many cases, the work of enemy agents in the United States consisted of procuring information about Confidential Department and bureau surveillance operations and sounding the alarm when appropriate to avoid arrests or preventing the process of intelligence gathering regarding seditious meetings altogether. A joint operation to uncover a significant stash of arms and ammunition along the border between Brownsville and Port Isabel was thwarted owing to leaked information that alerted a group of conspirators, headed by Gen. César López de Lara, that they were being watched. Agent de la Garza had made sure that the operation would be kept absolutely secret. This was to make sure, in the case that arrests were made, that "the scandal would not be repeated when Prieto Laurens and other rebels made the case . . . that I had bribed the American officials, etc., etc."[46]

This reference was to the July 1925 arrest and subsequent deportation of Abelardo Hinojosa. Hinojosa had been taken into custody by bureau agents and, while appealing his arrest, had been unceremoniously deported with the help of the immigration inspector, Capt. William M. Hanson. Prieto Laurens and others within the delahuertista circle started a letter-writing campaign that grabbed the attention of several congressmen in Washington. In the present operation, de la Garza had left little room for similar errors; secrecy was of utmost importance. Nevertheless, when de la Garza arrived at Punta Isabel, the individuals who were expected to host the seditious meeting as well as the arms and ammunition that he was looking for had disappeared. While de la Garza apparently never laid blame or speculated as to how his intelligence might have been leaked, the failure of this particular operation, which de la Garza took every precaution to conceal, suggests that the enemies of the Mexican government in exile were, in some cases, several steps ahead of their pursuers in the espionage game.

The Catholic contingent in exile also utilized their own spy networks to procure information about the activities of the Confidential Department in the United States. Just six days following the failure of the operation in Brownsville, de la Garza noted that the Catholic clergy in the United States had "a well organized secret information service that is supplied by individuals in the service of our government in various Ministries and Departments, especially by women who work in various offices, who, perhaps some, innocently, are taken advantage of by ill-intentioned experts to acquire . . . information that is then exploited by the enemy."[47] In San Antonio, de la Garza reported that the name of a Mexican government employee, one señorita Berta Ruíz, an employee in the Ministry of Education, had been used for the purpose of intelligence gathering by "a woman by the name of Perches to acquire information for the clergy."[48] The report referenced Señora Luz Franco de Perches, who served as the Catholics' and the felicistas' most important intelligence broker in El Paso. Carolina Ruíz was also identified in the report as Berta's sister, who was employed in the Department of Information within the Ministry of the Interior—another leak in the intelligence network. De la Garza's informants could not say with any certainty whether the intelligence provided by these women was provided with intent or procured via clever deception. However, evidence suggested that they had sheltered the occasional priest in exile.[49] Neither the nature of the information nor the method by which it was obtained is specified in de la Garza's report, but judging from the tone of the report, de la Garza was well aware of the capacities of the enemy element in exile for counterespionage operations. This was not the first instance of a major intelligence leak that would be of benefit to seditious exile elements, and de la Garza rightly feared that it would not be the last.

## CONCLUSION

Confidential agents working on the border engaged in a very dangerous and complicated game. Although the methods of intelligence gathering and the ways in which consular agents operated in the United States changed in the years between the fall of don Porfirio and the advent of the Calles administration, the work of espionage and counterespionage remained much the same. The various administrations that rose and fell between 1911 and 1929 utilized secret intelligence-gathering organizations to protect them from their enemies in exile. However, the Ministry of the Interior and the Confidential Department realized the need for professionalization in their ranks if they were to effectively combat the multitude of threats that took shape in the years immediately following the de la Huerta Rebellion and, poised along the border and supported by various financial and moral backers in the United States, threatened to destabilize the revolutionary state under the command of Calles and later Pres. Emilio Portes Gil.

Professionalization was, however, only one of the obstacles facing Francisco Delgado and the Confidential Department. Agents in the field were subject to internal administrative conflicts over proper payment as well as a level of unnecessary oversight, in their estimation, from the departments upon which they depended for their paychecks. They also functioned in a political and social landscape that was often unwelcoming and, at times, quite threatening as a result of the clash of federal interests with local political alliances along the border. Local law enforcement agencies in the United States could be supportive of confidential agents' labors or, at the most inopportune moments, could be simply obstructive when it came to their treatment of the agents of the Calles government. Combined with the fact that consular officials and confidential agents often worked at cross purposes with their US counterparts along the border and, in many cases, expected more from the US justice system than could be allowed, confidential agents were frequently frustrated in their efforts to provide sufficient evidence to prompt Bureau of Investigation agents to make arrests. Finally, the exile groups that plotted against the Calles regime had their own veteran intelligence officers in their ranks, and they expended much effort producing counterintelligence to throw the agents of the Mexican government off their trail. Some of the individuals had served previous revolutionary governments and had privileged knowledge regarding espionage operations that made them the formidable foes of Mexican consular officials, confidential agents, and US law enforcement alike. While the obstacles to intelligence-gathering operations were myriad and great, the professionalization efforts undertaken by the Confidential Department under the leadership of Francisco Delgado led to the creation of a relatively incorruptible force of secret agents loyal to the Mexican state, not simply the Calles government, and determined to root out all external threats to the stability of that state. While the de la Huerta Rebellion of 1923–24 tested Mexico's internal security services, it was during that conflict that many of the confidential agents who would serve the department in the years following the uprising gained their experience. That experience was put to good use in a concerted effort to secure the border against exile conspiracies—a border that had been, and would remain, beyond the reach of the nation-states that shared it. A combination of the religious conflict raging in Mexico, the military leaders in exile who found themselves on the losing side of the revolution, and the use they made of the border regions forced a reevaluation of state control of the border in the 1920s. However, it would be in exile that don Adolfo and others would prove much more difficult foes to combat. It is to de la Huerta's early years in exile that we turn in the next chapter.

# TWO

# *DELAHUERTISMO* IN EXILE, 1924–1926

Scholars of the de la Huerta Rebellion have asserted that in the chaos of so many revolutionary generals grabbing for power in December 1923, don Adolfo was swept up in events that he had not planned and was powerless to control.[1] As events transpired, violent action became the only option to prevent Calles's victory, and de la Huerta lost control of his supporters—namely, Gen. Guadalupe Sánchez, *jefe militar* for the state of Veracruz—but the support from men of influence in the United States also evaporated.[2] Indeed, de la Huerta's role in the rebellion was little more than that of a figurehead. As a result, de la Huerta has often been seen as a tragic figure—at best a well-intentioned but ultimately flawed political actor, at worst a dupe of the military interests that rebelled in the hopes of seizing power for themselves. When the dust of the rebellion that took his name had settled in Mexico, however, and don Adolfo found himself in a new political environment in the United States, he took his mission to topple the Calles regime as a personal crusade. He cultivated every political and business connection he could find. Most of these relationships remained intact from his tenure as the treasury secretary in Obregón's cabinet. He relied upon these political connections and on business and banking relations, and he boasted an impressive network of agents and operatives that spanned the whole of the United States, Cuba, and portions of Central America. De la Huerta also utilized the relationship with the Yaquis that he fostered during the period of his governorship in his home state of Sonora to take strategic advantage of the Yaqui Uprising of 1926–27.

Although de la Huerta utilized all the contacts in the United States that he had fostered through his connections to the Obregón government, he was unable to realize his political goals for the destabilization of the Calles regime from exile. The reasons for his failure are myriad; however, it was the coming high tide of Catholic political activism from the exile cohort that was to be his movement's ultimate demise. While de la Huerta was a political actor more in control of his movement than he had been during the rebellion that took his name as rallying cry, he could not remove the stain of revolutionary anticlericalism that distanced him from the interests of the Catholic contingent in exile, nor did he necessarily deign to do so. While he and his agents worked tirelessly to raise funds and seek out new sources for armament, the attention of newly arrived exiles from the religious conflict just under way in Mexico went to military leaders exiled to the United States in earlier periods, both before and after the Revolution.

## THE DE LA HUERTA REBELLION

De la Huerta had begun to fall from Obregón's favor very early on in the period following the rebellion of Agua Prieta of 1920, the military rebellion that ousted First Chief Venustiano Carranza and elevated General Obregón to power. One of his first acts as the provisional president in 1920 was to extend a spate of official pardons, most significantly to Gen. Francisco "Pancho" Villa, who on more than one occasion had ordered General Obregón's execution. De la Huerta's political approach was conciliatory and certainly much needed in a nation still suffering from the effects of more than a decade of fratricidal warfare. He undertook vital negotiations with the Yaqui Indians of northern Sonora, who had just borne the brunt of the revolutionary military's attempts to cripple them altogether under the command of General Calles. When de la Huerta's term was over and Obregón became president, he appointed de la Huerta as the secretary of hacienda (treasury). De la Huerta set about the task of settling Mexico's foreign debt with the International Banker's Committee and its head, Thomas Lamont, a prerequisite for US diplomatic recognition.

De la Huerta chafed under Obregón's reproach for his initial failure to gain US recognition through his negotiations with Lamont. He was further enraged by Obregón's acceptance of the Bucareli Accords of August 1923, in which the president agreed not to apply Article 27 of the constitution to US companies holding land in Mexico in exchange for US diplomatic recognition.[3] Obregón's concession was more generous than what de la Huerta had negotiated with Lamont, yet Obregón had reprimanded him for a lack of decisiveness in his own negotiations. Finally, when a contested gubernatorial election in the state of San Luis Potosí threatened social unrest, Obregón intervened, establishing a provisional government in the state. De la Huerta saw this action as an unwarranted federal intervention, and on 26 September 1923, he resigned from his post as the secretary of hacienda.[4]

When the Partido Nacional Coporatista (PNC) offered de la Huerta the opportunity to run for the presidency under their nomination, he gladly accepted. De la Huerta's candidacy provided military leaders in opposition to Calles an opportunity to intervene in national politics. However, de la Huerta realized quite quickly that he could not control the military forces that had been conjured by the moment of political instability presented by the delahuertista electoral challenge to Obregón's favorite, Calles. De la Huerta's supporters quickly began to solicit support from those members of the military who could not be counted among the callista ranks. Initially, de la Huerta renounced the possibility of armed action against Obregón. When an arrest warrant was issued for him and his key political associates, de la Huerta boarded a train for the port of Veracruz, where Gen. Guadalupe Sánchez ensured his personal safety. De la Huerta still opposed military action while those around him advocated rebellion. De la Huerta was reluctant, and he cautioned the general that Obregón counted a majority of the national military in his fold, that Sánchez could not count on the loyalty of his subordinates, and that the full weight of the military would be brought down on the rebels. As de la Huerta recounted in his memoir, someone present in the planning meeting said, "Don't be afraid, Sr. De la Huerta." He responded, "Let's go ahead," adding, "It is a bad step that is being taken because it is premature."[5] The rebellion proceeded immediately and was crushed in less than a year. De la Huerta lost control of the military rebellion and was forced into exile in the wake of its failure.

In May 1924, just two months after the end of the de la Huerta Rebellion in the northern regions of Mexico, don Adolfo was cultivating old relationships with corporations in both the United States and Great Britain, specifically the Pearson interests—the conglomeration of petroleum companies owned by Sir Weetman Pearson. There were, in the United States, personnel of several large oil conglomerates, such as Pearson, Standard Oil, and those owned by Edward Doheny, who believed that should Calles be elected president in 1924, he would make it his personal mission to destroy their power and influence in Mexico and take over their holdings under the provisions set forth in Article 27 of the Constitution of 1917. There were, in fact, any number of conspiracies among the various oil conglomerates in the United States to weaken the Calles administration during this period. There was a constant concern among those major US producers holding property in the oil regions in Mexico that the potential implementation of Article 27 could spell the decline of US oil interests in the country. As Linda B. Hall has noted, those conspiracies most often revolved around the aim of politically severing the oil regions from the rest of Mexico. It had been suggested on the part of the oil companies that in the event that those regions broke away from central government control, the companies would pay their taxes directly to the powers in those regions rather than to the authorities in Mexico City. The Confidential Department, the Ministry of the Interior, and de la Huerta were all aware of these conspiracies, and as Hall notes, "As these taxes amounted to millions of dollars annually, the prize was substantial and might well have provided economic support for a takeover of the entire country."[6]

Pearson believed that Calles had his eye on his "El Aguila" company, and he decided to defend his interests appropriately with a $400 million investment and plans to pay for a rebellion should Calles be elected president.[7] There were rumors that large amounts of arms and ammunition were being purchased and stored in Canadian territory at the behest of groups loosely associated with the Pearson interests for use in a rebellion planned for summer or early fall 1924. Two representatives of these "loosely associated" groups, a Canadian and a Mexican, boasted to a Mr. Vernon J. Rose while on a business trip to Detroit that they were there buying arms and ammunition and storing the caches in Toronto and Montreal. When Rose questioned their ability to get the armament into Mexican national territory, one explained that their network of "friends" along the Gulf Coast was quite large—so much so that they could bring in any sort of war material they wanted.[8] The informant also boasted the arrival of a large quantity of equipment for an army of 200,000 men and the support of "El Aguila," which, as he put it, "will spend 25 million dollars if necessary to overthrow Calles, or he will be killed."[9] According to Rose's informant, all the large oil companies were aware of the plan and the time for negotiating with Obregón and Calles was past, as "Obregon's [*sic*] days were numbered, as well as Calles' . . . and . . . they would have to be eliminated."[10] Further, Rose's informant claimed that the Canadian government was in league with the Pearson interests and that, as a result, a large portion of the arms and ammunition that was purchased was also stored in Canadian territory without hindrance.[11]

While the planned revolution of which Rose spoke never materialized, Adolfo de la Huerta was making sure that there was a steady flow of arms and ammunition going to the rebels still in arms in the southern portions of the republic. Confidential Department reports stated that de la Huerta had been in New York in early October 1924, registered at a local hotel under the alias Francisco Hernández. Intercepted correspondence between Prieto Laurens and de la Huerta revealed that on his next visit to Liverpool, de la Huerta was scheduled to meet with a highly regarded British company to contract a business deal. De la Huerta was also pursuing the finalization of a shipment of war material that he had already purchased in England. This material was to be sent to Tuxpam and then to various destinations in southern Mexico, and they were to be shipped in "El Aguila" oil tankers.[12] Again, on 5 November, de la Huerta was back in New York attempting to get financial support from the British. He was advised by a messenger from Prieto Laurens to get in touch with a Mr. Lyman Chatfield, who had been one of Prieto Laurens's financial contacts and had secured war materials for him previously—most notably, $50,000 worth of arms and ammunition, at the time stored at an undisclosed location in Hamburg.[13]

While de la Huerta was negotiating a deal in New York with the British, the rebel groups in El Paso and San Antonio had been making their plans based solely on de la Huerta's ability to secure funds. By 26 November, those groups had begun to take their places. Immigration Inspector J. A. Moss reported that "rebel groups are concentrating all along the border, particularly in El Paso, Tucson, Douglas, Bisbee, Laredo and Las Cruces."[14] He also reported that there had been rumors of plans that Prieto Laurens was to move an invasion force south through Matamoros and on to Tampico, that de la Huerta was to invade Mexico to the east, and that the delahuertistas had managed to contract six US aviators to fly rebel planes. These plans may seem somewhat fanciful, and there may have been some truth to the rumors that Prieto Laurens was planning to personally lead a revolutionary expedition into the oil regions, but the rumors themselves attributed a sort of influence and power that most Confidential Department agents, as well as Mexican consular officials, believed the delahuertistas and the US oil companies possessed.

It is not altogether clear why this particular movement, which appears in the confidential reports to have been quite large, did not happen. Perhaps de la Huerta's business deal with the British failed. If so, it would not have been the first, nor would it be his last failure to negotiate viable financial arrangements with business interests—businessmen who made their decisions based on the likelihood of the success of rebel movements rather than the passionate rhetoric of the exiles behind them. On at least one occasion, de la Huerta reprimanded his brother, Alfonso, because he had failed to provide an accurate accounting of the names of wealthy and influential individuals in Mexico who had offered their financial support to the cause. As such, don Adolfo lamented that Alfonso had made him look like a fool when meeting with potential financial donors in the United States, as he was unable to offer them these important details. He admonished his brother for clinging to the illusion "that here in New York money is gathered in spades or that

I possess a magic wand for opening bank vaults." He chided, "These men are 'Business Men' who, in order to hand over one peso, need to know the probability of success, everything down to the last detail. . . . You believe that these men are easy to deceive and you're wrong."[15] Perhaps the movement never got off the ground as a result of internal divisions or mistrust among the leadership along the border. That the movement did not materialize should not obscure the point, however, that de la Huerta was making active use of the contacts he had established during his interim presidency and through his position as the secretary of treasury in the Obregón administration as a means to acquire the political capital and military force to topple the Mexican government.

After the failure of the de la Huerta Rebellion, the delahuertistas were the first to set up the political apparatus for coping with their state of exile. While the delahuertistas were certainly cultivating relationships with military men, such as Gen. César López de Lara in South Texas, the Catholic contingent in the United States was almost exclusively looking at exiled members of the Mexican military to lead their planned movements. As early as May 1924, Juán Manuel Alvarez del Castillo, the "Chief of the Department of Foreign Relations of the de-facto Government of Mexico" in Washington, issued a letter to all the delahuertista agents in the United States. He meant to inform these agents of important events as well as to instruct them in their duties. Most importantly, the letter discussed the position of some North American businessmen who were believed to be sympathetic and interested in furthering their cause. Del Castillo asserted that the English, as well as some representatives of the US government were interested in the possibility of supporting de la Huerta. He included a list of points that would result in a favorable opinion among those Americans who were able to offer assistance. Among the main points were that the succeeding government would have the ability to meet the requirements of debt repayment agreed upon when recognition was granted, that potential donors would only deal with a representative of de la Huerta or de la Huerta himself, and that the movement would have to be unified and disciplined with a clear military leader. The main generals mentioned in the letter were Enrique Estrada, Pablo González, and

Guadalupe Sánchez. We can reasonably assume that Edward Doheny and the men at the helm of the American Smelting Company and the American Copper Company were behind the establishment of these conditions, having been the companies to which Alvarez del Castillo made specific reference.[16]

Indeed, as was the case for most if not all the rebel exile groups, the financial issue was of the gravest importance for de la Huerta. One of don Adolfo's chief financial advisors and managers from 1924 onward was Ismael Palafox. Palafox supported the de la Huerta Rebellion in Mexico and, as a result, found himself in exile along with so many of de la Huerta's other supporters in that struggle. The delahuertistas discovered quite quickly that even if they were to elicit donations from among the members of the exile community, even the extremely wealthy, they had little hope of generating enough capital to stage a full rebellion. The answer to the perennial cash-flow problem was to work to secure large loans from private individuals, banks, or corporations. While most of the exiles associated with the major factions may have been bankrupt or certainly functioning on greatly diminished finances, it was understood that they could always count on the well-established and business-owning members of the immigrant milieu for a loan, especially if it promised to pay off with success. As one of de la Huerta's representatives noted, there were many people who had established businesses in the United States "who [had] a greater capacity than [the exiles] to give a regular contribution."[17] Palafox was one of the key individuals involved in securing these loans as well as making decisions about where to store these funds.

Palafox had been with de la Huerta at least from early 1924 on, but he had not always been successful in financial matters. He experienced at least one very serious lapse in judgment when he chose to deposit a large amount of funds in a bank of questionable repute that turned out to be a front for a couple of swindlers, who subsequently absconded with the money. According to delahuertista agent M. C. Almeida, they had been unable to achieve any level of success "due to the inexperience of Lic. Palafox, who had the strange notion of depositing the funds that were trusted to him in a bank of questionable credit," having been influenced, according to Almeida, by "thieves interested in criminal business."[18] It seems that by July of the same year, Palafox was still trying to make a reasonable attempt at managing the financial matters of the delahuertistas despite his recent failings. He explained to de la Huerta that he had not ceased to search for ways to unify funding sources. Palafox suggested several key methods for achieving this goal. First, he offered to set up a line of credit for himself at the American Trust and Savings Bank of Los Angeles in the amount of $2,000, offering his own assets as collateral. Second, he suggested the possibility of taking out a much higher-interest-bearing loan from "the Doctor." This was most likely a reference to Dr. Agustín Escobar, who facilitated communication among the felicistas and also seemed to be in possession of large sums of money. Third, as Palafox put it, he would place himself in the hands of someone he referred to simply as "the Jew," who had not officially committed to offering a loan but intimated that he could not make a deal for less than 8 percent annual interest. Finally, Palafox suggested decreasing the total amount of the loan, $2,000, to a more reasonable amount and extending it at a later date.[19] Whether he felt responsible for his mismanagement of funds earlier in the year or was simply carrying out orders from de la Huerta, Palafox was willing to put up his own money and had the financial knowledge to be aware of the various options available to him to store the funds and to secure loans for the cause. More important, Palafox's financial dealings illustrate that very early on, the delahuertistas were hard at work fundraising. The fact that they were soliciting funds and planning for more permanent sources of income suggests that they had a degree of foresight and caution that the other exile groups in the United States did not yet exhibit.

## THE DELAHUERTISTAS AND THE CATHOLIC EXILE CONTINGENT

It was not one of de la Huerta's primary goals to seek out the support of the Catholic elite in exile. While some of his agents did explore this particular option and de la Huerta made the religious question part of his public statements on broader political and social conditions in Mexico, he did not openly espouse the Cristero cause. With the most vitriolic rhetoric emanating from the Catholic camp, specifically in El Paso and San Antonio, why would de la Huerta neglect to tap into this massive swell of discontent that was supporting the movement in Mexico with whatever pecuniary assistance it could muster? Military leaders in exile were much more willing to entertain the idea of working with the Catholic elite in San Antonio and El Paso than with de la Huerta. In fact, it was with the Catholics that dissident generals like Marcelo Caraveo, Francisco Manzo, and José Gonzalo Escobar had the most contact prior to their rebellion in 1929. These same military leaders seem to have steered clear of the delahuertistas in exile. The point here is that de la Huerta and his agents were interested in working with a different support system in the United States than that of the military leaders like Félix Díaz and others who would rebel later in the decade. Díaz and Estrada and later Manzo, Caraveo, and Escobar were interested in harnessing the wave of discontent that had carried the Cristeros through nearly three bloody years of civil war. Although the delahuertistas were hoping to win over some of the support of men like Manzo and Escobar, ultimately these generals would ally with the Catholics. One reason for this particular choice of alliance is that the major disagreements regarding the reconstruction of the postrevolutionary state coalesced around the religious question. Even if military leaders in exile did not espouse the Catholics' religious views of the nation, they could all agree that the anticlerical articles the Constitution of 1917 and their strict enforcement had led to a precarious situation that threatened to unravel the thread of the nation. For the Catholics, the problem was the anticlericalism inherent in the document. For the military, property owners, men of business, and political elites, the problem was that Article 27 threatened the economic and political footing of the Mexican nation.

While de la Huerta focused on the application of the principles set forth in the 1917 Constitution in those cases that affected foreign investment in Mexico (both British and North American) and the fact that the administration of constitutional anticlerical provisions had led to a devastating war, he never gained the favor of the Catholic contingent in exile. Although the documentary record bears few explicit clues as to why this may have been the case, the most plausible explanation is that de la Huerta's previous association with the anticlericalism of Obregón and Calles might have turned potential Catholic and clerical support away from his message. On the other hand, Félix Díaz, someone never associated with the anticlerical strains within the revolution, may have been a logical choice as an ally, along with porfirian intellectuals such as Ignacio Lozano, the publisher of the San Antonio newspaper *La Prensa* and the Los Angeles periodical *La Opinión*, and Nemesio García Naranjo, a journalist for *La Prensa* and a major Catholic supporter. De la Huerta may have been too closely associated with the secularizing tendencies of the revolution to have been on the Catholic radar. The bishop of San Antonio, Arthur J. Drossaerts, after having been approached by a delahuertista agent in March 1926, was quoted by a confidential agent as having made the statement "frankly and openly that although [the Catholic exiles] were actively working, and would continue to work for the overthrow of the present government [of Mexico], they would never align their forces with de la Huerta, or with any leader who had defended or defends the Constitution of 1917."[20] Drossaerts, of course, was a high-ranking member of the North American clergy, but we may assume that the same sentiments were shared by many among the Catholic elite in exile in the United States.

## THE STRANGE CASE OF DEMETRIO TORRES

De la Huerta was certainly able to use his contacts in the diplomatic realm to great effect when it came to finding sources of funding or greasing the wheels at certain ports of entry, but at times, other delahuertistas were able to utilize the language of exiles and refugees under the temporary jurisdiction of the US government to obtain a desired result. The case of Demetrio Torres (a.k.a. Chaparreras) is instructive, as it illustrates that well-to-do exiles with knowledge of diplomatic relations could do as much to destabilize political relations at relevant locales along the border as a well-placed counterrevolutionary expedition or a significant shipment of arms.

Demetrio Torres came to San Antonio with ex-general Francisco Coss in October 1925 with the aim of purchasing bomb-making materials. Torres was part of a gang that had derailed at least two trains between Mexico and Laredo, Texas, and in one of those bombings, a civilian and a soldier had been killed. The material they were trying to appropriate was intended for a train robbery to take place south of Piedras Negras around the first of November, when Mexican Customs was scheduled to move a large amount of currency from the border to Mexico City.[21] What Torres was looking for was an *explosor eléctrico,* a detonation device that was used in large-scale mining operations and, as such, completely legal to possess. American federal officials were watching Torres's and Coss's movements closely, and the consulate in San Antonio, as well as the Confidential Department, offered assistance.[22] On the afternoon of 29 October 1925, Torres, Coss, and several others were arrested in San Antonio on charges of violations of US immigration law. Coss was later released, as it was ascertained that he had entered the country legally. As Torres was charged with immigration law violations and not neutrality law violations, he was incarcerated in San Antonio and placed under the jurisdiction of the chief immigration inspector there, Capt. W. M. Hanson.[23]

As late as January 1926, Mexican officials were still negotiating the extradition of Torres to Mexico. The judges at the deportation hearing for Torres were reluctant to authorize his deportation, as there had been recent instances in which refugees had been deported and then executed at the hands of Mexican military officials as soon as they entered the country. Such was the case with Abelardo Hinojosa. Hinojosa had been part of a counterrevolutionary expedition in mid-1924 but had evaded capture until a year later. Captain Hanson assisted in the arrest. Hinojosa's deportation and subsequent execution became a rallying point for counterrevolutionary exiles in the United States, specifically the delahuertistas, and they made it a point to share their disgust with the press, members of Congress, and anyone in the Department of State who might listen.[24] In the case of Torres, Captain Hanson went directly to Washington to negotiate the particulars of his extradition. It was decided that the US government would concede to his deportation on one condition: Torres was not be tried and summarily executed by the Mexican authorities, "so as not to give a reason for the press to make a scandal as happened in the case of Abelardo Hinojosa."[25]

Perhaps more damaging for the Mexican authorities whose job it was to stop counterrevolutionary activities was that there were also individuals in political circles in Washington who offered advice and support to de la Huerta and his agents. The two names that appeared consistently in the case of Torres were Richard Cole and a man referred to simply as Captain Hopkins. Although not much is known about the latter, Richard Cole was an important resource in Washington for the delahuertistas, mainly in the realm of arms trafficking. It was their contact with Hopkins and Cole that really concerned Confidential Department agent Fernando de la Garza, as the possibility of influencing policy in Washington was more dangerous a prospect than any rebel attempt at fundraising. It was de la Garza's opinion that these gentlemen were not terribly important in terms of shifting policy in Washington, but they were sufficiently familiar with people in the US government who had daily contact with functionaries in the Departments of Justice, State, and Defense.[26] The delahuertistas not only continued, undaunted in their seditious activities; they made every attempt to use the contacts that they had in Washington to make themselves appear as the victims of persecution from both American and Mexican authorities.

The entire situation provided the delahuertistas with the perfect platform from which to petition the secretary of labor, James J. Davis, in defense of Torres. Jorge Prieto Laurens, Francisco Coss, and several other delahuertista signatories sent a telegram to Davis protesting Torres's deportation proceedings. The language that they used to address him is illustrative of their own ability to manipulate the discourse surrounding exiles, political refugees, and international relations. "We beg you to settle as quickly as possible," entreated the signatories, "the liberty of the Mexican Citizen Demetrio Torres, prisoner in this city [San Antonio] for involuntary violations of Immigration law, as a political refugee to whose honorability we can attest, who crossed the border fleeing the persecutions of his political enemies to save his own life."[27] In the delahuertista narrative of events, an exile known to have been responsible for the deaths of a civilian and a soldier in Mexico and the bombing of no fewer than three trains became guilty of "involuntary" violations of immigration law in the process of "fleeing . . . persecutions" in Mexico. When de la Garza became aware of the petition, he reported that American officials in San Antonio were of the opinion that officials at the Department of Justice and the Department of Labor would never take the petition seriously, as they were aware of the character of Torres and would immediately assume that if Prieto Laurens and his group were vouching for his honor, they must be cut from the same cloth.[28]

Despite Prieto Laurens's protests, they had come too late to save Torres. Captain Hanson and Agent de la Garza had already made plans to expedite Torres's deportation.[29] Hanson presented de la Garza with a plan in which Torres would be retrieved from his cell in San Antonio—ostensibly to make a declaration at the immigration office. Keeping him sequestered, he would then be spirited away in a car and dropped off a few feet into Mexican territory. Then he would be picked up by the relevant Mexican authorities and taken out of Nuevo Laredo, Tamaulipas, without being allowed contact with anyone apart from the members of the personal guard transporting him. The utmost secrecy was to be maintained at all times. These precautions were to be taken to prevent defense lawyers, the press, or anyone interested in Torres's safety from making definitive claims of wrongdoing on behalf of the American or the Mexican governments. The Confidential Department accepted the plan and put it into action quite quickly.[30] By the afternoon of 13 January, Torres had been handed over to the military garrison at Nuevo Laredo.[31]

Three US senators, G. H. Moses, Republican from New Hampshire; Hiram Warren Johnson, Republican from California; and William Henry King, Democrat from Utah, headed up the investigation into the case of Torres. At the investigation hearing, the argument that the officials in San Antonio made in their defense was that they did not know Torres would be charged in connection with his participation in the de la Huerta Rebellion. Senator Moses claimed that there was ample evidence to the contrary and that Hanson and Department of Justice agent Manuel Sorola acted contrary to the decision of the review board that tried the immigration case against Torres. The decision of the review board was that Torres should be deported to Cuba or Canada, and it was noted that the subsecretary of the Department of Labor approved the decision. Senator Moses's claim was that border agents ignored the decision and handed Torres over to the Mexicans knowing that his fate was already decided.[32] The committee also specifically went after Agent Sorola and Captain Hanson, accusing them of working directly with Mexican government officials to turn Torres over to his executioners. Hanson, Senator Moses noted, had personally driven Torres in his own automobile to the border to hand him to the military commander at Nuevo Laredo.[33]

The actions taken by Prieto Laurens and other delahuertistas in the case of Torres give a sense of the sort of damage they could do. They knew that if they made the right arguments about their own status as political refugees and made those arguments relevant in the field of international relations, their claims would be heard and perhaps acted upon. By the time the inquest was over, Captain Hanson was forced to resign his post. Ultimately, he could not withstand the political pressure from Washington, and his position in the Department of Labor had been greatly compromised. Manuel Sorola and his supervising agent, Gus T. Jones, managed to weather the storm, but de la Garza lamented the fact that Hanson, Sorola, and other officials in San Antonio had done such a service to the Mexican government by capturing dangerous individuals like Torres but had been treated so disgracefully by the US government, going so far as to refer to the senators involved in the investigation as "the enemies of Mexico." Meanwhile, the exiles who had been planning sedition in the United States were free to advance their own plans against the Mexican government.[34]

## DE LA HUERTA AND THE YAQUI UPRISING OF 1926

From the porfirian period onward, the restitution of Yaqui lands had always been one of the primary goals of the Yaqui. One of the main issues at stake in the parched desert state of Sonora had been access to water. The Yaqui and the other major sedentary indigenous group in northern Sonora, the Mayo, occupied those regions around the Mayo and Yaqui Rivers. As such, their lands had been prime targets for nonindigenous farmland dating from the seventeenth century, when Jesuit missions moved into the area. By the end of the eighteenth century, the Yaquis managed to hold on to most of their lands. By the time that Porfirio Díaz brought the railroads to northern Sonora in the late nineteenth century, however, the Yaqui ended up, in large part, landless, and many were shipped off to Yucatán as slaves on the henequen plantations.[35] They had rebelled on a number of occasions during the porfiriato and into the revolutionary period whenever prior agreements had been made to restore their lands had not been honored by succeeding regimes. In 1911, Francisco Madero, for example, reached an agreement to restore to the tribe those lands along the north side of the Yaqui River, but as Madero's administration was painfully short-lived and followed by the dictatorship of Gen. Victoriano Huerta, action was never taken.

Following Pancho Villa's 1915 raid on Columbus, New Mexico, and in part as a result of the resurgence of villismo resulting from Gen. John "Blackjack" Pershing's Punitive Expedition, the Yaqui tribes in Sonora rebelled once again. It was Obregón who placed the provisional governor of the state, Plutarco Elías Calles, in charge of the military campaign against the rebellion. Calles took this mission very seriously and aggressively pursued the goal of crushing this particular rebellion, but he also fully intended to cripple the Yaqui capacity to rebel altogether.[36] As governor of Sonora, it was de la Huerta, not Obregón or Calles, who managed to negotiate a peace settlement with the rebellious Yaquis in 1919, putting an end to Calles's military campaign against the tribe.[37] Despite Obregón's and Calles's prior acts of military aggression against the tribes, the Yaquis adhered to the Plan of Agua Prieta, which brought the Sonorans to national political power—in no small part due to the goodwill that de la Huerta had cultivated among the Yaqui.[38] Although President Obregón recognized Madero's previous 1911 agreement in 1921, the legal mechanisms by which land was redistributed in the postrevolutionary period delayed those restitutions indefinitely.[39] While the Yaqui continued to press for the restitution of their lands, President Obregón instead sought to shore up access to water for farmers and ensured water concessions to the Compañía Constructora Richardson to build irrigation works and hydraulic plants.[40]

On 12 September 1926, a group of Yaqui Indians hijacked a train that was carrying then ex-president Obregón from the city of Nogales to his farm in Cajeme. Presumably, the attack was meant as retribution for Obregón's growing land investments in the Yaqui Valley. Obregón, in the intervening years between the end of his presidency in 1924 and his bid for reelection in 1927–28, had returned to chickpea farming and had extended his productive lands into those previously held by the Yaquis. The Yaqui had been in open rebellion for two weeks prior to the attack, and they blamed Obregón and Calles for their sinking fortunes and disappearing lands. Obregón learned of de la Huerta's hand in fomenting the revolt when a set of letters from de la Huerta to Luis Matus, the leader of the rebellion, came into his possession. De la Huerta claimed that Obregón never had any intention of addressing the issue of restitution of Yaqui lands. To the contrary, he claimed that Obregón intended to steal their lands from them.[41]

Whether de la Huerta was using the Yaquis' penchant for periodic rebellion to his advantage or had a genuine interest in their centuries-old claims to land along the Yaqui River is unclear. However, the Yaqui Uprising of 1926–27 served his immediate goal, which was the cultivation of instability along the border between Arizona and Sonora and the eventual seizure of the border city of Nogales. In this sense, de la Huerta may have simply been compounding on more than a century of baiting Yaqui resistance by using the issue of access to land as a wedge to drive between the Yaqui and the Mexican government. Given the intensity of the government's campaign against the rebellion, there would have been much enmity toward Calles and Obregón among the Yaqui. The Mexican congress allocated $1 million pesos to the campaign, which by way of intense aerial bombing of Yaqui strongholds in the Sierra Occidental, pounded the combatants into submission by late 1927.[42] In light of de la Huerta's conciliatory attitude toward the enemies of the revolution (and specifically the enemies of Obregón, including Pancho Villa) during his six-month tenure as the provisional president, the Yaquis most likely saw de la Huerta as a defender of Yaqui interests, given that the other political actors in Sonora had used the tribe for military ends and then turned the regular army against them, pushing them farther into the Sierra de Bacatete. Whatever the motivation for the support that the Yaquis put behind de la Huerta in exile, the tribes had ready access to the unguarded recesses of the border between Sonora and Arizona.

On 7 September 1926, the chief and general of the Yaqui and Mayo tribes, Luis Matus, released a manifesto announcing that the Yaquis were in rebellion against the state and central governments, claiming as the patron of their rebellion Adolfo de la Huerta, asserting, "Don Adolfo de la Huerta . . . is the only one presently that could fulfill the interests of the fatherland, leading it down the right path of progress and peace."[43] The manifesto itself was not unusual in that it covered almost the same points that most manifestos and proclamations of the day did. It began by urging all Mexican citizens to join in the struggle against "the unworthy dictators, despots and tyrants" who were destroying the country and followed by asserting that the time had arrived to put an end to the "dictatorships that always divert us from progress and peace."[44] The opening of the manifesto certainly spoke to the rest of the Mexican people as compatriots. In the following paragraphs, Matus spoke for the Eight Governors and Eight Tribes, asserting that they "protest energetically, the arbitrary acts of an executive who has lost the path of democracy." He continued by making the claim that the Yaquis would not stand for any more presidential impositions or the trampling of "the principles of liberty of thought," and he proclaimed that when Mexico had a government that would respect the rights of every citizen, then that government would be respected.[45] In the manifesto, however, Matus never mentioned the restitution of Yaqui lands, which had been promised and deferred by Madero, Obregón, and Calles. Instead, the manifesto held as sacred those abstract concepts on the minds of almost all the opposition to the Calles regime, such as democracy, justice, and freedom of religion.

It is possible that Matus had only a minor role, or no role at all, in composing the manifesto and that delahuertista agents residing in Sonora penned the document. An agent for the Confidential Department, Agent 21, operating in Piedras Negras, Coahuila, reported that the seditious manifestos that had been circulating in the areas of Sonora and Coahuila and bearing the name of Gen. Luis Matus or distributed as anonymous had, in fact, been encountered along the entire length of the border. According to the agent, the most likely sources of the propaganda were two delahuertista agents named Rafael Múzquiz and ex-colonel Ramón Múzquiz, who were living in Eagle Pass but were known to have connections with the exile populations in El Paso and San Antonio.[46] Many of the manifestos that bore Luis Matus's name during the course of the Yaqui Uprising of 1926 contained elements of previous manifestos, as if they were being compiled from a larger collection of phrases and then sprinkled with various admonitions and denunciations of the Calles government as tyrannical and despotic, followed by calls for democracy, justice, and freedom. In another manifesto of 4 September 1926, titled "Alerta. Ciudadanos Mexicanos," the language is consistent with the sort of upper-class political rhetoric that would have been used by exiles such as de la Huerta or educated military leaders. It is reasonable to assume, as did Agent 21, that delahuertista agents were mass-printing manifestos in support of de la Huerta and putting Luis Matus's name on them. This manifesto specifically made the claim that Adolfo de la Huerta was the man that Mexico so desperately needed, without making any reference to the peace negotiations that led to the end of Calles's campaign against the Yaquis in 1916.[47]

It appears, at least, that de la Huerta was again negotiating with the Yaquis in September 1926 and quite possibly through the end of that year. The extent to which he or his agents in Sonora had committed to funding and arming the Yaquis, however, is not as clear. It is certainly possible that de la Huerta was using the rebellion to suit his desired end, which was the creation of instability in northern Sonora that might allow his forces to seize the city of Nogales. News reports during the course of the federal army's campaign to put down the rebellion of 1926 describe a fairly large Yaqui force, held up in the Sierra de Bacatete, in possession of what was perceived as a great deal of ammunition and armament. Yet because the ammunition was incredibly old and inferior to the equipment that the federal army was using, the Yaquis, according to the Mexico City press, did not stand a chance.[48] The federal army spent the months of September, October, and November establishing their presence along the northern frontier in preparation for the campaign, which began in December 1926. By all accounts, *El Universal* and *Excélsior* reported that the Yaquis were large in number and well armed but that the federal forces were much better equipped, far outnumbered the Yaquis, and would have no problem making short work of the rebellion.[49] News reports notwithstanding, there was a concerted effort on the part of delahuertista agents, both in Arizona and in Sonora, as well as among religious leaders in Sonora, to provide ammunition and moral support to the Yaquis.

In Ures, Sonora, Bishop Juan Navarrete had been a particularly thorny opponent for local officials and representatives of the central government. Over the course of seven years, the bishop had managed to establish Catholic support centers throughout the northern part of Sonora, each with its own leadership and fundraising structure. According to Agent 9, these associations, or *centros,* provided "funds for the Church, in different amounts according to the quotas of each association," and "the funds of these associations [were] destined for the maintenance of the religion, improvements to the Church etc." The agent went on to say that over seven years, this money, which all went to the bishop, would have amounted to a small fortune. When it came to investigating the bishop's role in fomenting the Yaqui Uprising, the agent pointed out that the bishop, for a period of eight months, had not missed one Sunday of saying the mass and giving conferences in the village of Cócorita, which was very close to Yaqui territory. He also pointed out that at the time of the Yaqui Uprising, the bishop was heard to say that the Yaquis had certain cause to rebel because the Mexican government had denied them every right, "among them, the freedom of religion, which was the most sacred."[50] The agent noted that this was an idea that was very prominent in the manifestos that had been attributed to Luis Matus and that this fact was simply evidence of the clergy's hand in fomenting the Yaqui Uprising. One of the priests serving in Hermosillo, Lauro Duarte, had even hosted a conference in the home of a local woman, Carolina de Martínez, where he reportedly made the claim that the Yaquis were true Catholics and deserving of God "because if Jesus had spilled his blood to save humanity from the clutches of the devil, the Yaquis would spill their own blood to conserve their religion."[51] As further proof of the hand of the clergy, the agent connected the bishop to two local officials—the mayor of Cócorit, Jesús Ceballos, as well as the local notary, Alberto F. Moreno—to the rebellion. The agent reported that volunteer guards were already being formed to defend against the Yaquis but that in Cócorit, the volunteers had ceased to offer their services because the mayor and the notary were suspected of having been very close to the bishop and were influencing the actions of the volunteer guards.[52]

For Agent 9, it was entirely clear that the clergy had a hand in fomenting the Yaqui Uprising and also that there were local officials who were either complacent or actively supporting the activities of the clergy in Sonora. However, he did point out that although he thought these details were sufficiently concrete and that other people he interviewed stated emphatically that the clergy was behind the events, they could offer no evidence to support their claims. The agent also admitted that there was little or no proof at all of any sort of connivance between Bishop Navarette and delahuertista agents. The only indication, according to the report, of delahuertista involvement was that one of the Yaqui leaders, Capt. Simón Espinoza, had disappeared unexpectedly, having gone to the United States. Two days after his return, the Yaquis began their rebellion.[53] This evidence might certainly be considered entirely circumstantial, but for confidential agents operating along the border, it was enough to suggest that there was something going on between Sonora and Arizona that was worth mentioning to their superiors.

Indeed, there were meetings between the Yaqui leadership and Adolfo de la Huerta in Tucson, Arizona, in early December 1926, as reported by Agent 2 in Ciudad Juárez.[54] There had been rumors in late 1926 of the arrest of de la Huerta. In his report, Agent 2 asserted that there was absolutely no truth to those rumors and that, in fact, the Department of Justice had provided Adolfo de la Huerta with a seven-man guard for his trip to Tucson. Whether this portion of his report was accurate is not clear.[55] The main point, however, was that the reason for de la Huerta's trip to Tucson on 6 December 1926 was to meet with "some of the Yaqui rebel leaders, who . . . were found a short distance from the border [near Tucson] with an escort of 200 men, to drive don Adolfo to the rebel headquarters by instruction of the Chief Matus."[56] According to the report, de la Huerta declined the request that he place himself at the head of the rebellion. He still had unfinished business in the United States, he claimed, and it would not be prudent for him to leave these things as they were because they were key to the larger plan of toppling President Calles. He, however, assured them that it would not be long before he would be in a position to take his place at the head of the Yaqui movement. All that was required was the successful Yaqui seizure of a prominent border city so that don Adolfo could enter Mexico without the risk of violating US neutrality laws.[57]

The agent's report is not the only one to claim that de la Huerta had made promises to the Yaquis with regard to his intentions of support. By 8 January 1927, the Yaquis themselves had claimed that de la Huerta had lied to them, asserting that they had been victims of delahuertista agents who told them that the populations along the northern border of Sonora were under the control of the delahuertista faction.[58] Perhaps de la Huerta was not directly fueling the Yaqui Uprising of 1926, but he was certainly hoping to use that rebellion to foment the sort of instability in Sonora that would allow him to enter his home state uncontested—at least uncontested by the United States government and all its agents along the border. It was not until May 1927 that what de la Huerta had seen as a logical plan to move into Sonora became a possibility when a small Yaqui contingent threatened to seize the border town of Nogales.

In the months between February and July 1927, members of the Yaqui tribe made frequent visits to Tucson, presumably to meet with de la Huerta or his agents. There were regular reports from the Mexican consul in Tucson, J. E. Anchondo, regarding the movements of small bands of Yaquis crossing the border unarmed with the intention of retrieving stashed arms and ammunition in Arizona. There were also several reports that Adolfo de la Huerta; Bishop Navarrete; José Gándara, who was "secretary of war" for the Liga Defensora Religiosa (LDR) in El Paso; and a well-known arms dealer named Esteban Borgaro were working (not necessarily together) to organize and equip a second rebellion with Yaquis who had been living and working in El Continental, a town thirty-five miles outside of Tucson. After the ultimate failure of this second Yaqui Uprising of 1927, Bishop Navarrete was tried in federal court in Tucson for attempted violations of US neutrality laws. He was arraigned and released on a $2,500 bond on 15 September. In Consul J. E. Anchondo's report of the arrest and trial, he pointed out that the bishop had been arrested in connection to the case in which Gándara, Borgaro, Luis

Gayou, Gómez Morentín, and Adolfo de la Huerta had been charged with inciting the Yaquis to rebel in May of the same year as well as providing them arms and ammunition for the rebellion.[59] For Anchondo, the arrest and trial was a boon for the Mexican government, especially in the eyes of the American public, as it proved, once and for all, that the Mexican clergy was actively attempting to topple the Calles regime.

De la Huerta attempted to put together his own Yaqui expeditionary force from his base in Tucson. Border Patrol officer A. T. Spence reported that as early as May 1926, de la Huerta had made promises to the Yaqui leadership. If they took up arms and fought for the overthrow of the Calles government, when de la Huerta took the reins of power, "their lands would be restored to them and . . . all the rights of a Mexican citizen would be given them."[60] Regarding the most recent Yaqui Uprising, Spence asserted that in February 1927, a Yaqui named Juan Frias had made his way from Tucson to the Yaqui River carrying a signed document from de la Huerta instructing him to go and recruit one hundred Yaqui soldiers to help carry a certain amount of arms and ammunition back to the river. If Spence's report was accurate, Juan Frias and the Yaquis of which he spoke probably were planning the assault on Nogales, Sonora, which was to take place in May 1927.

On 11 May 1927, the prosecuting attorney for the Yaqui case in Nogales, Arizona, submitted a report to the consul general in El Paso regarding the arrest and detention of forty Yaquis who had crossed the border into Nogales, Arizona.[61] The Yaquis had crossed into US territory on the morning of May 7 and were picked up by Border Patrol agents and immediately handed over to military authorities for detention. El Paso assistant district attorney E. B. Elfers and Consul Anchondo went to Nogales, Sonora, to have a meeting with Gen. Francisco Manzo, who was at the time the *jefe militar* of the state of Sonora and who had been the head of the campaign against the rebellious Yaquis. While they were meeting with General Manzo, Colonel Dougherty, the commander of American forces in Nogales, Arizona, came personally to inform General Manzo of the capture and detention of this small group of Yaquis. According to the colonel, there was only one of the forty Yaquis being held who claimed to speak any Spanish. This prisoner related that none of his fellow travelers had ever been on the US side of the border and that they all had spent their entire lives along the Yaqui River. He asserted that because of the Mexican government's relentless campaign against the Yaquis, they had all decided to move into the United States and leave Mexico forever. He further claimed that before they were captured, there had been ninety individuals in his group and that they had been under the charge of a man named Frias—presumably Juan Frias, the Yaqui that de la Huerta allegedly appointed to recruit one hundred Yaquis to transport arms and ammunition. As Colonel Dougherty himself asserted, they had been poorly provisioned with food but were carrying large amounts of arms and ammunition when they were captured.[62]

A Confidential Department report from 13 May posited that a group of ex-generals and loosely aligned delahuertistas, including Pablo González, Francisco Coss, César López de Lara, and Modesto García Cavazos, were planning large-scale attacks on Piedras Negras, Villa Acuña, Chihuahua, and Nuevo Laredo that were arranged to coincide with the Yaqui seizure of Nogales, Sonora.[63] If this report were accurate, it would suggest a high level of organization and cooperation among the exiles in the United States. This confidential agent asserted that Francisco Coss had received $4,000 from the revolutionary junta in Texas represented by Nicéforo Zambrano, Dr. Jesús Ibarra, Pablo González, and Félix Díaz and that although all of them wanted to be the chief, "most [were] inclined to name Adolfo de la Huerta."[64] Certainly, the Yaquis were planning to take Nogales in May 1927, and it is clear that Adolfo de la Huerta, if not planning the entire attack, was certainly hoping to capitalize on its success, as evidenced in statements that Luis Gayou and Alfonso Gómez Morentín made to Department of Justice agents.

When the Yaqui army was set to seize the border city of Nogales, Adolfo de la Huerta sent his private secretary, Luis Gayou, down to the border in order to prepare to ship in a quantity of arms and ammunition to refresh the Yaqui supplies. He was also to provide police and additional military security in the event that increasing hostilities threatened widespread instability. Gayou claimed that he had been ordered by de la Huerta, upon the news that the Yaquis were planning to seize Nogales, to ensure that events did not get out of hand, potentially resulting in an international scandal. Prior to having received the actual order from de la Huerta, Gayou informed Department of Justice agent A. A. Hopkins of de la Huerta's intent to send a delegate to the border in the event of the effective seizure of Nogales. As he indicated, de la Huerta had informed the proper authorities in Arizona as well. Gayou had been chosen for the task because he could speak fluent English, and in his statement he noted that he had been charged with three principal duties: First, he was to close down all saloons "and other centres [*sic*] of vice which [were] numerous in that town." Second, he was to ensure the safety of all noncombatants. Finally, and perhaps most important, he was to "endeavor to organize all public services, civil as well as military and which comprised the municipal police force to put into effect all the regulations that had to be dictated for the preservation of order and also to organize the immigration service and the fiscal guards which assist the customs department in the prevention of contraband."[65]

In order to maintain the peace, as Gayou described, one needed arms and ammunition, and it was the attempt to move these materials into Mexican national territory that ultimately landed Gayou in the custody of agents of the Department of Justice. As he asserted, "I realized that for the organization of the municipal police and the fiscal guards I was going to need arms and as these services had to be organized the first day of the occupation of the town by the revolutionary forces . . . I decided to secure the arms necessary for such services to be stored in Tucson in order to obtain at the opportune time the corresponding permission to take them out of this country."[66] Well aware of the fact that Calles had spies operating in Tucson and many other points on the border, Gayou worked closely with Alfonso Gómez Morentín, a well-known arms smuggler and delahuertista, to secure the war material. As Gayou explained, the shipments had come to him through the mail in a perfectly normal fashion; he had inspected the packages and had the materials stored at a location of which Department of Justice agents had prior knowledge. Again, it was important for Gayou to assert that all these activities were carried out in a perfectly legal fashion, being careful not to violate any neutrality laws. The proper authorities were made aware of de la Huerta's intentions, and he himself had a conversation asking two Department of Justice agents exactly what could and could not be done with regard to violations of neutrality laws. As it happened, one of the last shipments that Gayou received from San Antonio contained cartridges about which he claimed to know nothing. He maintained that at the time, he did not even suspect that it might have been an arms shipment, but as he was on his way to a local hardware store where he intended to store the shipment, he was arrested. Gayou closed his statement by asserting that de la Huerta had always been very careful not to violate the law and "had always recommended that we act in complete accordance with the authorities in this country."[67] One cannot ignore the flimsy veil of legitimacy that Gayou attributed to his and de la Huerta's alleged "services" that they proposed to offer to maintain law and order in Nogales, but more interesting was the notion that his claims might have somehow assuaged US officials' trepidation regarding a clear and undisguised attempt to ship arms and ammunition to the Yaquis, then in open rebellion.

## CONCLUSION

Adolfo de la Huerta and his agents and followers utilized every angle available to them in their quest to topple the Calles regime from the relative safety of the United States. If he had lost control of events during the course of the de la Huerta Rebellion, don Adolfo was entirely in control of his political and financial dealings in the United States and perfectly aware of the consequences of his actions. Far from the dupe of the military and political interests involved in the de la Huerta Rebellion of 1923, Adolfo de la Huerta's actions in exile in the United States, though they were unsuccessful, were those of a political actor determined to effect change in his home country. He was able to take advantage of political terrain with which he was already acquainted through his experience in international politics as Sonoran governor, interim Mexican president, and treasury secretary under Obregón. While the early years of his exile yielded scant tangible success, he was able to facilitate the movement of arms and ammunition into Mexican territory for a number of purposes, and he established himself as one of the most politically powerful exiles among the counterrevolutionaries active along the border. The political influence and agility of his agents in the case of Demitrio Torres presents yet another example of the power that exiles could wield when their energies were directed in precisely the right direction.

The actions of US law enforcement agencies along the border and the activities of agents of the Confidential Department were key in apprehending important members of the delahuertista circle. Many de la Huerta supporters were engaged in important fundraising and arms-smuggling operations, such as Esteban Borgaro and Luis Gayou. Others, like Capt. William Hanson, assisted the work of the Confidential Department in more extralegal ways, using deportation as a means of disposing of the militantly dangerous among the exile cohort in the United States. The influx of wealthy Catholic immigrants to places like El Paso and San Antonio after the summer of 1926 would also push de la Huerta out of the exile spotlight. The Catholic contingent in exile regarded don Adolfo as a political liability as a result of his association with the revolutionary anticlericalism of Obregón and Calles. The Catholic exile community would choose to put its support behind other men. At the same time, the advent of the Cristero Rebellion in mid-1926 and the flood of Catholic refugees across the border changed the landscape of counterrevolutionary activism for the rest of the decade, shifting the center of political power away from de la Huerta and toward a broader network of actors. This network included the aforementioned military leaders, the US Catholic hierarchy, Mexican intellectuals in exile, Canadian arms dealers, and the Knights of Columbus. It is to this story that we turn in the following chapter.

# THREE

# THE REVOLT OF THE LOSERS

## GENERAL ENRIQUE ESTRADA'S FAILED REBELLION ON THE CALIFORNIA-MEXICO BORDER

On the evening of 16 August 1926, a caravan consisting of armored trucks and numerous other makeshift military vehicles made its way through California's Imperial Valley toward Engineer Springs, approaching the international border separating Southern California from Baja California. Agents of the US Bureau of Investigation obtained reliable intelligence that an attempted border crossing was planned for this particular evening. As Special Agent Edwin Atherton was combing the routes in and out of Engineer Springs, he discovered a canvas-covered truck on the side of the road. The driver, Juan Estrada, the brother of Mexican general Enrique Estrada, was arrested along with a total of 104 conspirators who had also made their way toward the border and fallen into the agents' trap. There would be many more arrests to come over the course of the evening. By 10:30 p.m., the operation had yielded such a large catch that agents were forced to call teams of law enforcement officers from the surrounding area in order to make the arrests. By the end of the day, agents had apprehended a total of 136 men, including Gens. Ramón B. Arnaiz, Agustín Gamou, and Nicolás Rodríguez, one of Estrada's key recruiting agents.[1]

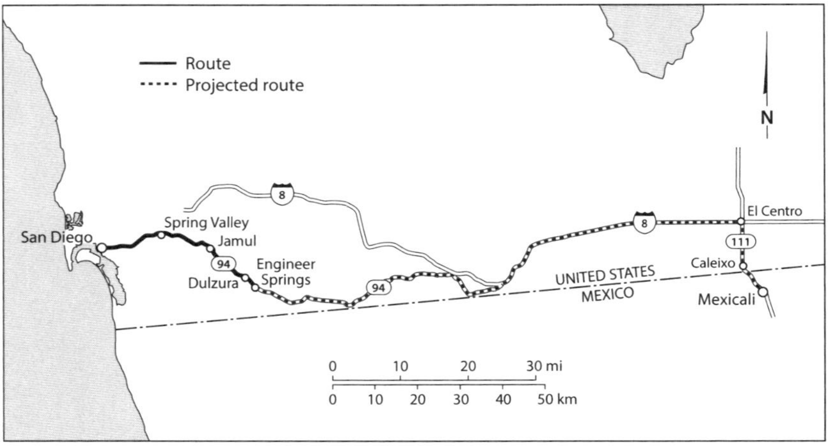


*Map of Gen. Enrique Estrada's route through the Imperial Valley*

Bureau agents at the Los Angeles branch were tipped off to the possibility of an attempt on Baja California when they learned that a local hardware firm, the Parker Hardware Company, owned by Earle C. Parker, had recently acquired 150,000 rounds of ammunition and 400 Springfield rifles. It was not uncommon for hardware stores in the early twentieth century to be involved in a certain level of arms trading, but according to Agent A. A. Hopkins, "The Parker Hardware Co. is a very small firm and could have no legitimate use for this number of rifles or amount of ammunition."[2] The intelligence that agents had collected suggested that large quantities of war material had been purchased from an important supplier in New York and then shipped to San Diego specifically for General Estrada's expedition. Agent Atherton's sources in Baja California also corroborated previously obtained intelligence—namely, that Estrada was involved in recruiting soldiers in and around Los Angeles and that he planned to carry out his expedition across the border "sometime between August 1st and 10th."[3] The exact date of the invasion had not been ascertained, but the border town of Compuertas was posited as the point of entry. Informants also claimed that there was a contingent in Mexicali prepared to take Gov. Abelardo Rodriguez captive and that there were troops in Chihuahua and Sonora that were prepared for rebellion.[4]

Estrada's rebellion failed miserably. It ended in the eventual arrest of all 150 members of the army that he had assembled from among the immigrant populations of Los Angeles's East Side as well as one of the largest federal trials of the era. The putsch failed, in part, because Estrada and his ranking officers profoundly underestimated the perceived apathy with which the Department of Justice and local law enforcement agencies along the border might look upon such cross-border military movements against a neighboring sovereign. However, it was successful in its organization, if not its execution, because the elite exiles involved in its planning understood the nature of the border as a space from which their plots not only would gain traction but could move freely across a boundary that, for them, as elite political actors, was little more than a revolving door.

This chapter examines the importance of the US-Mexico border in the immediate postrevolutionary period as a place of refuge and regeneration for the Mexican Revolution's losers. Most of the revolution's enemies, as well as the revolutionaries who had been pushed out of the country from 1915 to 1924, ended up along the US-Mexico border, and they were all involved in one way or another in schemes to overthrow the Calles regime. The international border in the 1920s was littered with the revolution's enemies. At the same time, a vigorous political Catholic movement had taken root in Mexico City as well as in the center-west region of the republic that had allied with Estrada and other more dangerous exiles in the United States. The initiation of the Cristero Rebellion in 1926 heightened rebel exile activities and allowed for the cultivation of new alliances based on Catholic loyalties and a shared perception that the Sonoran victors of the revolution were bent on implementing constitutional reforms that did not benefit the majority of the population in Mexico. It was a network of exiles, both new and old; arms dealers; and political Catholics in Mexico City who made Estrada's expedition possible. As impressive as the effort was, the importance of its assemblage is that it represented one of the strongest and best-organized expeditions to take advantage of Catholic financial and political connections, in both the United States and Mexico, even before many of those involved in the plot ended up in exile. The enemies of the Mexican state sought out connections, sympathies, and loyalties on both sides of the international boundary. The vista of counterrevolution on the border offers a window into the connections between liberal anticlerical revolutionaries working from the borderlands and political Catholic exiles fomenting resistance to the revolutionary state in Mexico City—unlikely bedfellows, to be certain, but the alliances served a larger shared goal: to put an end to the Calles government.

After the failure of Adolfo de la Huerta's Rebellion in 1923, Estrada and several of his confidants and supporters from the state of Jalisco were forced to flee Mexico for the safety of the United States. Estrada found himself in Southern California, and his fellow rebels fled to New York, New Orleans, and Havana, Cuba, among other locations. Soon after Estrada arrived in San Diego, he began to plot a new rebellion with the intent of unseating President Calles. In less than a year, Estrada obtained enough munitions and men to stage a modest but nonetheless threatening invasion of Baja California. By the time the case against Estrada went to trial in US Federal Court in January 1927, the web of conspirators involved grew to include Mexican ex-patriots living in Los Angeles and San Diego, political Catholics in Mexico City, and US citizens from New York to San Diego. In all, Estrada obtained 3 armored trucks, 150,000 cartridges of ammunition, 400 Springfield rifles, 2 high-caliber machine guns, 100 pipe fittings for bomb making, and 4 monoplanes, as well as the support of 150 combatants from in and around the Los Angeles and San Diego areas.[5]

Of the four regional rebellions that constituted the de la Huerta Rebellion, the activities of Estrada in Jalisco were the most dangerous for President Obregón.[6] Estrada was one of the most successful military leaders under Obregón's command during the years of the revolution and had occupied the important post of secretary of war in Obregón's early cabinet before being assigned the post of chief of the second division of the national army, a position that placed him in charge of a six-state territory, including Jalisco, Zacatecas, and Nayarit.[7] Unlike some of the generals who rebelled against the state in 1923, Estrada did not enter the fray necessarily because of discontent over the choice of Calles as Obregón's successor. For Estrada, the reorganization of the Mexican military and Obregón's attempt to reduce

*Gen. Enrique Estrada as secretary of war under the administration of Pres. Álvaro Obregón, 1921*

*FAPECFT. Fototeca Archivo Fernando Torreblanca (AFFT), fondo Álvaro Obregón, Oficial (FFAOO), serie:* Material para un Libro, 1920–1921. *Imagen 44, inventario 741.*

the local autonomy of military leaders were the main motivations for his uprising. According to historians Fidelina Llerenas and Jaime Tamayo, the "military leaders felt effected by measures such as reducing the region under control of each caudillo and increasing the number of military chiefs in each region."[8] Obregón's measures were an attempt to reorganize the military and reduce the possibility of a rebellion against his government. In the case of the de la Huerta Rebellion, however, Obregón's strategy had the opposite effect, sparking a conflict that involved 40 percent of the Mexican military's officer corps.[9]

From the moment of Estrada's arrival in California, he insisted that he would take no part in violating US neutrality laws while he resided in the United States. He did, however, make it clear that he considered himself an enemy of the Calles administration and that "should a formal movement occur at any time, having for its object the overthrow of the Calles government, he would join any reputable leader."[10] Estrada certainly knew that he was being watched by bureau agents. Interestingly, in a period in which the issue of illegal immigration was heating up in the southwestern United States, the Bureau of Investigation and the newly established Border Patrol concerned themselves with stopping 150 Mexicans from *reentering* their home country. Estrada's failed rebellion must be examined in the context of the early twentieth-century expansion of federal law enforcement agencies as related to the issue of illegal immigration in the US Southwest.

Mae Ngai has examined this particular period in US immigration history and argues that it was in the mid-1920s that Mexicans, who unlike immigrants from Europe had avoided numerical quotas, became the quintessential "illegal alien[s]."[11] While the Johnson-Reed Immigration Act of 1924 placed numerical quotas on many European populations seeking entry into the country, it did not place similar quotas on Mexican immigrants. It did, however, institute specific documentation requirements for Mexicans crossing the border into the United States. According to Ngai, "The regime of immigration restriction remapped the nation in two ways. First it drew a new ethnic and racial map based on new categories and hierarchies of difference. Second, and in a different register, it articulated a new sense of territoriality, which was marked by unprecedented awareness and state surveillance of the nation's contiguous land borders."[12] The desire to regulate the flow of immigrants via quotas, combined with the expansion of federal law enforcement along the US-Mexico border and new restrictions on Mexican migration, sheds light on the Department of Justice's preoccupation with Estrada and his army. Estrada came to California after the failure of the de la Huerta Rebellion in 1924, the same year as the unveiling of the Johnson-Reed Immigration Act. By 1926, there was a fully functioning Bureau of Investigation, Border Patrol, and Immigration Service. All these institutional arms sought to regain control of the nation's borders under the pretense of regulating the flow of Mexican immigrants. Moreover, the mandate for these law enforcement arms went beyond policing the physical boundaries of the nation; they were also charged with surveillance of the Mexican exile communities throughout the United States. This directive meant that the investigative arm (the Bureau of Investigation) had a duty to keep an eye on exiles like Estrada and anyone else who might, at one point or another, decide to conspire to do away with the Calles government in Mexico.

As stated earlier, as of 1924, there were no numerical restrictions placed on immigration from the Western Hemisphere. Demand among the agribusiness interests in the US Southwest dictated access to an unrestricted source of cheap seasonal labor, the sort provided by seasonal migration from Mexico. The labor demands of southwestern ranchers and commercial agriculturalists ensured that the numerical quotas instituted for European immigrants would not affect their largely Mexican labor supply.[13] This is not to say that there was a dearth of voices clamoring for the restriction of Mexican immigration. Between 1910 and 1920, a demographic shift was taking place along the border, caused in large part by the Mexican Revolution. As a result of this influx of immigrants from Mexico, a head tax of $8.00 and literacy tests were implemented in 1917.[14] The migrants spilling across the border to escape the violence of the revolution caused an upswing in already racist attitudes in the US Southwest, and demands to restrict the flow of people from the south became more pronounced as the image of the impoverished, diseased, dirty, indolent Mexican took pride of place in the North American imagination.

These migratory influxes, along with the end of the First World War, led to a drive to secure the nation's boundaries beginning in the 1920s.[15] While there had been various law enforcement arms that policed the border prior to the 1920s, it was in May 1924 that the US Border Patrol was established as a new federal arm of the US Immigration Service. However, far from operating in the interests of the federal government, Border Patrol agents in the 1920s were operating on their own understanding of local conditions, "individual interests and community investments."[16] Moreover, the Border Patrol at its inception was essentially a local arm of law enforcement with a vague national mandate to protect the nation's borders in the name of immigration control. As an arm of the US Immigration Service, which was already poor and neglected, the Border Patrol was also woefully underfunded.[17]

The annual reports of the commissioner general of immigration for the period under consideration serve as an excellent source of information regarding overall expenditures on immigration control as well as policy recommendations from the commissioner general of immigration to the secretary of labor. In the report narratives, the commissioner general also included reports from the districts on the US-Mexico border, in which the everyday problems experienced by district inspectors were detailed. As such, they help differentiate between the legislation driving policies on the border and the actual problems with the implementation of that legislation on the local level. In the annual report for 1923, for example, the commissioner general lamented the fact that the introduction of the quota limit act of 19 May 1921 had led to an increase in the incidence of illegal border crossings in all the districts along the border. One of the main concerns for the commissioner general was that the quotas placed on "less desirable" European newcomers were leading to an increase in the number of cases of surreptitious entry and contraband smuggling. In the words of the commissioner general, another, "and in this instance a most troublesome, development of the year has been the growing tendency of inadmissible European aliens to attempt to enter the country surreptitiously, which in turn appears to have led to increased activities on the part of professional smugglers engaged in the business of assisting such aliens to enter over the land and water boundaries."[18]

Worse than the increase in smuggling and illegal entry was the fact that the US Congress had as yet failed to allocate the funds that the Immigration Bureau needed to protect the nation's borders. The annual reports indicate that more often than not, the district immigration inspectors and officers were completely overwhelmed. The San Antonio district officer expressed the tremendous difficulty he and his force had with combating coyote-assisted crossings of southern and eastern Europeans, groups that were restricted by the quota laws of 1921. In his estimation, the San Antonio district could only deal with these crossings by adding a significant force to patrol the border.[19] The El Paso district inspector reported that even after repositioning checkpoints in order to further strengthen these illicit points of entry, the new immigration law had placed an additional burden on immigration officials, increasing the amount of time that each immigration inspector was required to spend working with an arriving alien. Further, the fact that the law increased the workload but provided no additional personnel or funding curtailed the normal preventative policing associated with inspecting incoming migrants. As a result, "because of the smallness of the immigration appropriations . . . the force is now inadequate to keep abreast of the work of inspecting arriving aliens."[20] Aside from the difficulties presented by inadequate funding, the El Paso district inspector cited the terrible danger that officers put themselves in every day because of the meager federal expenditures for the protection of the border. Officers were shot and badly beaten on occasion by unscrupulous coyotes and illegal border crossers, because instead of sending officers on patrol in groups of four, as it should be, the El Paso district inspector was forced to send them out in pairs, compromising their safety. There was also a hint of contempt for the relatively higher expenditures at the Ellis Island point of entry. As the inspector put it, "The expenditure of vast energy and huge sums of money in guarding the portals at Ellis Island against the entry of the proscribed seems a vain and futile thing so long as the back-yard gate swings loosely on its hinges."[21]

The immigration inspector in Southern California reported that smuggling aliens across the border by automobile had become increasingly difficult to combat despite the existence of "mounted guards of this service stationed at strategic points on automobile highways in southern California." The problem was not that there were no patrols in the area; the problem was that "the number of these guards is pitiably insufficient, there being but 14 in all southern California."[22] The Southern California district inspector also lamented the undesirable result of the elimination of regular patrol launches along the coast, which caused a resurgence of smuggling by sea. As he noted, the lack of patrol launches left the coast completely undefended, and his district was doing everything in its power to control the flow of traffic over land. In closing, however, he further noted that "as the bureau well knows . . . not even an approximately effective organization against the illegal introduction of aliens . . . by land and sea can be hoped for until Congress makes sufficient appropriation for a defensive force."[23] Even following the creation of the Border Patrol in May 1924, the total force along the US-Mexico border consisted of five hundred men with limited modes of transportation. The commissioner general of immigration noted that there were "certain patrol districts where a force of 10 men are called upon to cover a territory of approximately 300 miles."[24] In this space of three hundred miles, there were so many well-traveled smuggling routes that to "attempt to place guards at each of them would not only be futile, as their identity and location would become a matter of common knowledge, but the number of men that would be required to maintain an adequate protective force renders such a plan impracticable."[25]

The immigration issue of the early twentieth century is only one component of this story. In the 1920s, both the Border Patrol and the Bureau of Investigation were fledgling law enforcement arms, short on funding and prestige. Rhodri Jeffreys-Jones points out that in the 1920s, the Bureau of Investigation was emerging from a period in which its agents represented a small corrupt clique that acted on its own authority.[26] Reform was the order of the day, and in 1924 the bureau gained a fresh young director named J. Edgar Hoover. One of Hoover's recent biographers has asserted that it was his personal goal to reorganize and professionalize the young bureau.[27] The Border Patrol in the 1920s suffered from the same underfunding and disorganization that the bureau had suffered in the 1910s. It is possible that the main law enforcement organizations involved in the capture and trial of

Estrada made a show of the whole affair because they needed the publicity. It was not enough that at the height of the era of prohibition in the United States, J. Edgar was in the spotlight in the fight against the mob; there was also the state of the nation's borders to consider. Of course, the Bureau of Investigation had as its mission only internal law enforcement and was not intended to work in an international context. However, the massive arrest of what appeared to be a small army and the across-the-board charge of violations of US neutrality laws meant that the Bureau of Investigation could now make a claim for the importance of increased funding for the protection of the border between the United States and Mexico. In other words, the arrest and trial of Estrada and his army proved that the border needed to be secure.

## ESTRADA'S "ARMY": CONSPIRATORS AND RANK AND FILE

The various US citizens involved in Estrada's expedition, such as Earle C. Parker, may have been assisting Estrada for sheer profit motive as opposed to any real identification with the general's cause. The legal sale of arms to Mexican insurgents had ended with the United States' diplomatic recognition of the government of President Obregón in 1923. Pres. Calvin Coolidge was holding fast to the promise of neutrality and enforcing an arms embargo on Mexico. Illegal arms sales and trafficking were, therefore, a potentially lucrative business. Arms trading and smuggling had been a very profitable, and often political, practice during the years of the revolution even from the moment that Francisco I. Madero was planning to confront the dictatorship of Porfirio Díaz from the safety of San Antonio. As the decade of revolutionary violence progressed, the political positioning of the United States shifted, and even the possibility of legal trade in arms was subject to open for some factions and close for others. Whatever the case, there were always methods for procuring arms and ammunition—provided military leaders could muster enough money, appropriate contacts north of the border, and adeptly use a sparsely patrolled international boundary.[28]

The motives of the Mexican residents of Los Angeles who joined Estrada's army and assisted in the preparation of his war material are somewhat clearer than those of arms smugglers like Parker. Prior to the trial, a large number of the rank and file entered pleas of "not guilty." These individuals were interviewed, and a statement was taken from each regarding what they were to testify in court. The most interesting aspect of the testimonies is that nearly all the rank and file tell the story of being recruited—by Rodríguez or some other Estrada officer—with the knowledge that a cross-border rebellion was to be the goal of their activities and that they were told by the recruiting agent there would be no problem because the US Department of Justice had sanctioned the operation. According to their testimonies, these men all willingly participated in an activity that, although they believed it had been sanctioned, could still have cost them their lives. They were all aware that the act in which they were going to take part was an invasion of Baja California staged from US soil. The men chosen to participate in this invasion all came from sections of Los Angeles that hosted dense and fairly close-knit Mexican immigrant populations. According to one bureau agent, Los Angeles had been a hub for quite a few of Mexico's most notorious rebels, and it was that same community from which the latest recruits had been plucked.[29]

Carlos Alcantar, recruited as an armored truck driver, reported that Nicolás Rodríguez told him that they were planning an invasion of Baja California and "assured him that everything had been arranged with the Department of Justice and that they would not be bothered."[30] Another witness, Felipe Araujo, was assured that the troops on the other side of the border would support them when they crossed over and that "they would be given money and everything they needed."[31] Louis Alvarez testified to the fact that he was approached by an Estrada agent and was told that they were planning to attack Baja California and that it was a safe operation because it had the blessing of the US government. He even produced a document that was believed to be the authorization for the rebellion direct from the Department of State.[32] These men were also lured by promises of military rank after the success of the rebellion. They were all told that they would receive steady and substantial pay, which they could then send to the families they might still have in Mexico. Baldemero Aguilar, apparently homeless, was paid one dollar per day until the initiation of the expedition, and when Francisco Chavarria asked how much he would be paid, he was told "they would give [him] whatever I needed to send [his] family and after that they would pay [him] $5.00 per day."[33]

Although none of the witnesses were asked why they had participated in the attempted rebellion or if there had been some sort of religious motivation, the barrios in which the recruiters were working were heavily Catholic and the participants were well informed on political events in their home country and willing to fight for the Catholic cause. Ricardo Romo points out that the communities that were established in East Los Angeles were quite devout. Romo suggests that because of the combination of the religious persecution in Mexico and a general disdain for the Calles administration among the immigrant population in Los Angeles, Estrada was able to assemble his supporters from among this disgruntled population. Although Romo misinterpreted Estrada's role in the uprising as "the leader of the Catholic faction," his observations about the correlations between immigration patterns and the religious persecution in Mexico are useful.[34] He notes that between 1926 and 1928, roughly 1,200 immigrants made their way to Los Angeles from the town of Arandas, located in the heart of Cristero territory in Los Altos de Jalisco, quite possibly fleeing the violence of the Cristero Rebellion.[35] It is difficult to ascertain how many Mexicans fled the region in the years prior to the outbreak of hostilities, but we can assume that there must have been a great amount of support in Los Angeles among the Catholic community for Estrada's activities, whether the rank and file expressed adherence to the cause or not.

The areas of Los Angeles from which Estrada's recruiters pulled their soldiers were those same barrios that contained large populations of long-established immigrant communities. These communities were home not to a transient or seasonal population; they were inhabited by long-standing residents, which meant that these communities had been in existence well before Estrada and his officers entered the country between 1921 and 1924.[36] Pedro Castillo asserts that these communities had come into existence beginning in the mid- to late nineteenth century.[37] The barrios between North Spring Street and Mission Road were the areas most heavily targeted by Estrada's

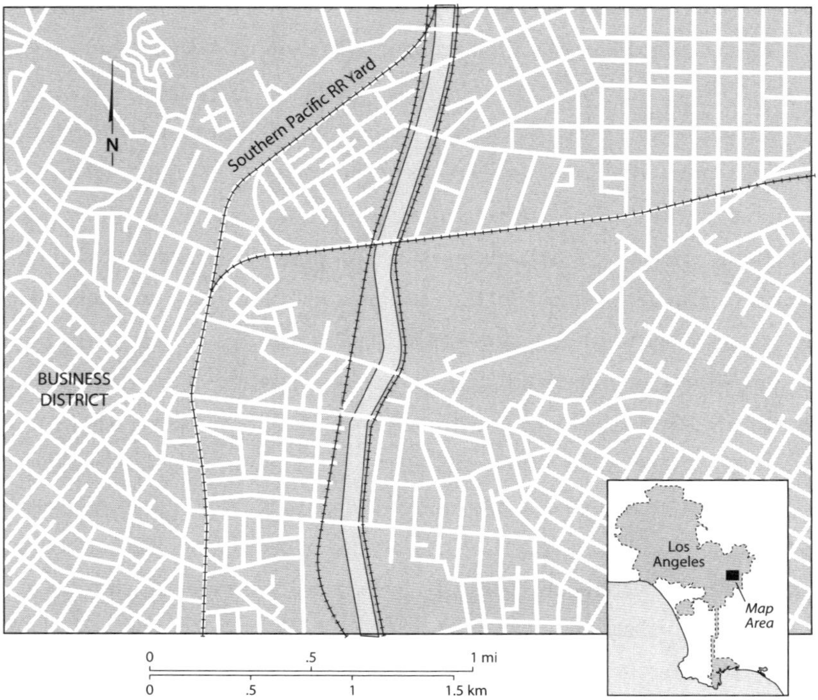


*Map of East Los Angeles*

recruiters, while a still significant amount of recruiting took place in the areas around the old Plaza District and south into the Business District.[38] The neighborhoods located east of the Los Angeles River were home to a 30 percent Mexican immigrant population. The neighborhoods on the west side of the river and bordering the Southern Pacific Railroad yards were home to a 58 percent Mexican immigrant population. And before the rise of the Business District, just south of the Old Plaza District, the west side was the epicenter of Mexican settlement in the early 1900s.[39] These three regions were prime territory for Estrada's recruiting activities.

Estrada's recruiters covered a wide range of territory within the Los Angeles area. In all, there were a total of seventeen recruiting agents. Among them, Nicolás Rodríguez, Petrolinio López, Juan Pardo, Nicolás Barajas, Jesús

Castro, and Gen. R. B. Arnaiz were the most active. These men had backgrounds in military service and aviation and some civil engineering training (part of their military training) in Mexico before they departed for the United States. Like Enrique Estrada, they were well educated. Estrada, in addition to having earned the rank of general of the division and having served in Obregón's early cabinet as secretary of war and marine, had been a civil engineer before the revolution. All the leaders had clean criminal backgrounds, except for Nicolás Rodríguez and Carlos López, who had both been arrested but not convicted on prior attempts to violate neutrality laws in El Paso (Rodríguez was arrested in 1922 and 1923; López was arrested in El Paso in 1923). A safe assumption would be that the two were working together in 1923. These men were successful at convincing many residents of the East and West Los Angeles barrios that it was necessary to wage war against the Calles government in order to affect change in Mexico.

It is clear that the leaders of Estrada's rebellion, at least those with revolutionary experience, could not be counted among what anticlerical reformers would have referred to as religious *fanáticos*. Indeed, Estrada and those in his immediate circle considered themselves liberal anticlerical revolutionaries. However, when it came to rallying recruits to their cause, they had to use the language of outrage over the perceived religious persecution that was occurring back home under Calles, a leader who claimed the same liberal heritage that they espoused. Of course, a claim of liberal anticlericalism did not necessarily conflict with an individual's own personal identification as Catholic. While anticlericalism had manifested itself in varying and, at times, radical ways during the revolution, the majority of revolutionaries were quite moderate in their anticlerical fervor. They channeled their vitriol into the cause of extricating, for example, the influence of the clergy from public education.[40] For Estrada, one of the problems with the Calles government was that in the president's anticlerical zeal, he had lost his liberal compass. As a result of this loss of direction, the president had done just as much a disservice to the nation by restricting the rights of the clergy as instituting a theocracy and curtailing the rights of secular citizens would have done.[41] Estrada's position meshed well with the cries of dictatorship and bolshevism being hurled at Calles from both big oil interests in the United States and political Catholics and the clergy in Mexico.

## MILITANT CATHOLICS AND GENERAL ESTRADA'S CONSPIRACY

As mentioned earlier, it is possible that at least some of the participants in Estrada's rebellion might have been motivated by their own connections to the church in Mexico—or perhaps by solidarity with Catholics across the border. It was believed that in Los Angeles and the surrounding areas, there were regular meetings between delahuertistas and old carrancistas including Enrique Estrada; Cutberto Hidalgo; Gens. J. M. Robles, J. Francisco Arnaez, Pablo Ortega, Nicolás Rodríguez, José López Zuazua, Manuel J. de la Vega; and an extensive list of other conspirators. They were believed to have held their meetings in San Bernardino and Hollywood, California. At one point, they were suspected of congregating in the home of Estrada's uncle, Rafael Corcuero.[42] According to reports, the conspirators, although they had very little money, were waiting for funds "from the Archbishop of Guadalajara Dr. Francisco Jiménez Orozco [*sic*], who, in a recent letter had offered Gral. Estrada a large sum which was to be delivered by representatives of a banker from Guadalajara named Salvador Ugarte."[43] According to the report, the conspirators' main sources of funding were exiles in Havana, landowners in Mexico, and the Mexican clergy. With regard to the relationship between Estrada and Archbishop Orozco y Jiménez, the report stated that Estrada had "the very powerful support of the Archbishop of Guadalajara, Orozco Jimenes [*sic*] who is a very valuable element within the Mexican Clergy [*sic*]."[44]

Not only was the archbishop implicated in the plot on the US border; elite women in the ranks of the Liga Nacional Defensora de la Libertad Religiosa (LNDLR) were apprehended in the Federal District just a few days after the capture of General Estrada. On 18 August 1926, the *Los Angeles Times* published a story linking the Estrada conspiracy in California to a group of political Catholics in Mexico City: "The Chief of the secret [*sic*]

Service, José Mascorro, declared tonight that his investigations have revealed that the plot for uprisings in various parts of the republic on Sunday last was largely organized by Catholic women and definitely was connected with the revolutionary movement of Gen. Estrada, near the Mexican border in California."[45] The women involved were identified as Señora Josefina Novoa and Señora Luz de Perches. The two women were high-ranking members of the Liga Nacional Defensora de la Libertad Religiosa (LNDLR), and in addition to the señoras, one Fr. Octaviano Rodríguez was also arrested for possession of antigovernment propaganda.[46] The charge of possessing Catholic propaganda is not surprising, as one of the main functions of the LNDLR was to disseminate antigovernment and pro-Catholic propaganda. Since the arrest of Estrada in California, the number of arrests in Mexico City had peaked at sixty possible conspirators, who were "charged with being 'suspected of having revolutionary propaganda in their homes.'"[47] In the immediate wake of the arrest of Estrada and his army in Southern California, more than seventy people had been arrested in the Mexico City area on charges of plotting to overthrow the established government. Officials were clear that the plot was to be carried out in unison with that of Estrada in Baja California but that Estrada's capture had derailed those plans.[48]

The fact that these individuals had connections to the LNDLR is important in the broader border element of this story. In June 1926, the political battle between the church and the revolutionary state in Mexico had come to a head, resulting in the decision of Archbishop José Mora y del Río to suspend all services administered by the Mexican Catholic Church. The LNDLR was the organization that took charge of the lay propaganda campaign against the anticlerical policies of the Calles government. In the aftermath of the arrests in Mexico City, some of the more prominent leaders of the organization made their way north to the United States to seek support from the exile community and also from the North American Catholic Church. Señoras Perches and Novoa, mentioned above, served a brief ten days in prison, and upon their release, Perches went into exile in El Paso, Texas, and soon established contact with Guillermo Rosas Jr., the private secretary of Félix Díaz, as well as the Knights of Columbus.[49]

A conspiratorial triangle developed in 1926 among the supporters of Estrada, Félix Díaz, and high-ranking members of the Liga, the organization that would, by the end of the year, come to lead the armed insurrection against the Mexican government. The various plots to overthrow Calles, hatched in exile after the arrival of throngs of political Catholics along the border, would grow to include defected delahuertistas—such as Gen. César López de Lara, a particularly mercurial but influential Mexican exile in South Texas—as well as military leaders in charge of border garrisons in Mexico. The threat to the process of state reconstruction in Mexico should not be understated. If the de la Huerta Rebellion, the Cristero Rebellion, or any one of the smaller border rebellions had succeeded, the door to power might have opened for a politico such as Félix Díaz or any one of the many contenders for power in exile. Men like Díaz would not have been content with simply assuming the presidency. Enrique Estrada made clear in his statements to the Justice Department his disdain for the anticlerical provisions of the 1917 Constitution and, more specifically, the Calles administration's handling of the religious question. Félix Díaz constantly insisted that the demise of the Mexican republic would be Article 27 of the 1917 Constitution and that the Constitution of 1857 was the document that best ensured the stability of the nation and the welfare of the Mexican people.[50] If successful at toppling the Calles government, they might have fundamentally altered the development of the postrevolutionary state.

The felicistas, a rough grouping of Mexican exiles rallied around the figure of Félix Díaz, claimed as their banner the Constitution of 1857, the document that the revolutionary Constitution of 1917 replaced. The old constitution was devoid of the guarantees of rights for workers; protections for Mexico's natural resources and restrictions on the power of the church and clergy were contained in the 1917 Constitution. The 1857 document guaranteed, instead, the rights of foreign property owners and foreign capital. Félix was instrumental in the toppling of the Madero regime in February 1913, and after Madero's assassination on the order of Gen. Victoriano Huerta, he worked closely with Huerta, the newly minted dictator, to pacify the country. When Pres. Woodrow Wilson refused to recognize the new regime, cutting off the supply of arms that Huerta needed to restore order and roll back the gains of the revolution, Félix utilized his contacts in the United States to smuggle the requisite arms and ammunition. His relationship with Huerta, however, went awry when he planned to run for the office of president in 1913. Like Félix's uncle, Huerta refused to relinquish power and allow Félix, heavily supported by the porfirian old guard, to run for the presidency. For his part, don Félix refused to take a stand against Huerta, and as a result, many of his supporters switched sides to become huertistas.[51] Díaz went into exile in Cuba and later the United States before the fall of the Huerta regime. After Huerta's demise at the hands of the constitutionalists commanded by Venustiano Carranza, Díaz began to rebuild his old base of political support from the United States.[52] The carrancista revolution again offered Díaz the opportunity to regain some of his lost power and prestige. But with the exception of a particularly poorly planned and, as such, unsuccessful expedition against the carrancistas in the state of Veracruz in February 1916, Díaz spent the better part of the rest of his life in exile in New Orleans, Louisiana.[53]

Still, Díaz accumulated a vast network of supporters in the United States. Many had backed his presidential bid in 1913, but there were also old delahuertistas, estradistas, and a whole conglomeration of other "*-istas*" in exile north of the border. There were so many *-istas*, in fact, that as early as September 1924, there were already calls from prominent exiles to "put an end to the ismos and the istas and to form one great party that will put itself to the sole task of national reconstruction."[54] The felicistas and many other exile groups saw in Estrada's expedition, and in the Cristero Rebellion, opportunities to reassert their power and reinstitute the old order in Mexico. Even as early as June 1924, on the eve of the presidential election, the sense among some felicistas in the United States was that no matter the outcome of the presidential contest, the winner would set about the initiation of a new revolution, "and the result, perhaps, will be the triumph of our cause."[55]

In December 1923, felicistas in exile hoped that their chance had arrived with the initiation of the de la Huerta Rebellion. With the pronouncement of open rebellion by Guadalupe Sánchez and de la Huerta's manifesto to the nation of December 1923, felicistas in the United States viewed the rebellion as serendipitous. One of Guillermo Rosas Jr.'s confidential informants reported that when General Sánchez declared himself in open rebellion against the Mexican government, the possibility of rebellion presented "the supreme moment for the Jefe [Díaz] given the disillusion of the government and the state of revolution in the country, without even considering the other powerful factors that determine the stance . . . of the White House."[56] The exiles were also watching the political events that led to the rebellion itself, including the subtle but serious conflict between de la Huerta and President Obregón that precipitated de la Huerta's resignation from the president's cabinet in September 1923 and his subsequent bid for the presidency in the 1924 election. The breakdown of what had appeared to be a solid and unified Sonoran political machine represented, for the revolution's enemies in exile, the opening for which they had hoped. The moment in which de la Huerta split from Obregón's cabinet was also significant in that it followed official recognition from the US government. Many felicistas saw official recognition as a major impediment to their activities against the Obregón administration. Recognition meant that it would be more difficult to topple the Mexican government because the flow of arms to Obregón would resume and would be restricted to others. One prominent felicista pointed out that more than at any moment since the rebellion of Agua Prieta, which brought Obregón to power, the "rupture of the triangle of Agua Prieta will offer us, in a few days, the best opportunity to carry out our patriotic projects."[57]

There was only one problem for the potential rebels and their "patriotic projects." They lacked the essential unity they needed to make their move against the Mexican government, and few really trusted de la Huerta—certainly not Díaz's and Rosas Jr.'s closest supporters. The felicistas were loath to view de la Huerta as anything more than a collaborator in the Sonoran triangle, part of the same Sonoran clique that ousted Carranza in 1920. As Federico García y Alva put it, de la Huerta was a potential usurper, in his opinion, much like Obregón and Calles. The de la Huerta Rebellion, according to García y Alva, not only did not have the nation's best interests at heart but was led by "a faction of the same nucleus that has ripped it [the nation] apart with its personal and base ambitions."[58] With regard to the rebellion of Estrada, the felicista camp, although interested in Estrada's activities, did not place much faith in the general's abilities. Dr. Julius Zeigner Uríburu, the informant for the Bureau of Investigation in Los Angeles, commented in a letter to Rosas Jr. that after a meeting with Esteban Cantú, former governor of Baja California, and José María Maytorena, it was generally agreed upon that Estrada was really not capable of directing a successful rebellion.[59] However, by December 1925, Uríburu changed his mind. He claimed that his informants led him to believe the US government would back any rebellion led by capable generals, such as Díaz, and that it might be the opportune moment to act.[60] Shortly thereafter, Uríburu arranged a series of meetings with Rosas Jr. and Estrada.[61] These meetings gave Estrada the confidence to approach Díaz about the possibility of contributing financially (or otherwise) to his rebellion. Díaz agreed to support Estrada's activities. To what extent is difficult to tell, but Estrada wrote the porfirian general a glowing letter in February 1926 thanking Díaz for his collaboration and lauding the value of his influence within the exile community.[62] One can only imagine how difficult it must have been for Estrada to address Díaz in such a deferential tone, having been among the throngs of revolutionary soldiers who had fought and died to unseat his uncle, don Porfirio.

Díaz's assistance was useless, it would seem, as other members of the exile community commented, that the failure of Estrada's rebellion owed to the confidence that Estrada had placed in Uríburu and bureau agents' assurances that he would not be prevented from crossing the border. The suspicion in the felicista camp was that Uríburu had conspired with Agent Emilio Kosterlitzky to entrap Estrada.[63] This notion, if accurate, would lend some weight to the idea that bureau agents allowed Estrada to build his army and gather his war material only to capture him and publicize his trial. Regardless of the intentions of Uríburu, or even Kosterlitzky, the fact that Díaz offered his assistance and his influence to Estrada in 1926 suggests that the old porfirian general thought, or at least hoped, that Estrada would succeed.

Mexican officials viewed the capture of Estrada by bureau agents as a sign that the US government was dedicated to the protection of the border and to the health of the Mexican state by way of solidifying the border. The implication for this vision of the relationship between the two nations was that not only did the United States support Calles in the Estrada case, but perhaps the religious conflict that had exploded in the summer of 1926 could also be dealt with much more easily. The United States could take a more hands-off approach regarding the internal affairs of its neighbor to the south. The actions of the US government in preventing Estrada's army from crossing the border had hardened the Calles administration, and as the *New York Times* put it, "any further attempts to start a revolt will merely strengthen the Mexican Administration's determination to continue its present policy in the conflict with the Catholic Church until the Church accepts all the [anticlerical] regulations."[64] The Mexican government was under quite a bit of pressure from Catholic organizations in the United States to change its policies toward the Mexican church. Likewise, political Catholics relied on their brothers and sisters north of the border for solidarity in their cause. By demonstrating that the United States would not allow insurrections to foment on its side of the border, the US government was sending a clear message that it would not interfere with policies within Mexico. Further, the capture of Estrada made explicit the warning that Catholic militants would not be able to use the US-Mexico borderlands as a staging ground for further rebellions.

President Calles was publicly silent regarding the failed rebellion in Southern California. Minister of Foreign Relations Aaron Saenz, however, did release a statement to the US press. Saenz expressed his pleasure that the United States was upholding its promise of strict neutrality in the internal affairs of Mexico and that the Estrada case would lead to a stiffening of the border between the two nations. The foreign secretary also claimed that the Mexican government was continuing and increasing its surveillance of key Mexican exiles. Saenz sent orders to all the Mexican consuls along the border to keep watch for other attempts at rebellion and to report on anything that might come to them regarding the activities of "the dissatisfied elements in the United States who have renewed their activities lately."[65] The statement made by Saenz suggests that beyond the immediacy of the Estrada affair, the secretary of foreign affairs was well aware of the fact that there were more individuals like Estrada plotting along the border. Because of the presence of these conspirators, perhaps the US neutrality laws took on a new importance. The public silence on the Estrada affair was accompanied by almost daily reporting on the religious conflict that had engulfed the country. We might assume that compared to the headaches with which Calles was dealing in his own national territory, he had little time or energy to pay attention to a rebellion in San Diego staged by a washed-up obregonista. But the failed rebellion on the border was not simply ignored by the Mexican administration; there was a renewed campaign to secure the major entry points along the international boundary under the supervision of Calles's secretary of war and marine, Joaquin Amaro.[66] Thus the arrest of Estrada and his army was accompanied by a refortification not only on the US side but also on the Mexican side.

## CONCLUSION

While the threats to the revolution from within the boundaries of the Mexican nation were substantial in 1926, they were not limited in scope by the international border between Mexico and the United States. They sought out connections, sympathies, and loyalties on both sides of the international boundary. The US-Mexico border, from California to the Gulf of Mexico, was home to a strange cast of disgruntled reactionaries, revolutionaries, and political Catholics—the revolution's losers—who held as their goal the ruin of the government of Plutarco Elías Calles. Although the arrest and trial of Estrada were accompanied by a refortification of the border, the failure of General Estrada's rebellion also marked a shift in the way in which the revolution's losers viewed their use of the border. The advent of the Cristero Rebellion gave these same exiles hope of the possibility of a renewed offensive. The religious conflict would allow for new alliances and fresh inroads for the felicistas and the more dangerous elements in the exile community. Estrada and his higher-ranking officials, for their trouble, received prison sentences and stiff fines—for Estrada himself, one year and nine months in federal prison and a $10,000 fine for violation of the US Neutrality Law.[67] While Estrada's expedition failed, it ultimately resulted in the arrival of many more of the Cristero

Rebellion's exiles to San Antonio and El Paso. They would then lend support to other counterrevolutionary plots and intrigues throughout the remainder of the decade. The failure of Estrada's rebellion thus marked a turning point in the fortunes of many of Mexico's enemies in the United States and began a new period of exile activity focused principally on the Catholic contingent in exile. Prior to the summer of 1926, law enforcement agencies in the United States, consular officials, and the agents of the Confidential Department had approached the prevention of seditious plots with a certain confidence that exiles such as de la Huerta, Estrada, Díaz, and López de Lara, among others lacked the resources necessary to constitute a legitimate threat. The Cristero Rebellion forced a reassessment of those threats and a concentrated focus on the activities of Catholics in exile. The members of the Liga in the United States continued to collaborate with Díaz, the Knights of Columbus, and other important members of the exile community.

As the intensity of exile activities began to increase, more and more Catholic exiles began to join the ranks of the rest of the revolution's losers in the United States. New fears regarding the formation of more powerful alliances and broader networks involving US Catholics, for example, led the Mexican government and the Confidential Department to investigate more closely the cross-border connections that they had previously discounted. The resources that the Catholic contingent in exile could summon were much more extensive than those to which de la Huerta and Estrada had access. Moreover, the Cristero Rebellion raging in Mexico conjured images of massacres in villages of the faithful in the countryside at the hands of the Mexican military. While few in the US public could identify with the cause of a group of military and political elites like Estrada and de la Huerta, images of Cristeros hanging from telegraph poles stirred the hearts of even the most lukewarm among the Catholic community in the United States. The Catholic contingent in exile utilized public opinion and the support of the Knights of Columbus, the North American Catholic hierarchy, ex-members of the military already in exile, and a broad network of arms smugglers to achieve their ends. The initiation of the armed phase of the Cristero Rebellion and the connections in exile that nourished it thus sparked fresh concern regarding border security and the stability of the Mexican state. The longer the Cristero Rebellion continued to drain military resources and national finances, the slower the progress of state reconstruction and the more Calles's image in the United States would deteriorate. Most alarming for the Mexican government were the connections that the Catholic contingent in exile might seek among the military leaders in the northern states of Sonora, Chihuahua, and Tamaulipas. As we will see in chapter 5, those connections would find their ultimate manifestation in the rebellion of José Gonzalo Escobar in March 1929. It is to the activities of Catholic exiles, the Knights of Columbus, and the North American Catholic hierarchy that we turn in the next chapter.

# FOUR

# CATHOLIC EXILES AND CONSPIRATORIAL NETWORKS

In the early years of exile organizing—from 1924 to 1926—it was nearly impossible for the various factions to negotiate any sort of alliance or agreement regarding the future course of action against Calles. As a result, each faction operated on its own internal logic of action. The delahuertistas, as we saw in chapter 2, took the diplomatic road in assembling support for their cause and in attempting to affect public opinion, via the Spanish-language press, against the Calles regime. The various high-profile prelates in exile were similarly utilizing their contacts in the US chapters of the Knights of Columbus and the North American hierarchy of the Roman Catholic Church as well as the North American press to achieve their goals. The felicistas were reaching out to all the military contacts they could find and were beginning to establish relationships with elite political Catholics. Finally, the estradistas made their own plans for immediate action, resulting, as we saw in the previous chapter, in a complete failure and a reassessment among the exile community of what was and was not possible in the field of counterrevolutionary activities in the United States. None of the various factions could achieve the unification they needed for success, and as a result, none were entirely successful in their individual endeavors. Here I posit that the capacity of distinct exile groups to make amicable alliances increased when the Cristero Rebellion began in the summer of 1926. It was not simply renewed Catholic activism that inspired hopes of uniting the various factions in exile; it was the prolonged social and political instability that provided the space and opportunity for a broader range of alliances among the exiles in the United States. The significance of the persistence of the conflict and the potential for a deterioration of border security and state stability was not lost on the Mexican government or the Confidential Department. The conflict also gave rise to a more vigorous strain of American Catholic activism not limited to propaganda but involving more bellicose activities undertaken by high-ranking members of the Knights of Columbus and others working to circumvent US neutrality laws to get valuable arms and ammunition to the Cristeros in the field.

The spark that ignited open hostilities between the church and the Mexican state came in February 1926, when the archbishop of Mexico, José Mora y del Río, publically denounced the anticlerical provisions of the 1917 Constitution: "The Episcopate, clergy, and Catholics do not recognize, and will combat, Articles 3, 5, 27, and 130 of the present Constitution. We cannot for any reason change this position without betraying our Faith and our Religion."[1] In retaliation, Calles stepped up his attacks on the church, banning religious processions, deporting foreign priests, closing church schools and monasteries, and making it a requirement for all Mexican priests to register with local magistrates. In order to put pressure on the Calles government, the archbishop of Mexico initiated a church strike—maintained for the duration of the conflict—during which time no masses were held. The implications of the strike for the people of Mexico were tremendous, particularly in the central-western states of Jalisco, Nayarit, Michoacán, Zacatecas, and Queretaro. Those aligned with the church organized guerrilla armies and waged war on the secular state and its supporters, peasants who were the beneficiaries of the state's agrarian reform program, or *agraristas*. The conflict was the bloodiest and most protracted that the postrevolutionary period would see. The Cristeros as well as the federal army were guilty of outrageous atrocities during the conflict. The guerrillas burned down the secular schools and murdered teachers, and the federal army attempted to kill one priest for every teacher murdered and looted churches across the Cristero heartland.

Just as the revolution produced its own set of exiles, so too did the Cristero Rebellion. These Catholic exiles consisted of priests and lay Catholic political leaders from organizations such as the Liga Nacional Defensora de la Libertad Religiosa (LNDLR) and other Catholic action groups in Mexico. The popular rebellion in the countryside was, in large part, directed by the Liga. The Liga was at the top of a hierarchy of groupings that included the Asociación Católica de la Juventud Mexicana (Mexican Catholic Youth Association; ACJM) and the Damas Catolicas (Catholic Ladies). These organizations comprised the elite of Mexican society and the most vociferous defenders of the church and clergy in Mexico, and they produced the most active and militant members of the Catholic contingent in exile.[2] The felicistas and other factions in the United States saw in the Catholic contingent a golden opportunity to renew their efforts against the Mexican government. While the failure of Enrique Estrada's expedition in Southern California at the hands of US Bureau of Investigation agents may have seemed a demoralizing defeat for some, it did not dash the hopes or the activities of the Catholic elite in exile. This chapter will trace the efforts of the Catholic elite to unite the various factions within their own community, to solicit the assistance of the North American Catholic hierarchy and the US government, and to search for an appropriate military leader in exile to guide them to their ultimate goal, the defeat of the Calles regime.

Before addressing the relationships and conspiracies forged within these exile communities, it is important to consider carefully the state of exile and the ways in which these communities operated in the specific context of the tumultuous 1920s. Those who I referred to as the "revolution's losers" in the previous chapter shared certain important characteristics in terms of their social standing, political careers, and military experience that made them dangerous in ways that other exile groups in the twentieth century were not. They were all forced into exile in the wake of a bloody revolution that seemed to have no end; some, such as the religious leaders that made their way to the border, were extremely adept at tapping into longer-standing exile communities from the early years of the revolution. They were able to establish new networks of communication and maintain old ones on both sides of the border that they used to great effect, and they were all well-to-do exiles. Among their ranks were newspaper editors such as Ignacio Lozano, owner of San Antonio's *La Prensa,* and porfirian intellectual Nemesio García Naranjo, a regular contributor to Lozano's editorial columns. There were educated men and some well-seasoned political actors, such as Adolfo de la Huerta, former congressman Jorge Prieto Laurens, and the president of the Liga Defensora Religiosa (LDR) in the United States, René Capistran Garza. There were also men, like César López de Lara, Enrique Estrada, Candido Aguilar, and Pablo González, with nearly lifelong military experience that prepared them for clandestine operations, cross-border espionage, and most important, arms smuggling.

Prior to the beginning of the Cristero Rebellion, no single exile group was considered by the US or Mexican authorities as terribly dangerous. Adolfo de la Huerta and the delahuertistas were perhaps the most threatening of the exiles, but only until the outbreak of the Cristero Rebellion. The felicistas had generally been considered a joke among most law enforcement agencies and Mexican consuls in the United States until the possibility that the felicistas might come to an arrangement with the Catholic element in exile became more likely. This possibility became more and more of a reality as the number of Catholic dissidents along the border began to rise after the summer of 1926. Even with the increased potential for alliances between the felicistas and the Catholics, Díaz himself was never a major negotiator after the failure of Estrada's rebellion. Instead, other elements within the felicista camp, such as Díaz's personal secretary, Guillermo Rosas Jr., made their own deals according to their ambitions. It must be noted as well that the felicistas cannot be said to have had as coherent an organizational structure as the delahuertistas or the Catholics. Instead, other exile groups cherry-picked the alliances they wanted to make within the felicista camp. A prime example was Gen. César López de Lara, in Laredo, Texas. While he may have considered himself a delahuertista when it was most advantageous, the new opportunities for success that were presented by the energy and power of Catholic exiles led him to offer his services to the felicistas and anyone else who might make use of them. Eventually, the Catholics and the felicistas would win the favor of rebel generals in Mexico, and López de Lara was well positioned to lend his support to them as well. If anyone respected the foundations of their alliances, López de Lara was too much of a pragmatist to do so himself. Thus identifying key alliances within the exile milieu is often difficult when one takes into account the myriad personal and group interests as well as political and military ambitions at work among and within the individual factions.

Alan Knight's concept of the "logic of the revolution" seems an appropriate application to exiles' approach to alliance building. Regarding the revolutionary process in Mexico, Knight posits that "as the Revolution unfolded it evolved a logic of its own, which cannot be precisely related to the social origins or ideologies of participant groups."[3] As the revolution progressed, competing programs clashed, revolutionaries adapted and turned on each other, and political alliances shifted in ways that confounded the revolutionary process. In similar fashion, exile groups were forced to make seemingly contradictory alliances as a result of their condition of exile. While there may have been very clearly stated goals among the Catholic contingent, they were beholden to the forces in which they sought support: prerevolutionary porfirians, who held the Constitution of 1857 as the document by which Mexico should be ruled; revolutionaries rejected by the post-1920 regimes because of personal ambition or dissenting views on fundamental political ideals; old villistas, now mercenaries with military contacts in Mexico hoping to exact revenge on a revolution that robbed them of what they believed to be their just rewards; and a network of Anglo smugglers, gunrunners, politicians, Catholics, and commercial elements hoping to topple Calles for their own interests. For example, the alliance between López de Lara and the forces of Gen. José Gonzalo Escobar in March 1929 was the product of Catholic organizing, felicista and delahuertista connections, and individual initiative among key military chiefs on the Mexican side of the border—in Chihuahua, Sonora, and Tamaulipas, specifically. But these networks and alliances could not have been developed without well-informed and politically active negotiators and spies.

One of the most important of these links between the various interests involved in counterrevolutionary activities was Señora Luz Franco de Perches. Indeed, the contribution of women to the Catholic cause in exile in the United States was one of signal importance. From the early 1920s, Catholic women participated in social organizations such as the Damas and, as Patience Schell has asserted, served as intermediaries not only between the church and the home but also between the church and Mexican society.[4] According to Schell, "The damas católicas realized that the revolution was officially anticlerical, but they also saw that 1920s Mexico was still in flux and that they could lobby for a Mexico that allowed for a socially and politically active church."[5] For elite women, it was their duty to promote the model of Catholic feminine piety. The most important result of their efforts to organize Catholic women was the emergence of Catholic women's labor unions that served as the basis for resistance to the anticlerical policies of the revolutionary state. Catholic militancy and Catholic social action went hand in hand.

Luz de Perches was one of the most militant and involved Catholic activists in Mexico City in the 1920s. Her son, José Perches Franco, was the private secretary to Archbishop José Mora y del Río throughout the decade, both in Mexico and in exile in El Paso, until the archbishop's death on 22 April 1928. De Perches was also a prominent member of the Damas but later became involved in the Liga. The reader will recall that she was one of the participants in the August 1926 plot in Mexico City that was to coincide with Enrique Estrada's expedition into Baja California, and she spent ten days in prison for her participation.[6] Shortly after her release, she left Mexico for exile in El Paso. De Perches was well connected to the Catholic community as well as the felicistas in exile, and she worked tirelessly to inform Díaz and his private secretary, Guillermo Rosas Jr., of every aspect of political and military happenings in Mexico and in the United States. She was a key node of communication and information between Mexico and various exile groups—Catholics, Liga Nacional Defensora de la Libertad Religiosa (LNDLR) members, felicistas, as well as military leaders also plotting rebellion from the Mexican side of the border.

Although the content varied and some portions of the intelligence may have been less useful than others, de Perches offered a plethora of information regarding casual contacts that may have been of use to Díaz, information about the successes of the Cristero troops in various parts of Mexico, and on occasion, news of troop movements and rumblings of discontent in the garrisons in the north—mainly Chihuahua and Coahuila. The reason that de Perches was so well informed was that she was able to tap into several of the communications networks corresponding to the various factions. She was in constant contact with high-ranking members of the Knights of Columbus in the United States as well as various high-profile North American clergymen. She was also in close contact with Gen. Marcelo Caraveo's wife, Manuela. Caraveo, one of the generals who would later connive with the Catholics in El Paso, was an ex-villista, a revolutionary general under Obregón, and the governor of Chihuahua from 1928 to 1929. He maintained his ties to the military and boasted the full support of the garrison in that state. Finally, de Perches enjoyed seemingly unimpeded contact with René Capistran Garza, the executive chief of the Cristero Rebellion in the United States; Félix Díaz; and Guillermo Rosas Jr. Thus the number of lines of communication that intersected with de Perches placed her in a unique position as an intelligence broker for the Catholic contingent in exile.

With regard to the search for an acceptable leader that might unite Catholic interests with other political exile groups that boasted military backing—one of the long-standing requirements for financial support from that nebulous business-political axis in Washington and New York—Luz de Perches was equally well informed. While exiled factions in the United States had been seeking some sort of unification since well before Estrada's failed mission in August 1926, finding a suitable candidate was a challenging proposition because the Catholics who held positions within the Liga were hoping to keep the leadership of the organization in the United States in their own camp rather than branching out into the available military leadership in exile. Ultimately, the Liga presented René Capistran Garza as their candidate to lead the rebellion from exile. Capistran Garza had been a high-ranking member of the Liga in Mexico City and was one of the most active members of the Catholic community in the United States. As pointed out in the case of the earliest counterrevolutionary attempts at organizing, the problem for the anonymous financial contributors to the cause was that they required an individual or group of individuals who were guaranteed to be able to obtain the support of the Mexican military. Capistran Garza, as de Perches pointed out, had absolutely no military experience or connections.[7] She nonetheless sang his praises, asserting that he was a good, honorable, and valiant man; a wonderful speaker; and perhaps most important, "a good fervent Catholic, easily influenced so that high-ranking Catholics have someone to obey them blindly."[8] De Perches also pointed out that Capistran Garza had, in fact, made important connections with the old elements of the porfirian federal army residing in New York. Of course, these contacts would have meant nothing to potential financial contributors to the cause. They wanted current military leaders who would still have contacts in Mexico, not porfirian military leaders who could no longer count on support within the revolutionary military. De Perches took seriously the goal of unifying the various factions in exile because she understood that the only way to gain the financial backing and influence of the elements in the oil and mining industries, as well as key politicians in the US government, was to demonstrate without a doubt that all their prerequisites had been fulfilled. Despite his shortcomings, she believed that Capistran Garza had the capacity to make that unification a reality.

However, Capistran Garza could not stay in the good graces of the Catholic contingent for long. As the pressure for results from various camps mounted, several Catholics, including those handling the money, were disappointed in Capistran Garza's performance as leader of the Catholic cause. As of January 1927, there were already calls to remove him from his position if he did not soon deliver a viable movement. There were others aside from Capistran Garza, more militant and willing to use military force than he, who were favored by the Catholics and felicistas alike, such as José Gándara, one of the leaders of the Partido Católico (Catholic Party) and a staunch supporter of the LDR in the United States. After meeting with prominent Jesuit priests exiled in San Antonio, de Perches pointed out that the priests, the Gándara family, and their constituency in El Paso were "very disgusted with Capistran."[9] While Capistran Garza may have had the moral and personal qualities considered necessary to lead the Catholic contingent among the exiles, there were other aggressive elements that could deliver immediate action, meaning they were willing to forge ahead with their own plans for rebellion. José Gándara was not only a dedicated adherent to "the cause" in Mexico; he had been chosen by the LDR in the United States to serve as their minister of war. He was a tireless activist who concentrated most of his energies on gunrunning and organizing cross-border rebellions. As a result of his activities, he came under the scrutiny of the US Department of Justice, leading to a two-year federal prison sentence for violation of US neutrality laws.

Gándara was a photography studio owner in El Paso and had lived in that city for most of his adult life. He was a Mexican emigrant from Chihuahua, and his father had been a lawyer for the American Smelting and Refining Company for thirty years.[10] Gándara was quite well situated to assist in the Cristero cause, being conveniently located in the city that became the greatest hot spot of Catholic and anticallista fervor along the border. But he also had a strong reputation among the business classes and men of politics in El Paso—a reputation, in part, passed down from his father, also a well-respected and pious member of the Mexican resident community there. Gándara was also linked to the greater Catholic network in the United States, holding membership in the Knights of Columbus as well as the Asociación Católica de la Juventud Mexicana (Mexican Catholic Youth Association; ACJM). After a visit with key Mexican prelates in Mexico City in September 1926, Gándara claimed to have received full authority to carry on in the United States all fundraising and organization activities necessary to further the Catholic cause in Mexico. Gándara enjoyed substantial support from the local Catholic population, the bishop of El Paso Anthony Schuler, as well as the Knights of Columbus. After he and Capistran Garza released a manifesto urging Mexicans across the republic to rise in arms against the Mexican government under the banner of Cristo Rey, Catholic exiles in El Paso were hopeful of a successful revolution led by one of their own. By this time, there were widespread rumors that

Gándara was busy purchasing arms and ammunition and recruiting a large fighting force for that purpose.[11]

As Capistran Garza began to lose ground within the LDR, the ties between him and Gándara also loosened; Gándara began to look elsewhere for potential support. This he found in the persons of Bishop Schuler, a Jesuit named Cruz Garde, and the exiled bishop of Sonora, Juan Navarrete. Bishop Navarrete, as we saw in chapter 2, was involved in conspiring with the delahuertistas to foment rebellion among the Yaqui Indians. Around the same time—mid- to late 1926—he was in negotiations with Gándara. Fearing that the constant squabbles and infighting among the exile Catholic action organizations over fundraising were doing more to harm than good, Gándara came to the conclusion that it was time for action whether the funds were sufficient or not. It was among the Yaqui tribes that Gándara began recruiting.[12] It is clear that there was very little consensus among the Catholic exile organizations in the United States and the Liga in Mexico City as to the exact manner to proceed with any belligerent act against the Calles government. Although the LNDLR would choose as its military leader Enrique Gorostieta Velarde—a porfirian military officer turned mercenary—in 1928, as of 1926 and into 1927, there was hardly any agreement regarding the choice of military leadership. Further, the propensity to utilize the forward momentum of the Yaqui Uprising in Sonora was not limited to the delahuertistas. Perhaps more accurately put, the Catholics were willing to negotiate with anyone, regardless of principle, when an alliance seemed possible.

Gándara's plan had been to cross the border into Ciudad Juárez, where he would be joined by bands of Yaquis. Upon the successful seizure of the city, the Catholics would use Ciudad Juárez as their base of operations in the campaign against the government. However, as in the case of Enrique Estrada's failed rebellion in Southern California, Department of Justice agents were watching Gándara's activities. Gándara had been buying arms from a dealer in Tucson who was already known to bureau agents as having purchased and shipped arms to Mexican rebels (mainly Yaquis in Sonora) in previous months, Esteban Borgaro. Borgaro was arrested and soon incriminated some of his associates, including Gándara. Having seen the writing on the wall, Gándara turned himself in to police in Tucson in June 1927.[13] Just one month before Gándara's failed rebellion, Adolfo de la Huerta had attempted to utilize the Yaqui Uprising to his advantage in much the same way. Indeed, it was in May of the same year that Luis Gayou, Adolfo's brother Alfonso de la Huerta, and the de la Huerta's purchasing agent, Francisco Ferriz, were arrested. Although there is no direct evidence that these various groups of exiles were involved directly in negotiations with each other, they must have known that there was a common end to which they could strive in providing arms and ammunition to the Yaquis.

The case of José Gándara illustrates the complex nature of alliances and power brokering among the exile factions in the United States. It is not clear whether any of these individuals were communicating with each other or whether they were making their best efforts to rebel across the border, unaware of the plans of others. This case also illustrates the divisions and differences of opinion among the elements in the Liga and the LDR organizing the effort that was ultimately intended to bolster the fortunes of the Cristeros in Mexico. There was never any certainty that the various factions in the United States would work with each other; they operated on their own schedules and according to their own internal loyalties. Certainly they remained abreast of news of the other factions' activities and failures, but aside from occasional cross-factional meetings to discuss the possibility of unification, the main groups remained reluctant to cooperate. The delahuertistas, most of them soldiers or politicians from the revolution, reached out to the felicistas, but don Félix would never entertain an alliance with the same revolutionaries who threw him out of the country in 1914. The Catholics were never interested in flirting with de la Huerta because of the stain of revolutionary anticlericalism. The nature of the networks that actually *were* formed in exile, for the most part, followed these factional lines. Delahuertistas tended to gravitate toward military leaders with revolutionary credentials, such as Enrique Estrada and César López de Lara. Felicistas allied with the Catholic contingent and the porfirian element in exile, among them Ignacio Lozano, Nemesio García Naranjo, and don Porfirio's old minister of foreign relations, Francisco López Carvajal.

It was not just within the Mexican Catholic, ex-porfirian, or ex-military circles that the Catholic rebels found support; the US-Mexico border, as has been discussed at length, was a place beyond the effective grasp of both the Mexican and US governments. The existence of Mexican confidential agents, dedicated Mexican consuls, and the varied US agencies along the border certainly attest to a clear attempt to gain some control. But control of the border and the people who inhabited it would remain elusive for the rest of the decade and, indeed, beyond. In Laredo, for example, Díaz and the Catholic contingent could count on quite a bit of support, certainly equal to that found in San Antonio or El Paso. Moreover, Laredo, Texas, shares its border with Nuevo Laredo, Tamaulipas. It was in this particular zone that much of the contraband arms and ammunition made their way into Mexico. It was also the main zone of operation for the famed tamaulipeño Gen. César López de Lara. There was constant rebel activity in and around Laredo, and certain US officials were at the center of that activity. In addition to the throngs of exiles from the porfirian period residing along the border and points north, there were American citizens who, like the old porfirians, longed for the stability that they believed had been ensured by the Constitution of 1857. Some—mercenaries, arms dealers, detective agencies—were in it to make a profit from the chronic political instability in Mexico. Others, such as Laredo district attorney John A. Valls, Supreme Knight James A. Flaherty, and Washington, DC, attorney Chandler P. Anderson saw a real and dangerous parallel between the Mexican revolutionary state and the Soviets—in the religious as well as the political and social fields. Whatever their motivation, these individuals operated as key elements of support for the felicistas and the Catholics. We should be clear about the nature of their activities. These individuals were not simply writing inflammatory letters to their legislators or peacefully protesting the policies of the State Department in Washington; they produced propaganda, personally purchased and carried arms and ammunition into Mexico, knowingly violated US neutrality laws, and traversed not just the Mexico-US border but also the US-Canada border. In this sense, the networks that the counterrevolutionary exiles utilized in their quest to topple the Calles government spanned the entire continent of North America and two international boundaries.

John A. Valls, the district attorney for the jurisdiction of Laredo, had a bad reputation in the region for being unpredictable and mercurial but was also very powerful on the local level. While Valls had a reputation for bully tactics and questionable ethics, his favorite targets were Mexican consular officials and Confidential Department agents. On 6 February 1926, José García, a Mexican Confidential Department agent, made his way back across the border between Nuevo Laredo, Tamaulipas, and Laredo, Texas. He had planned to pay the Laredo sheriff a visit before settling back down in Laredo. Valls was in the sheriff's office at the time and asked García to accompany him to his office. In his report, García attested to being browbeaten and treated in a despicable manner. Once in Valls's office, Valls upbraided the agent for carrying a sidearm, for which he had documented and signed permission from Special Agent in Charge (SAC) Gus T. Jones in San Antonio and from Capt. William Hanson, immigration inspector at Laredo. Valls, not satisfied with García's response, took the pistol, accusing him of having been an assassin for the Mexican government.[14] García protested, but when he realized that his defense would get him nowhere with Valls, he asked to be permitted to talk to his consul, to which Valls responded, "I don't give a fuck about your Consul, I'm the only one in charge here."[15] He then went on to question García regarding the Mexican government's actions in the case of Eugenio Bianquini, an individual wanted for the murder of a local sheriff's deputy and suspected of hiding out in Northern Mexico.[16] Far from assisting in Bianquini's apprehension, Valls accused the Mexican Secret Service of doing everything in their power to protect him. When Valls asked García why Bianquini had not yet been apprehended, García replied that the failure had been the result of "the indiscretions of the American Police." The statement was perhaps ill advised, as it was at that point that Valls threw García in the lockup.[17]

As the case of the altercation with Agent García illustrates, Valls was an imposing figure. He was aggressive, hostile to Mexicans—particularly the agents of the revolutionary government—and operated in Webb County virtually unchallenged by other political officials. According to Garcia's report, it was a well-known fact that all the officials in the county were terrified of Valls because he had a reputation for putting people in jail simply for having a difference of opinion.[18] Throughout his tenure, Valls was anything but cooperative with confidential agents and Mexican consular officials. He made it his mission to obfuscate and complicate matters for the representatives of the Mexican government. He maintained ties to the reactionary element, and his activities certainly earned him the title of "enemy of the Mexican Government."

As if the Mexican authorities needed any more evidence of Valls's reactionary connections, Consul Alfredo Vásquez in Brownsville confirmed the district attorney's connivance with the Díaz faction. In early April 1927, Díaz made a two-day visit to Laredo, where he met with Valls at the Robert E. Lee Hotel, a popular gathering place for counterrevolutionary exiles. According to the consul, Valls promised Díaz "that in case [Díaz] decided to lead an armed movement against the Government of Gral. Calles, [Valls] would assist him with his political influence in order to move arms and ammunition that he would need for the revolution through the jurisdiction of Laredo."[19] The consul went on to say that Valls had actually promised Díaz quite a bit more. Valls pledged the services of the Laredo police force as a personal guard during Díaz's visit to that city and promised to protect him from agents of the Mexican government, who Valls referred to as the "spies of the bandits in Mexico." Valls also pledged that he would work out deals with hardware stores with which he had good relations and could count on for the arrangement of shipping arms and ammunition and that he would undertake an extensive propaganda campaign in support of Díaz in the regional presses—mainly *La Prensa* in San Antonio.[20] According to the report, Díaz did not take the offer but promised to think it over very seriously. It is doubtful that Valls was plying the general with promises that he could not deliver; he was most likely fully prepared to provide exactly the assistance he had offered. Moreover, it was reported that Díaz held a very strong affinity for Valls. The two had been seen together chatting frequently around Laredo, and according to one of the consul's contacts, Díaz had mentioned to those of his friends who came out to say good-bye at the station that "a group of men like Valls would be sufficient to change the government in Mexico."[21]

Agent Fernando de la Garza confirmed Vásquez's report of Valls's meeting with Díaz, pointing out that although there was no written record of the meeting, there were multiple reliable witnesses to the fact that Valls had met with Díaz in his hotel room at the Robert E. Lee.[22] De la Garza verified the fact that Valls had promised to offer his support to Díaz but that he even went so far as to volunteer to organize a fundraising campaign for a rebellion, should it be necessary, assuring Díaz that all the local official agencies, "rangers, police, etc. far from persecuting him, would care for him, watch his back, and give him all of the necessary support so that the rebellion spreads into Northern Mexico."[23] Verified or not, De la Garza knew that if the Mexican government were to take any legal action against Valls, it would certainly fail. People were so terrified of Valls that there was no one willing to testify against him.[24] As late as September 1928, Valls was still making injurious statements against the Mexican government in the *San Antonio Light*, a Hearst publication, and *La Prensa*, Ignacio Lozano's publication, also of San Antonio. In this case, Valls had not limited his vitriol to the Mexican government but had made insulting remarks regarding the US Department of State in reference to the handling of the Mexican situation. As a result of his comments and prior association with men like Díaz, there had been a movement in the Republican Party to get rid of him.[25]

Valls was a perfect example of a local elected official who was free from the intervention of the US government to put into practice personal policies that would support his own hostility toward the Calles regime in Mexico. He was enabled by a local regime of threats and political bullying that made opposition undesirable, if not impossible. In reference to the assistance that Mexican agents received in Laredo in the apprehension of dangerous exile elements in 1929, Consul Rafael de la Colina mentioned R. L. Bobbitt, the attorney general in Webb County, as being very helpful and sincere in his relations with the consul. Bobbitt was Valls's replacement in that year. However, de la Colina added that there was no doubt in his mind that Bobbitt could find himself in a difficult position if he were to make enemies of those who had been politically dominant in Webb County for years, "headed by the Attorney John A. Valls" and who had "always harassed, directly or indirectly, our government and its functionaries."[26] Even after Valls's term as district attorney, he remained a political force with which to be reckoned. In fact, shortly after his appointment, District Attorney Bobbitt was promoted to the office of Texas district attorney, and Valls was returned to his post in September 1929.[27]

## THE NORTH AMERICAN CLERGY AND THE KNIGHTS OF COLUMBUS

While the North American clergy was somewhat divided with regard to supporting the Catholics both in Mexico and in the United States, there were certain American prelates, such as Archbishop Arthur J. Drossaerts, who took quite a militant stance on the responsibility of the United States government in the matter. The bishops in question did not involve themselves in the arms-smuggling activities of the interested parties already discussed, nor did they make public statements condemning such practices. In fact, it was Drossaerts who stated proudly that Catholics were engaged in a movement to put an end to the Mexican government and, as such, would not ally with Adolfo de la Huerta "or with any leader who had defended or defends the Constitution of 1917."[28] While many of the Catholic exiles and others were producing vicious propaganda for print in newspapers such as *La Prensa* and the *San Antonio Light*, the bishops put in their fair share of condemnation of the Calles government as well as that of the United States in the hopes that their voices might sway readers by educating the public on the situation in Mexico. As scholars have quite rightly pointed out, the activities of these North American prelates, and others in the American hierarchy, had an effect on public opinion in the United States but were ultimately ineffective on the level of US policy.[29]

Archbishop Drossaerts was one of the most outspoken and vituperative opponents of the Mexican government. He was incredibly well positioned in San Antonio, which in the 1920s had become a gathering place for exiled

Catholics and, more generally, political exiles from the revolution. Along with El Paso, San Antonio had become a hotbed of Catholic activism, and any individual who had the will and the money to put together a propaganda campaign or a rebellion could find their most influential contacts there. San Antonio was the adopted home of exiled bishop of Mexico José Mora y del Río and the bishop of Aguascalientes, Ignacio Valdespino, both of whom died later in their state of exile in that city. San Antonio was also home to many of the exiled members of the LNDLR such as René Capistran Garza, a hub for political exiles like Jorge Prieto Laurens, and the home of *La Prensa,* a notorious and unapologetic supporter of the full spectrum of Calles's opposition in the United States. Archbishop Drossaerts was one of the opposition's loudest supporters.

The Mexican consul in San Antonio, Alejandro P. Carrillo, upon having met the archbishop for the first time in March 1926, found Drossaerts to be a frank, cordial, and honorable man. They discussed the allegations that some of the exiled priests residing in San Antonio (mostly Spaniards and Italians) had been producing anonymous propaganda unfavorable to the Mexican government. Drossaerts claimed that although he was aware of the existence of the propaganda, he had no knowledge of it being produced by exiled priests.[30] In a very amiable conclusion to their meeting, the archbishop expressed to Carrillo that it had been a pleasure to meet him and that because of the many good references he had received, he felt as if he had known Carrillo for a long time.[31] Four days after his meeting with Drossaerts, Carrillo met with the editor of the *San Antonio Light.* The local paper had printed some commentary from Drossaerts regarding the religious question in Mexico along with some of the anonymous editorials that had concerned Carrillo in the first place. The editor and some of the correspondents for the paper refused to take credit for the editorials. The consul was then convinced that the negative press the Mexican government was receiving in the United States was the direct result of clerical influence. He reported that he had come to understand that the propaganda in the local press was being "influenced by the Catholic element . . . as unfortunately there are some periodicals that agree with their ideas, they have no qualms in printing what pleases them [the Catholics]."[32]

Drossaerts, like many of his cohort, objected to the Calles regime on the grounds that the government was suppressing the Mexican people's right to free and open religious worship. On a deeper level, however, and mimicking the admonitions of the US oil and mining interests, they equated the Obregón and Calles governments, and later the Cárdenas administration, with bolshevism. They looked to Soviet Russia and made the argument that the suppression of religious freedom was simply the first step in a process that would, if not stopped by the United States, result in the spread of bolshevism across the border. Drossaerts, more than any other American prelate, made this correlation very clear in his writings. In the foreword to Fr. Michael Kenny's famed 1935 publication on the Mexican persecution, *No God Next Door,* Drossaerts lamented, "One must be blind not to detect the intense menace to our own free institutions, to our democracy and liberty in the Calles and Cárdenas policies. Moscow has its laboratory, its efficient workshop in Mexico. And it is not so much a distracted Mexico they want to conquer; they are after bigger game: the Colossus, our own United States is what they wish to bag in their relentless war against God and Christian civilization."[33] Indeed, widely distributed pamphlets produced by the American hierarchy and the Knights of Columbus in the 1920s boasted titles such as "Red Mexico: The Facts" and "Mexico: Bolshevism the Menace." Father Kenny himself wrote, "'Russia on the Rio Grande' and 'Our Bolshevist Border' first sprung to mind as proper captions for a frank description of Mexican Government today. Soon, however, these were found inadequate to picture an administrative system more ruthlessly planned and executed and in most important essentials more destructive of law and liberty and every elemental right . . . than the reddest and rawest that Lenin and Stalin have so far inflicted on humanity. Nor would any title be adequate that ignores our share in this development."[34] For religious leaders like Drossaerts, the association of anticlericalism with the revolutionary government in Mexico was best translated into protests directed to the State Department and White House against what was perceived as open support for a bolshevist state. Drossaerts in particular made the argument that the recognition of the Mexican government represented a fundamental contradiction, as the United States had not recognized the Soviet government.[35] While Archbishop Drossaerts and other religious leaders limited their activities to public pronouncements and the production of propaganda, the Knights of Columbus under the direction of Supreme Knight James A. Flaherty were engaged in more sinister activities.

Historian Matthew Redinger has suggested that the activities of the Knights of Columbus, and those of the North American Catholic hierarchy in general, were focused on aggressive political protests and peaceful propaganda campaigns meant to sway public opinion in the United States against the established government in Mexico. More specifically, Redinger makes the claim that in all the fundraising activities undertaken by the Knights of Columbus, none of the money went to support the Cristeros in Mexico.[36] While he quite rightly notes that there were myriad approaches that the American clergy took with regard to the perceived religious persecution in Mexico, his claim that the hierarchy and, more specifically, the Knights of Columbus refrained from getting involved in the violence in Mexico must be scrutinized in light of Mexican sources that tell a different story regarding the Cristero Rebellion. Funds collected by the knights were allocated to the relief of exile families, political refugees residing in the United States, and many of the exiled prelates as well as to intense anti-Calles propaganda campaigns. However, the Knights of Columbus, under the direction of Supreme Knight Flaherty of Connecticut, were also involved in a network of arms smuggling that spanned the United States, Canada, and Mexico. The network operated with the expressed purpose of sending arms and ammunition out of British Columbia, down the Pacific Coast, and into Mexico's Pacific ports—mainly Mazatlán. The armament was most certainly destined for the Cristeros in the field, and as such, the Knights of Columbus were actively supporting the Cristeros in battle.

Flaherty, much like Drossaerts, was openly critical of the Calles government and also of the perceived indifference of the US government toward what he viewed as religious persecution in Mexico. The Knights of Columbus more broadly had made it the organization's mission to influence the policy of the US government with regard to the religious persecution in Mexico. Their primary desires, however, were the lifting of the arms embargo and the withdrawal of recognition of the Calles government. These goals had been agreed upon in a resolution drafted at a national conference of the knights in Philadelphia on 5 August 1926. The resolution was then sent to Pres. Calvin Coolidge and Secretary of State Frank Kellogg. After discussing the matter, Coolidge and Kellogg took the position that there was no justification for US intervention in church-state relations because US citizens had not been affected.[37]

Flaherty then contacted President Coolidge to arrange a formal meeting, and Coolidge immediately referred him to Secretary of State Kellogg. Kellogg made it clear that the United States was not in the position to intervene in the affairs of Mexico and would not lift the arms embargo under any circumstances. Having been thoroughly unsatisfied by the results of the encounter, Flaherty sought a meeting with Coolidge. He was interested in talking to the president not just because he had not obtained the desired result from the secretary of state but also because he felt that there had been a fundamental misunderstanding of the position of the Knights of Columbus on the Mexican situation. He believed, quite rightly, that the secretary of state understood that the knights were pushing for direct intervention in Mexico—certainly the knights had publicly stated this position since August. Flaherty now insisted that the organization had been misunderstood. He only wanted to clarify to the president that the knights were not seeking US intervention in Mexico and would be satisfied "if this government will rigorously protect American lives and property whenever they are involved in Mexico."[38] Flaherty dropped all the knights' demands for a lifting of the arms embargo and the withdrawal of recognition of the Calles government. Perhaps Flaherty curbed his public vitriol in order to avoid drawing attention to his organization's activities.

In September 1926, a high-ranking knight suggested to Flaherty that there should be a fund to assist exiled priests and other refugees from the conflict and to produce Catholic propaganda mainly as a means of stemming the "bolshevist" tide sweeping Mexico by generating anti-Calles public opinion in the United States. Flaherty established what quickly became a $1 million Mexican fund.[39] The supreme knight asserted that the money that was being raised was in no way being used to foment any rebellion in Mexico or to fund the creation of a Knights of Columbus "army" there, an accusation that had been raised in the Mexico City press. The funds were intended to "aid the nuns and priests driven out and to spread propaganda which may lead the Mexican government to change its policy or the American government to do something about it—possibly in the way of withdrawal of recognition."[40] Flaherty's covert activities, uncovered by Mexican confidential agents, evidence an entirely different attitude regarding the use of the knights' funds for the Cristero cause. In September 1926, an informant for a local Los Angeles newspaper editor reported to the Mexican secretary of foreign relations, Aaron Saenz, that the collection of funds for a revolution in Mexico was "a done deal" and that the Knights of Columbus had been collecting money, "close to a million dollars . . . in order to start a press campaign to foment a revolution in Mexico to which the funds collected were destined."[41]

Flaherty's involvement went much further than the informant knew at the time. He was involved in a complex arms-smuggling network that consisted of a group of diverse players, at the head of which was a prominent New York and Washington, DC, attorney named Chandler P. Anderson. Anderson was also the American commissioner of the Mixed Claims Commission dealing with the German sinking of the *Lusitania* who, just the previous year, settled a claim of $217,337.14 for individuals and corporations in California.[42] Anderson was the organizational head who set up the connections in Canada and established the network of intermediaries in the United States and Mexico that acquired, shipped, and received the materials. In the supervisory position was a veteran liquor (and all-around contraband) smuggler named George Merrill. Merrill made sure that shipments went out on time and maintained contact with intermediaries and suppliers in Canada and Mexico.[43] The intermediaries were supplied with personnel by the New York–based Eagle Detective Agency.[44] Moreover, some of the agents of the Eagle Detective Agency who were serving as nodes of contact between Canada and Mazatlán were residing in Mexican national territory the entire time. However, de la Garza had been unable to identify them. In fact, de la Garza suggested that because the evidence on the Canadian side was accurate and they had the identities of the northern component of the operation, it should be the goal of the Confidential Department to shadow the known agents and follow them to their contacts in Mexico, thus attacking the network at its terminal points.[45] There is no indication, however, in the documentary record that the Confidential Department ever followed through with the proposal. The problem was that de la Garza knew he was not dealing with a bunch of petty smugglers. The connections they were utilizing would have relied on relationships with local officials who could grease the wheels at major ports to make sure that the contraband made it into the country unmolested.

George Merrill had been involved in smuggling arms and other contraband materials for some time, but it was just after the arrest of Enrique Estrada in August 1926 that he was associated with Anderson.[46] The two were in constant contact regarding the state of the supply of armaments available for purchase as well as the methods for managing the operation. Merrill did not hold a very high opinion of the Mexican exiles who had worked with Estrada, nor did he believe that Mexicans were capable, in general, of carrying out the sort of operation they were undertaking—at least not unsupervised. When Anderson authorized Jésus Rodríguez, who had previously worked with Enrique Estrada, to go to Canada to see if Merrill needed any help, Merrill became agitated, stating, "I trust no Mexican, no matter how good he might be, and while some of them may be alright to carry out orders within the Mexican territory, I would not let them know too much about our activities in the U.S. or Canada."[47] Merrill further noted that he had to change his location because a man named A. Merrill (no apparent relation) had checked into an adjoining room and began asking the front desk staff questions about him. He requested that Anderson not contact him through their normal channels but to wait for him to call from a location outside the hotel.[48] Merrill's complaint suggests that the surveillance on Mexican exiles extended beyond the border between the United States and Mexico, across the country, and across the US-Canada border. It is also quite clear that the smuggling and conspiratorial networks spanned the whole of the North American continent as well as Central America.

Of the approximate $1 million collected by Flaherty and the Knights of Columbus, a total of $86,896 went to be managed by Anderson for the month of November 1926. The list of expenditures was submitted to Flaherty directly from the office of Anderson in early October of that year. The most important lines in the fiscal report were to George Merrill in the amount of $3,748; to "General Agents" (no doubt of the Eagle Detective Agency): $9,827; to Enrique Estrada: $5,000, perhaps for legal counsel; and for "purchase of material": $47,450. Anderson himself was paid in the amount of $1,500, and interestingly, the Knights of Columbus provided "our people in San Antonio" with $8,500.[49] The notation "our people in San Antonio" most likely referred to the Catholic contingent under the leadership of the Archbishop Drossaerts. It was through the efforts of the consul general in New York, Arturo Elías, President Calles's half-brother and political confidant, and the Confidential Department that this particular plot was uncovered. However, the information and the circuitous route it took on its way to the hands of Mexican officials suggests that the Knights of Columbus' conspiracy to help unseat Calles through Catholic rebellion was fraught with international intrigue and espionage and a transnational network of interests that did not always work toward the same end.

In November and December 1926, Agent Fernando de la Garza was charged with a very special investigative mission at the behest of Consul General Elías.[50] The consul general had come into possession of a set of documents that detailed the activities of Anderson and Merrill and wanted de la Garza to investigate their validity.[51] The process by which Elías came to the documents was questionable at best, but the story is intriguing. An international spy known as Doctor J. Notsovitzki (a.k.a. Richard Williams) was involved in the arms network and generated and maintained an extensive documentary record regarding his activities and associations with Anderson, Merrill, and Supreme Knight James Flaherty. It was Notsovitzki who sold the documents to Elías. As de la Garza put it, Notsovitzki was a very active international spy who, because of his prior affiliations with enemies of the Mexican government, could not be trusted and should be handled with the utmost care.[52] Throughout the investigation, de la Garza uncovered a much more extensive conspiratorial network involving well-known bankers, such as George Fisher Baker, director of the First National Bank of New York, who had been providing a large proportion of the funds necessary for purchasing arms. Additionally, de la Garza discovered that the documentation contained details that clearly implicated other individuals who were engaged in activities that were "out of the reach of our Department to counteract."[53] De la Garza never mentioned these individuals in his report, but considering the extent of the arms network and the connections in Washington that Merrill, Anderson, and Flaherty boasted, it is not unreasonable to conclude that the "other elements" of which de la Garza spoke may have been prominent political figures in Washington and New York or prominent oil men. As de la Garza pointed out, Chandler Anderson was the director of the claims commission and "the man with the most influence with the White House and above all with the Department of State."[54] Indeed, the most interesting aspect of this particular case is that although Arturo Elias, Fernando de la Garza, the Confidential Department, and President Calles all were in possession of such damning evidence, no action was taken against Anderson, Merrill, or Flaherty. In fact, Flaherty was elected for another two-year term as supreme knight and later was elected to a higher commissioned status within the organization. Even more surprising is that the documentary record ends without resolution. There is no indication that a single agent of the Eagle Detective Agency was ever arrested or that any member of the conspiracy involved below the level of Flaherty or Anderson was ever charged with violations of neutrality laws. It is most likely that Anderson's position on the Mixed Claims Commission and his connections in the Department of State and the White House made him untouchable. It could also be that the information, while valid, came from such an unreliable source as Doctor Notsovitzki that the evidence could never be sufficient to accuse—much less convict—a high-ranking and respected member of the US political community. In any case, there is no further evidence in the files that the network continued to ship arms and ammunition to Mexico after its discovery by Mexican agents—at least not under the supervision of Flaherty or Anderson.

## CONCLUSION

The Cristero Rebellion in Mexico had a profound impact on the ways in which alliances were formed among the exile communities in the United States. Whether porfirista, felicista, delahuertista, or other, alliances formed in the years after 1926 took on a more Catholic tinge and became more viable than they had ever been before. Those who made no explicit statements regarding the religious question or maintained the stain of revolutionary anticlericalism, such as Adolfo de la Huerta, fell out of favor with the new Catholic exiles. Others who could find common cause with the Catholic contingent gained their favor. The conflict in Mexico not only increased the possibilities for more favorable alliances among the exiles; it also heightened concerns among Mexican consular officials and Confidential Department agents along the border that interests among the exile communities were coming together in dangerous ways. On a third level, the Cristero Rebellion initiated a new stage of American Catholic activism, most of it as benign as public pronouncements and editorializing on the religious situation in Mexico. While consular officials and confidential agents certainly considered the pronouncements injurious to the prestige and honor of the Mexican nation, it was the covert activities being undertaken by the likes of the James A. Flaherty, Chandler Anderson, George Merrill, and others working to circumvent US neutrality laws that seemed most threatening. While smugglers like Merrill, interested in profit, had been involved in operations in Mexico for years before the Cristero Rebellion, Flaherty had a mission that went well beyond the drive for personal gain. The upsurge in violence and the perceived persecutions of Catholics had created a desperate situation for men like Flaherty and Archbishop Drossaerts, and much like the counterrevolutionary exiles, it forced Flaherty into making strange alliances in order to achieve his end. While the Catholic contingent in the United States considered its alliance with the felicistas useful for the moment, don Félix lacked the military connections they needed within Mexican national territory. No matter how many rifles, machine guns, bombs, or cartridges made it across the border, the rebellion still lacked the military leadership it needed to make a genuine attempt against the Calles government. As a result of this deficiency, the ranking members of the Liga and the leaders of the LDR in the United States began to reach out to some of the already discontented chiefs of the northern Mexican garrisons, such as Gens. Marcelo Caraveo, Francisco Manzo, and José Gonzalo Escobar, as well as old porfirian generals, such as the famed Enrique Gorostieta Velarde.

These fresh alliances with the active military in Mexico posed the biggest threat to the Mexican government. The Cristero Rebellion and the constant intrigues among the exile groups in the United States had taken a toll on the resources of the fledgling Mexican state. The longer that conflict was left unsettled, the more unstable the political and military elements along the border would become. Moreover, the assassination of president-elect Obregón in July 1928 at the hands of José de León Toral, a Catholic fanatic, would drive a wedge between obregonistas and callistas, complicating the already troubled relationship between the Mexican state and the military along the border in the northern states of Sonora, Chihuahua, and Tamaulipas. The rebellion of José Gonzalo Escobar sought to utilize the energy of the Cristero Rebellion and the Catholic contingent in exile to intervene in national politics and to prevent the installation of Calles's choice for interim president, Emilio Portes Gil. Thus the military rebellion did not occur in isolation from the broader complex of contestation regarding the process of revolutionary state building. The same set of fundamental issues that drove the de la Huerta and Cristero rebellions and the revolt of Gómez and Serrano gave rise to the Escobar Rebellion. It is this conflict that the final chapter will treat.

# FIVE

# CATHOLIC CONSPIRACY AND THE MEXICAN MILITARY

Military historians have asserted that throughout the 1920s, the Mexican armed forces were no more unified or professionalized than they had been during the previous decade of revolutionary violence.[1] While the Adolfo de la Huerta Rebellion certainly allowed Álvaro Obregón and Plutarco Elías Calles to eliminate the least trustworthy military leaders from the ranks, it also required that the positions once occupied by those disloyal officers be filled by potentially more inexperienced, corruptible, or politically ambitious men. The officers who took part in the rebellion were local chieftains who enjoyed a substantial level of political and military might. They could, as Robert Carriedo points out, "support particular administrations, rebel against others, desert former allies, and create new alliances with one-time enemies, all on a personal whim."[2] At least some of these generals had subordinates who were of the same mind or who expected the same benefits of the position that their seniors boasted. Carriedo also quite rightly observes that while Obregón's practice of bribing generals for their loyalty might have worked in the short term, the approach had no lasting effect on the ultimate loyalty of individual military men to the government. That three of his generals, owing their rank to support of Obregón in 1920, rebelled against him in

1923 indicated the limits of his $25,000-peso *cañonazos*.[3] In the case of the de la Huerta Rebellion, Obregón and Calles were able to make short work of the rebellious generals. Those who were not killed in battle or executed beat a hasty retreat to the US side of the border. What of those who remained loyal obregonistas? The general level of political and social insecurity meant that a future rebellion could potentially claim those officers as well.[4] Despite the victory over the delahuertistas, there were other officers who expressed their loyalty but contented themselves with watching and waiting to see if Obregón and Calles would be capable of holding on to national power. While many generals remained genuinely loyal to Obregón, their fidelity to Calles was never secure. That the remaining officers who did not participate in the de la Huerta Rebellion would remain loyal was even less certain. Thus "Obregón continued to seduce them with his 25,000 peso 'cannonades,' new automobiles, and other benefits."[5] Military dissent constantly threatened the revolutionary and postrevolutionary governments, and it was for this reason that the reorganization and professionalization of the armed forces was such an imperative for the administrations of Obregón and Calles.

Corruption in the officer corps was one of the by-products of bribery and graft. That Obregón continued his strategy of plying officers with money and big-ticket items in exchange for loyalty meant that the most trusted among the officer corps were often the most incorrigible. The tale of Gen. Guadalupe Sánchez having been rewarded with $50,000 pesos and a car in exchange for the assassination of a fellow general is legend, as is that of secretary of war Gen. Francisco Serrano's payment of his $80,000-peso gambling debt using funds from the national treasury.[6] Even into the late 1920s, there were serious deficiencies in the professionalization of the officer corps, and it is clear that their fidelity was never sufficiently guaranteed. Moreover, rather than producing concrete results, the reorganization and professionalization of the military that Calles had been undertaking along with Secretary of War Joaquin Amaro ruffled the feathers of some of the more powerful generals in the northern states. In the case of other military conflicts in the course of the revolution, the generals who rebelled against the state were almost always driven by personal ambition and a desire to defend against any encroachment upon their own local power. The same was true for José Gonzalo Escobar's rebellion of March 1929. The case of the Escobar Rebellion illustrates that along the border and in the states that lined it, the governors, the military, and the political machines that ruled those areas resisted the centralizing efforts of the Calles regime. That the northern states remained fiercely independent and had connections to the Catholic contingent in exile made those military commands prime targets for the Catholics, the delahuertistas, and the felicistas in their plots to overthrow the Mexican government.

While confidential agents, the US Border Patrol, and the Department of Justice were able to shore up specific problem areas along the border, many regions were not secure enough to prevent continued relations and communications between sympathizers in Mexico and exiles in the United States. It was one thing for the Mexican government to exile its Catholic dissidents, obstinate priests, and their collaborators; it was a much more difficult task to cut their lines of communication back to Mexico. There was a tremendous concern among the various Mexican state agencies and military garrisons along the border that Catholic sedition in the United States could be carried, much like a virus, by Mexican citizens traversing the border to attend religious services administered by known enemies of the Mexican state. The case of Fr. Pedro Centurioni and his parishioners in Eagle Pass, Texas, is illustrative of the difficulty of tracking and controlling human movement across the international line in one of the more loosely controlled stretches of the border in the 1920s.

Pedro Centurioni was among the religious leaders considered by border officials and agents to be most inflammatory in his rhetoric regarding the religious conflict in Mexico. In late April 1927, Centurioni had been observed berating his parishioners for not doing their duty to help the cause of Catholics in Mexico, calling his male parishioners "cowards, bad Mexicans, and false Catholics" because they had not joined the war against the Calles government. He then turned to the women in the congregation, deeming them "ignorant and bad Christians" for not having urged their husbands and their children to take up arms and fight against the government, which had, as its aim, the destruction of the Catholic faith in Mexico.[7] According to the chief of military operations in Piedras Negras, Coahuila, Jesús Fuentes Dávila, the real problem with the antigovernment rhetoric Centurioni was spouting was that many of the members of his congregation were, in fact, residents of Piedras Negras, not Eagle Pass: "As a large number of his Mexican parishioners come from Piedras Negras, being those whom he commands to declare themselves in rebellion . . . I suggest . . . that orders be issued that the Immigration Office at Piedras Negras prohibit Mexican citizens of both sexes resident in [Piedras Negras] from going to Sunday services at the Catholic church in Eagle Pass." If parishioners still wanted to attend the services in Eagle Pass, Fuentes suggested, they could renounce their citizenship and remain on the US side of the border. They would, at that point, be considered enemies of the Mexican government.[8] Fuentes considered Centurioni's remarks inflammatory and feared that parishioners coming back to Piedras Negras might rise up against the Mexican government as a result of the sermons in Eagle Pass. He proposed that the government should prevent them from attending the services, and should the parishioners resist the prohibition, they would not be allowed to reenter, having chosen exile over dedication to the patria. The concern was well founded, given the arms trafficking of other counterrevolutionary groups such as those under the command of Gen. César López de Lara in South Texas. It was not long before the immigration office in Piedras Negras took Fuentes's suggestion and put it into practice.[9] The case of Pedro Centurioni and his flock illustrates that the level of concern along the border was quite high when it came to policing movement across the line that might involve any connection to Catholic "sedition" in the United States.

Calles was well aware that there were serious deficiencies in the loyalty of the military to his administration, and according to one historian, it was because Calles felt uneasy about the state of the army that he began his intensive professionalization campaign, including an overall reduction of the military.[10] One of the major problems with professionalization, in addition to the issue cited previously, was that revolutionary generals simply had always been involved in local politics; they saw it as one of the benefits of their position as *jefes militares*.[11] The very weakness of the postrevolutionary governments of Obregón and Calles meant that they could not effectively arbitrate local conflicts, and it was this weakness that gave certain military generals such a prominent place in local political affairs. The local authority that they enjoyed was a holdover from the days in which "First Chief" Venustiano Carranza utilized military leaders as proconsuls in regions that the constitutionalists secured during the war between the factions (1913–20). Notable examples were Gen. Salvador Alvarado in Yucatán and Manuel Diéguez in Jalisco. In the 1920s, many of the generals who maintained their local political power were loyal obregonistas who supported the rebellion of Agua Prieta. Because the central government in the 1920s was weak and contested, it was difficult to convince these generals, especially those along the border, to relinquish their authority. It was only in the period following the de la Huerta Rebellion that we see an attempt on the part of the Calles administration to begin to centralize power in Mexico City over the various state entities. As Calles began to crack down on local officials, both military and civilian, conflicts erupted over local power configurations that were disrupted when callista governors were favored over more independent obregonista governors, as was the case with José Guadalupe Zuno in Jalisco.

Zuno was a staunch obregonista and used his position as governor of the state of Jalisco to support a host of labor unions that remained stubbornly independent of the Confederación Regional de Obreros Mexicanos (Regional Confederation of Mexican Workers; CROM) under the leadership of Luis N. Morones, Calles's secretary of industry. Moreover, the Catholic labor unions in the state, particularly in Guadalajara, were always in conflict with Zuno's secular labor syndicates, and on more than one occasion, fighting had erupted in the streets of Guadalajara.[12] A number of members in the Cámara de Diputados, representatives of the state of Jalisco, carried out a smear campaign against Zuno with the approval of Calles and Morones, claiming the governor had been in league with Enrique Estrada, Manuel Diéguez, and Salvador Alvarado during the de la Huerta Rebellion. It mattered little that Zuno was innocent of the charges. During the conflict, he had been forced from the governorship and went into hiding among his supporters in the city. Zuno knew that Calles's ultimate goal was to force impeachment proceedings against him, a process that would permit the national congress to appoint an interim governor. In an adept political move, Zuno resigned rather than allowing Calles to remove him—in effect, preventing the president from installing his own provisional governor and putting the Jalisco legislature in a position to appoint its own candidate before holding a new gubernatorial election.[13] The same pattern was repeated throughout the remainder of the decade, though not on the same scale. Other incidents consisted of municipal leaders being accused of delahuertismo by opponents who had a political ax to grind.[14]

After the assassination of president-elect Obregón in July 1928, Calles made a now famous speech before the national congress, asserting that Mexico had to move beyond the era of caudillos and one-man rule to become a nation of laws and institutions.[15] The generals in various regions of the republic who had enjoyed nearly limitless power then began to feel the squeeze of Calles's plan to reduce the military.[16] The president gave a separate speech to the officer corps at the National Palace on 5 September in which he bluntly told the officers present that their participation in politics would almost certainly become a detriment to the stability and welfare of the nation. For any one of these local strongmen to put in their bid for the presidential elections would, in Calles's opinion, result in further violence and bloodshed and would only serve to accelerate the growing rift within the military and threaten to tear asunder the entire "revolutionary family."[17]

Paradoxically, the general in attendance most opposed to military leaders involving themselves in local or national politics—and most vocal in this regard—was Gen. José Gonzalo Escobar, who pledged that he would "answer the president with all loyalty and honor" and that "all of the *divisionarios* have the obligation to do the same."[18] He professed that they should place their complete confidence in the president and Secretary of War Amaro and promised that "the military uprisings, the hostility, etc., have now passed into history . . . these words should not be heard among us" because he believed the army had been "definitively purged of those shameful elements." He went on to say that the assembled military chiefs should "no longer allow the word 'cuartelazo,' it should be absolutely forbidden."[19] Escobar and several other key generals, however, had no intention of placing all their trust in the executive or

*Gen. José Gonzálo Escobar giving a speech at a banquet in honor of provisional president Emilio Portes Gil at Chapultepec Castle, 1928*
*FAPECFT. Fototeca Colección de Álbumes Fotográficos de los Archivos Plutarco Elías Calles y Fernando Torreblanca (AAPECFT), fondo (AFFT), álbum 3:* Historia Politica de México, 1920–1928. Volumen III. *Fotografía 876, inventario 73.*

erasing the word *cuartelazo* from their vocabularies. All the while, the Calles government utilized agents and members of local government to investigate where various military leaders' loyalties could be counted, if at all. By September 1927, it was entirely unclear what position Gen. Marcelo Caraveo, the *jefe militar* in Chihuahua, might take toward the Calles government and whether he could be trusted to remain loyal. Later that same month, Caraveo left for Ciudad Juárez to meet with General Escobar. Escobar had already made deals with a group of military officers in Mexico City that was to be headed by Gen. Eugenio Martínez. They were planning a rebellion for 15 September, but the rebellion was never realized because Martínez rescinded his support.[20] As the evidence suggests, it was a daunting task to ascertain, from one day to the next, whether Calles could count on the northern generals to behave as loyal soldiers or instead to declare war on his government.

While they remained relatively silent, many of these military leaders did not appreciate the way in which Obregón and Calles dealt with the opposition to Obregón's reelection bid presented by Gens. Arnulfo Gómez and Francisco Serrano. In the wake of Obregón's presidential candidacy, a division between the main supporters of Obregón and the supporters of Calles became readily apparent. However, many of Obregón's past followers remained loyal simply because they were more anticallista than obregonista. When Obregón launched his candidacy in 1927, the obregonista/anticallista factions, the Partido Antireelecionista and the Partido Nacional Revolucionario (not the PNR created by Calles in 1929) presented their own candidates—Gómez and Serrano, respectively—directly challenging Calles's and Obregón's control of the national political machine.[21]

When it became clear that the presidential contest was stacked in Obregón's favor, Gómez and Serrano joined forces and rebelled simultaneously in Veracruz and Morelos. Both of their movements failed. Serrano was executed along with a dozen or more supporters in Huitzilac, Morelos, on 6 October, and about a month later, Gómez met a firing squad in Coatepec, Veracruz.[22] Justified or not, the executions of Gómez and Serrano certainly did not endear Calles or Obregón to the remaining men within the military still capable of pooling enough resources to put together a rebellion. A confidential agent in Chihuahua reported the news that the "death of General Francisco Serrano caused profound discontent among the military men in Chihuahua, principally in General Caraveo, who did not try to hide his anger for what he called an assassination. However, General Caraveo stated that it was already done and therefore there was nothing to do [about it]."[23] While the Norteño generals were not happy with the way in which Obregón and Calles handled their political opposition, they remained silent until the time was right for action.

Well before confidential agents were able to ascertain the attitudes of specific military leaders in Mexico regarding the exiles across the border, Señora Luz de Perches, the felicistas' and the Catholics' eyes and ears in El Paso, knew that the Knights of Columbus were interested in funding a rebellion and that the military leader they considered most agreeable to lead it was General Caraveo. The knights had chosen him because he had a privileged political and military position in Chihuahua, and his position at the border made him a prime candidate.[24] De Perches commented to two of her contacts in the Knights of Columbus that she believed "it was impossible that Caraveo would make a move while Calles was in power" but that Caraveo was also a devout obregonista who had enjoyed free rein to do as he pleased in Chihuahua under Obregón.[25] The insinuation was that he might have been loyal to Obregón but not to Calles. Luz de Perches's statement was somewhat prophetic, as indeed, Caraveo would wait until the interim presidency of Emilio Portes Gil to pronounce himself in league with the escobaristas.

## THE CASE OF GENERAL MARCELO CARAVEO

General Caraveo's story is complex. He had served in the revolutionary armies of Pascual Orozco in Chihuahua in 1910. He later served as a commander of orozquista rural forces against Madero in 1912 and received the rank of brigadier general for his service in the huertista coup that ousted Madero. He commanded federal troops against the constitutionalist forces in Chihuahua and, upon the fall of Huerta, fled to Havana and later the United States, presumably El Paso, but this portion of his personal story is unclear.[26] Caraveo returned to Chihuahua, ostensibly to offer his military services, when threats of US intervention were rumored in 1916. Upon his return, Gen. Jacinto Treviño, then military commander of the state, had him thrown in prison, and he was later transferred to the military prison of Santiago in Mexico City. He soon escaped with the help of some of his supporters in Chihuahua and soldiers who had served with him in the orozquista campaigns. He immediately joined the felicistas in Veracruz under the command of Gen. Manuel Peláez, fighting against First Chief Venustiano Carranza. Caraveo had even been one of the signatories of a manifesto denigrating the new Constitution of 1917 and proclaiming the ultimate validity of the 1857 document.[27] Although the details are not entirely clear, Caraveo managed to find his way onto the winning side in the rebellion of Agua Prieta, which resulted in the triumph of the Sonorans, the interim presidency of Adolfo de la Huerta, and the subsequent presidencies of Obregón and Calles. After serving as chief of military operations in Durango and the state of Mexico, Caraveo returned to Chihuahua in the same capacity in 1925.[28] The general's personal trajectory would suggest that if he was loyal to anyone, it was to Gen. Marcelo Caraveo exclusively.

In January 1927, Caraveo was forced to answer accusations of connivance with the felicistas and the exiled Catholics. Nicolás Pérez, a member of the Chihuahua state legislature and a strong supporter of Caraveo, had received information from an anonymous source that the general had been seen meeting with known felicistas in El Paso. Specifically, he was accused of attending meetings with Señora Luz de Perches.[29] Caraveo evaded the accusation by arguing that this was precisely the expected strategy for the enemies of the Mexican government in the United States to take against him, and he highlighted the criminal activities of de Perches in Mexico prior to her exile as proof of her questionable character.[30] Despite his protests, it was true that Caraveo's wife, Manuela, had been corresponding with de Perches regarding a number of matters—none more important, or damning, than troop movements and general morale in the Chihuahua border garrisons.

Caraveo attempted to cover up what was now a known connection between himself and the rebel exiles by asserting that perhaps on one visit to El Paso with his wife, they might have happened to meet the señora while shopping. Understanding that she was from a well-established family, he had no choice but to greet her in a fashion deserving of her social rank. Perhaps it was because of this chance meeting, Caraveo suggested, that Pérez's anonymous informant got the impression that he was in league with the felicistas.[31] He went on to point out that he had always been a strong supporter of Calles. His record served as the only proof necessary to defend his honor, he averred, and he was scarcely concerned with what anonymous writers said about him, because these were the typical tactics that the enemies of the government would use to generate dissension in the ranks. However, the reality was that someone with special intelligence in El Paso discovered the connection between Caraveo and the felicistas, and the general was forced to make a quick and decisive defense.

It was not entirely clear, as of January 1927, if Caraveo was committed to working with any of the exile factions in the United States. It was clear, however, that he had been contacted much earlier on the matter and that he was considering it. In March 1926, Luz de Perches contacted Manuela Caraveo because she desired to return to her home in Mexico City. Manuela offered, on behalf of her husband, to try to intervene with Calles and convince him to allow de Perches to come back to Mexico. In the meantime, de Perches probed Manuela regarding Caraveo's allegiance to Calles, and she explained that her husband supported the president. De Perches urged her to convince him to reconsider his position, cautioning, "An opportunity could be presented to your husband in the future that won't come around twice." As de Perches related in her report to Guillermo Rosas Jr., no matter what she said, she could not get Manuela to budge.[32] While it is important to remember that Caraveo remained loyal to the government, as did Escobar—even after the executions of Gens. Arnulfo Gómez and Francisco Serrano in October 1927—it did not mean that they were happy about the way in which Obregón and Calles handled the rebellion. It is reasonable to assume that men such as Caraveo, Escobar, and Gen. Francisco Manzo in Sonora would have been closely monitoring the political and military landscape, paying even closer attention to the general mood among the officer corps in the northern zones. Whether Caraveo was testing the waters with de Perches or seriously discussing his position in the future rebellion, being discovered caused a very serious problem for him.

Many within the Mexican intelligence community, as well as in the Calles administration, never truly trusted the generals who held commands along the northern frontier, least of all Caraveo. Confidential Agent (CA) 2 in Ciudad Juárez expressed concern that Caraveo was allowed to continue in his position as military chief of the state of Chihuahua given that his exact loyalties were unknown. It was certainly true that in the course of the preceding decade he had been an orozquista, huertista, anticarrancista, *and* felicista before ingratiating himself with Obregón. Moreover, the agent explained that Caraveo was a close friend of Gen. Francisco Serrano and speculated that had Gómez and Serrano's rebellion not erupted so quickly and spontaneously, they might have been able to count on much support from Chihuahua.[33] More alarming was that the Partido Liberal Progresista Chihuahuense (PLPC), at the behest of General Caraveo, was purging from the state and municipal levels all vestiges of obregonismo and replacing them with antireelectionists (in opposition to the reelection of Obregón), ostensibly preparing Caraveo's path to the governor's palace and closing out all the opposition that might be presented by Obregón or Calles.[34] Caraveo, indeed, had nearly total control of the state of Chihuahua, and it was clear that Obregón and Calles could hardly count on his loyalty to the federal government.

Of course, the felicistas had their eyes on Caraveo, but it is also evident that the Catholics were in agreement that don Marcelo was a very solid choice for their support to the military on the border. The Chihuahuan border was an area that was experiencing high levels of political instability, and it became the focal point for potential rebel exile activities. As early as mid-1926, key figures within the exile community such as Perches, Guillermo Rosas Jr., and Francisco López Carvajal, secretary of foreign relations under Victoriano Huerta, were already very interested in the possibility of recruiting General Caraveo into their counterrevolutionary camp. A gubernatorial crisis in the state involving the sitting governor, Jesús Antonio Almeida, and the PLPC provided an opportunity for the felicistas to cultivate a relationship with General Caraveo. In November 1926, Governor Almeida and his political cohort—specifically, his candidate for the governorship for 1928, Luis Esther Estrada—had accused Caraveo of an earlier attempt to use military force to push Almeida out of office. As Luz de Perches put it, Almeida and his cronies were undertaking a campaign to discredit Caraveo, and they had plans to replace him as the head of military operations in the state with officers more supportive of their leadership.[35]

De Perches contacted Manuela Caraveo once again in reference to the smear campaign against her husband in Chihuahua, making the argument that this was how Calles would repay Caraveo's loyalty to his government. Manuela responded by misguidedly pointing out that it was true that there was a campaign afoot to discredit her husband, but it was not Calles who was supporting it. Manuela related that although "she and her husband [were] well aware that power [was] not eternal, they [were] and [would] be with the government, and if it [fell], they [would] fall with it."[36] De Perches speculated that Caraveo and Manuela were only feigning loyalty to mislead Calles into thinking that Caraveo would support the government in the event of a military rebellion. She ultimately dismissed the theory, positing that the general considered the fall of Calles only a remote possibility. If Caraveo were to entertain the potential for rebellion at such an uncertain moment, it could cost him his properties in Chihuahua, not to mention his position of local power. The Caraveo family simply had far too much to lose. This caution did not mean, however, that Caraveo was unable or unwilling to involve himself in local politics in Chihuahua.

In April 1927, the minority party within the Chihuahua state legislature, the PLPC, managed to remove Governor Almeida from office. On the morning of 7 April 1927, members of the PLPC went to Almeida's residence to demand his resignation. Almeida fled for Ojinaga, but just outside the city, members of the military garrison, who were operating on orders from the local military authorities, stopped him. Almeida was forced out of the state and spent the rest of his life engaged in commercial enterprise in Mexico City.[37] The case of Governor Almeida illustrates the reach and influence that Caraveo, the PLPC, and other antireelectionist parties in Chihuahua had on local politics, but it also illustrates the fact that the Chihuahuan political machine remained out of Calles's and Obregón's control.

A letter that Caraveo wrote to Divisional Gen. Juán Andrew Almazán defending his position after the ouster of Almeida confirms that the political conflict had gotten out of hand and that don Marcelo was under quite a lot of fire. In Caraveo's opinion, it was a miracle that Almeida had not been removed earlier due to the fact that he and Luis Estrada had been so incredibly unpopular in the state. He assured Almazán, nonetheless, that the military had absolutely no part in the events that led to the governor's fall.[38] According to Caraveo, it was the governor and Luis Estrada who had been obstinate in their pursuit of local power: "Perhaps the President is already aware of the unpopularity of this entire group led by Luis Esther Estrada, but that of which he is undoubtedly unaware is the treachery with which these men have conducted themselves, abusing the magnanimity with which I have been working, to avoid provoking a conflict."[39] Almeida and Estrada, for their part, accused Caraveo of using his position as the military chief of the state to stir up trouble because the general wanted the governorship for himself, an accusation that Caraveo roundly denied. In a disingenuous but patriotic declaration in his defense, Caraveo claimed that he would only have accepted the high office of governor if there were no men of better character available than those who had just been removed from office. As if to place the final nail in Almeida's coffin, and in an attempt to deflect suspicion regarding his own activities, Caraveo claimed that it was a good thing the governor and his cronies were ousted because they were working with the clerical element and the Knights of Columbus in the state. Having removed these elements, Caraveo assured Almazán that he could "have complete confidence in the State of Chihuahua, and trust that . . . we [the state government] are with him [Calles] in punishing the false revolutionaries whenever necessary."[40]

The felicistas in exile had decided that they should reach out to the northern generals to assess the possibility of convincing some of them to support the rebels in the United States. Francisco López Carvajal spoke very highly of Caraveo, having been on the same steamer that had taken him to Havana in 1914.[41] López Carvajal advised Guillermo Rosas Jr. not to waste any time negotiating with any general without first speaking with Caraveo. "I can assure you," asserted López Carvajal, "that in honesty, loyalty, valor, and patriotism, there is no better."[42] He speculated that it was probable that Caraveo was only serving the Calles regime out of shame "and only because his vocation is to be a soldier and he doesn't have anything else to do."[43] With regard to the other candidates that the felicistas were considering, they were, by López Carvajal's standards, selfish and ambitious and could not be trusted. Rosas Jr., however, could have complete confidence that Caraveo would accept the offer to lead the felicista counterrevolution and would not let don Félix down.

Taking López Carvajal's advice, Rosas Jr. contacted Caraveo, lauding the general's credentials.[44] Rosas Jr. gushed, "It is you señor General, the man that destiny has placed in a position to rise to the height of duty. I do not doubt your background as an honorable man, patriot, and fighter."[45] He then asked, in no uncertain terms, for Caraveo to join the struggle of the felicista Ejército Renovador de la Revolución to save Mexico and to help overthrow the Calles government. It seems that Rosas Jr.'s ploy proved attractive, and

Caraveo had at least one meeting with the felicistas in January 1928. CA Fernando de la Garza had obtained evidence regarding meetings between Rosas Jr. and Caraveo in El Paso. According to the report, a Mexican exile named Pedro A. Gutiérrez had been made a colonel by Díaz and Rosas Jr. and had been placed in charge of the planning and logistics for an attack on Ciudad Juárez. Gutiérrez had connections with Mexican customs agents, members of the local military garrison, and some of the local merchants. His background included service in the revolutionary forces of Pascual Orozco under the command of General Caraveo in 1912.[46]

According to Gutiérrez, Díaz and Rosas Jr. were planning to take Ciudad Juárez, and they were going to get a lot of assistance from customs agents and the military to do so. Gutiérrez told de la Garza's informant that in meetings with Rosas Jr., Caraveo initially expressed that he was ready to join the movement, but it appeared that he changed his mind due to a later meeting he had had with Obregón. Obregón had confronted Caraveo and accused him of taking a large bribe from the clergy. The accusation was enough to prompt a cooling of Caraveo's attitude regarding his potential support of rebel activities on the border. It must have been at this point that Caraveo saw the felicistas' position as far too untenable to participate in the sort of intrigues that they had proposed. This particular case illustrates that Obregón and Calles had a major problem with which they had no effective way of dealing. They had a general in a major border garrison who was clearly having meetings with rebel exiles and who they suspected (or possibly had definitive proof) of having taken large bribes from the clergy. Caraveo received a stern warning, it seems, from Obregón, and the general backed down from the immediate plan of assisting with the attack on Ciudad Juárez. There was, however, no other action taken against Caraveo. The plan did not come to fruition simply because it was clear that the Mexican authorities knew about it and had taken preventative measures against it, and the key general who had agreed to offer assistance had experienced a sudden change of heart.

Marcelo Caraveo was not the only borderlands warlord in which the Catholic contingent and other rebel exiles had taken an interest. Gen. Francisco Manzo, military chief in Sonora and one of Calles's most trusted generals, was also an important potential recruit for the counterrevolutionaries across the border. As the Knights of Columbus and other elements were shopping around for the most likely military candidate to further the struggle against Calles, Gen. Francisco Manzo and Mexico City chief of police Gen. Roberto Cruz were at the top of the list.[47] By June 1928, Manzo was beginning to show signs of a particular independence of action in Sonora directly before the reelection of Obregón in July. Manzo had ignored no fewer than three orders from the secretary of war to present himself for a meeting in Mexico City. In response to Manzo's behavior, it had been necessary to send one of General Amaro's representatives to Sonora in order to bring Manzo to heel. The obstinate general threatened the representative and ordered him to return to Mexico City.[48] By the end of the month, it was reported that "the rumor continues that General Manzo, in the State of Sonora, maintains a rebellious stance, refusing to turn over command of the forces in his zone . . . claiming that he only obeys orders from General Obregón."[49] It is likely that Manzo's declaration of loyalty to Obregón and Obregón alone was his personal protest regarding all the centralization and professionalization attempts undertaken by the Calles administration. As Calles's rule came to a close and the reelection of Obregón drew near, Manzo may have been looking forward to a return to some semblance of normalcy to military operations on the border under the direction of his old mentor. Whatever Manzo's motivations, it was clear in mid-1928 that the general did not count himself among the loyal supporters of Calles's government—perhaps less so after the executions of Gómez and Serrano. The assassination of the president-elect on 17 July of the same year would highlight the divisions among the remaining members of the revolutionary family.

## EMILIO PORTES GIL AND THE OBREGONISTA-CALLISTA SPLIT

Obregón's reelection bid, the political maneuvering required to amend the Constitution of 1917 to allow reelection, and Obregón's victory all highlighted the political chasm between callistas and obregonistas. In fact, from early on in Calles's presidency, those in the military and in political positions who had been obregonistas since the rebellion of Agua Prieta considered themselves staunch opponents of Calles despite the fact that Calles relied on Obregón's backing and council for the remainder of his administration. While obregonistas such as Gilberto Valenzuela and Alberto J. Pani served in Calles's cabinet, the influence of the CROM through the ministry of labor head Luis N. Morones overpowered that of the obregonista contingent in the cabinet. The assassination of the president-elect was something that Calles had certainly not foreseen or orchestrated, as many of his detractors originally posited. It did, however, drive a wedge between the callistas and the obregonistas in such a way as to make reconciliation impossible, particularly after Emilio Portes Gil, Calles's minister of the Interior and a prominent figure in Mexico's oil regions, was chosen to be the new interim president.

At least one scholar has argued that the nomination of Obregón for reelection and the selection of Portes Gil for provisional president in 1928 were intended to provoke a division within the military as a means of forcing potential rebels or disloyal generals into action against the government.[50] National elections throughout the revolutionary period had done just that. Venustiano Carranza's choice of Ignacio Bonillas as his successor sparked the rebellion of Agua Prieta in 1920. Obregón's choice of Calles as presidential candidate in 1923 provoked the de la Huerta Rebellion. Finally, Obregón's candidacy in 1927 gave rise to the rebellions of Arnulfo Gómez and Francisco Serrano. It is unlikely that political leaders were actively provoking military rebellion; however, the consistent reactions from military quarters had certainly allowed Obregón and Calles to separate the proverbial wheat from the chaff. Portes Gil's selection for the provisional presidency came down to a political compromise. Although he served as Calles's minister of the Interior, he was a civilian obregonista with agrarian party ties in Tamaulipas and thus was acceptable to a broad cross section of the political influences—principally agraristas, obregonistas, and the military.[51] However, the supporters of the Sonoran favorite for the office, Gilberto Valenzuela, as well as the military leadership, among whom obregonismo still represented stern opposition to any political maneuvering that smacked of callismo, would not accept Portes Gil as a legitimate candidate.

By June 1928, Sonora was in the middle of a political crisis over the question of succession. General Manzo had routinely ignored orders from the secretary of war, responding that he would only obey orders from General Obregón; there were serious political conflicts over the battle for the provisional presidency in the wake of Obregón's assassination, widespread discontent over Portes Gil's selection for the interim presidency, a negotiated settlement between the state and central governments in February 1929, and open rebellion less than a month later. Many of the northern generals had been obregonistas and, if not obregonistas, certainly anticallistas. Congressman Gonzalo Santos, a staunch callista, had made public and inflammatory remarks to the effect that the entire state government of Sonora—particularly the Sonoran obregonista/anticallista bloc's favorite for the provisional presidency and author of the 1920 Plan of Agua Prieta, Gilberto Valenzuela—was "of a most revolutionary nature and that Sonora was in a state approaching open rebellion." The congressman's comments alone nearly caused a rebellion, according to the press, which reported that as of 14 February, a crisis between Portes Gil and his opponents in Sonora had been averted, but it was "generally accepted" that "Sonora was contemplating resistance if an agreement could not be reached . . . by many in official positions . . . on the border."[52] In very much the same way that local politics in Chihuahua were showing the signs of strain caused by the widening gap between the callista and obregonista camps in 1927 and 1928, so too was Sonora suffering the effects of the political vacuum left in the wake of the assassination of president-elect Obregón.

The crisis in Sonora at the outset of 1929 had deeper roots than Santos had initially indicated. Valenzuela was a Sonoran-born lawyer who had left Calles's cabinet position as secretary of the Interior for a post as Mexican minister to England in 1925. Regarding his departure, he noted that there were two reasons that a cabinet minister might resign his post: in the event that the president had lost faith in the minister or in the event that the minister had lost faith in the president. The latter was his justification for resigning.[53] Santos, on the other hand, was a callista and a supporter of Portes Gil's interim presidency. Once more, as in 1920, the specter of imposition loomed large over national politics. The Sonoran obregonista/anticallista bloc, as well as military officials in the border states of Chihuahua and Sonora, favored Valenzuela for the interim presidency and fully expected to run their candidate against Portes Gil. Calles sent his chief of police and close confidant, Gen. Roberto Cruz, to talk with some key senators to convince them to select Portes Gil, effectively shutting out Valenzuela.[54] After Portes Gil was sworn in, there was little to do about the situation until the official election was held in 1930. The remarks made by Santos were taken as slanderous in the worst possible terms and as an attempt to discredit the candidacy of Valenzuela, thus ensuring a callista victory in 1930. The *Douglas Daily Dispatch* reported the following:

> The situation which contained a marked degree of intensity and seriousness was brought about by reason of the fact that the northern states of Mexico had endorsed Gilberto Valenzuela as a candidate for the presidency and had then declared, through their spokesman that they intended to see that Valenzuela was permitted to run for office without being interfered with by accusations of treason or otherwise. The substance of the situation, according to Sonorans [*sic*] is that . . . Nogales demanded of the federal government in Mexico City that they eat the word of the hot headed [*sic*] senator [Santos] and mind their tongues in the future.[55]

The report went on to highlight the distrust of those in Sonora who had previously supported Calles and indicated that they had officially withdrawn their support for him: "They have sent him notice in a friendly and diplomatic way that he has served the republic well and long enough . . . and have tacitly suggested to him that he should release the reins and should retire to private life."[56] Moreover, the Sonorans and the Chihuahuans (especially those in the military) had favored an agreement with the church on the religious conflict since at least early 1927. Valenzuela and his supporters in Sonora also vowed, on their part, to negotiate a peaceful settlement to the conflict as part of their general political program.[57]

As for General Manzo, he made a valiant effort disprove the various reports that he and others in Sonora—particularly the governor of the state, Gen. Fausto Topete—were in open rebellion against the federal government. The press in Mexico City also made it very clear that by 19 February, there was absolutely no threat of military rebellion in Sonora. Manzo wrote directly to President Portes Gil, asserting, "I read published reports that my visit to Nogales was with rebellious intent toward the government you preside over with such distinction. I immediately denied the reports categorically and emphatically beg to communicate same to you."[58] Meanwhile, *La Prensa* published the report of the Mexican consul in San Antonio, Enrique Santibáñez, to the effect that "the news reports that have circulated regarding the outbreak of a revolutionary movement in the State of Sonora are entirely false. The said State is in a state of calm and maintains good relations with the federal government."[59]

The political conflict between Sonora and the government of Portes Gil was averted less than a month before the rebellion that took José Gonzalo Escobar's name would erupt along the northern border. The Escobar Rebellion was one in which Manzo and Topete took active parts. The two must have openly denied the intent to rebel against the federal government with deceit already in their minds. There would have been no chance that Manzo was unaware of what Escobar was planning. Moreover, Manzo, Topete, Escobar, and Caraveo had all been in communication with the Catholic rebels in El Paso and San Antonio since as early as the summer of 1926 and as late as mid-1928. They must have realized the potential of a military rebellion that could utilize the forward momentum of the religious conflict to achieve success, whether they agreed with its principles or saw it as an opportunity to advance their own agendas. Most important, the Escobar Rebellion highlighted the old obregonista/callista divisions that had been brought into such sharp relief with the selection of Portes Gil for the interim presidency. The generals who joined Escobar were all obregonistas who called for the overthrow of Portes

Gil—principally as a puppet of Calles, who ruled behind the scenes. Thus as Jürgen Buchenau has quite rightly asserted, the Escobar Rebellion was "an essentially anti-Callista movement."[60]

The escobaristas were keen to harness the social discontent caused by the religious conflict in order to coax the Cristeros over to their side—or at least to work in unison to topple the government of Portes Gil. An anonymous circular directed to the Cristeros and their supporters urged Catholics to keep faith because the military had taken up the cause of their defense of religious liberty. The author identified with Mexican Catholics, claiming that the military too had suffered "the bitter privation of its most noble and justified rights" and had "sympathized with" them. Catholics were also encouraged to fight with the army in a just war to protect the fatherland, protect liberties, and fight for God.[61] Despite the absence of a signature, it is most likely that this document was produced by the escobaristas in an attempt to channel the forward momentum of the Cristiada into the military rebellion. Moreover, the timing of the call of support for the military came at a moment when the administration of Portes Gil, the apostolic delegate from the Vatican, the North American hierarchy, and the US secretary of state Dwight Morrow were negotiating a peaceful conclusion to the religious conflict. It may have been a last-ditch effort to weaken the Mexican government's position in the negotiations. Indeed, at the very moment of the talks, the federal military still loyal to the government was carrying out an intense bombing campaign in Torreón and other regions in the north as well as in the Cristero-held territories in the center west. Regarding the bombing of Torreón, Gen. Mariano Montero Villar, one of many of the rebel representatives in New York, pronounced to the press that it was an unnecessary and vulgar display of force, taking the lives of few combatants and many more civilians. "The first result of the sending of arms to Mexico is that Torreon, an unfortified city, filled with thousands of defenseless Mexicans and hundreds of foreigners, was badly damaged by bombs, which killed one Foreigner and four Mexicans, including one child. If the Mexican Government," asked Montero, "as stated by the official bulletins, is sure the rebellion will be ended within two weeks, why does it bomb and destroy an unfortified city?"[62] After some initial successes in the military rebellion, both conflicts seemed to be coming unraveled, and it is likely that the escobaristas reached out to the Cristeros in order to bolster their fighting forces.

The escobaristas also courted *campesinos* (peasant farmers or agrarian laborers) in an attempt to curry favor from groups that would have otherwise identified as agraristas, aligned with the interests of the state. To the *campesinos* of the nation, Escobar promised in the name of his Ejército Renovador that the government that would be founded upon the triumph of his movement would protect the land already distributed under the Obregón and Calles governments, continue to distribute lands, expand those *ejidos* (state grants of communal village lands) already in existence, and create new agricultural credits.[63] A separate handbill was addressed to the Cristeros, asserting a well-worn claim that in its anticlerical quest, the Calles regime went from being liberal to dictatorial and tyrannical. "For this reason," the handbill asserted, "the Revolution . . . in its proposal to establish a national government instead of a sectarian government, a liberal government instead of an intolerant government, proclaims the urgency of ending the fratricidal war provoked by the religious question."[64] Thus the handbill proclaimed that the first act of the incoming government would be to repeal the articles of the Constitution of 1917 dealing with the clergy. There were no terribly radical departures in the platform of the Ejército Renovador with regard to land reform or the religious question. The escobaristas vowed to maintain the constitutional articles that made land reform possible and gave workers key advantages over labor, and they promised to, quite simply, put an end to the religious violence by erasing the constitutional articles most offensive to the church. The latter had been a topic of discussion in Norteño circles since at least mid-1927; however, the fact that this promise was at the top of the list of priorities suggests that perhaps the military had had enough of the chronic violence that weakened the nation and created unnecessary levels of instability along the border. It also illustrates the power of personal ambition and Escobar's capacity to seize upon the issue of religious violence and to use it to further his own ends.

For all of the organization, sound, and fury of the escobaristas and the Cristeros, the rebellion only lasted a few short months before being doused by loyal federal forces under the command of General Calles and the secretary of war, General Amaro. As the rebellious generals lost their battles, they too, like their fellow nationals before them, had to flee for the safety of the United States and Canada. General Escobar retreated to San Antonio before moving farther north to Vancouver, British Columbia, where he settled with his wife and children. The Mexican consul in Vancouver confirmed, in June 1929, that Escobar was living in the suburbs of Victoria. The consul also pointed out that several other Mexicans had crossed into Canada with proper passports and visas recently on the pretext of vacations, but these were actually Mexican secret agents.[65]

The following month, Escobar's financial standing was reported to the Mexican attorney general. Escobar had more than $100,000 deposited in the Bank of Montreal as of 28 February 1929, just six days prior to the initiation of hostilities. Records also showed that on 31 March, more than $50,000 had been deposited in an account held by Escobar at the National City Bank of New York. The money seems to have been the spoils of Escobar's exploits in Torreón, when he had stolen large qualities of gold and cash and deposited it in various banks with the help of Jesús Cueto, one of the general's business associates.[66] It was Calles's hope that with the intervention of Amb. Dwight Morrow, those funds could be retrieved. It is unclear as to whether the money was recuperated, as the documentary trail ends with the reporting of Escobar's financial holdings in Canada. Even after the rebellion was long over and Escobar was residing in Vancouver, the Mexican surveillance apparatus was hard at work keeping tabs on these latest exiles.

Caraveo too fled for El Paso in the wake of the defeat, but not before petitioning the administration of President Portes Gil for a peaceful conclusion to the conflict. Caraveo and Nicolás Pérez approached the Mexican consul in El Paso in mid-March, just ten days after the initiation of hostilities, to express their desire to meet with Portes Gil and put an end to the bloodshed in the republic, providing the government would make dignified proposals to the revolutionary movement. President Portes Gil replied that "the government of the Republic has nothing to discuss with the rebels, who, disregarding their duties and . . . every principal of loyalty, [had] provoked an armed movement that [placed] them beyond not only the decorum that they allege, but also outside the law."[67] Despite the snub from Portes Gil, Caraveo continued on in the rebellion, but by early May, the ex-general was residing in El Paso along with many of his supporters.[68] Realizing that the rebellion was quickly disintegrating, and having suffered a crippling defeat in Mazatlán, Francisco Manzo and fifteen members of his general staff fled for the safety of Nogales, Arizona, on 12 April. US immigration officials there took him and his men into custody, and Manzo made Arizona his temporary home until, in 1935, Pres. Lázaro Cárdenas offered a general amnesty to all political exiles still in the United States. In the interim, the Mexican government seized all of Manzo's properties in Sonora and Mexico City.[69] Gov. Fausto Topete and his brother Ricardo both spent years in exile in the United States, as did ex-chief of police Roberto Cruz.

## CONCLUSION

It was nearly impossible for Calles to secure the loyalty of the military or the governors in the border regions for the better part of the 1920s. Gen. José Gonzalo Escobar's rebellion in March 1929 revealed the dangers of years of military involvement in local politics and autonomy of action that had its roots in the very revolution that the Calles regime sought to protect and fortify. The political and military discontent that marked the final years of the decade along the Mexico-US border opened yet a final window of opportunity for the Catholic contingent and the felicistas in exile just across the line, and the military commands in Sonora and Chihuahua became prime targets for these exiles in their plots to overthrow the Mexican government. In the 1920s, one of the greatest challenges to the process of state reconstruction proved to be the Mexican military. Large numbers among the officer corps, many of them major figures in the revolution from the day of its outbreak, were reluctant to relinquish the local political powers that they felt they had fought for and, further, considered part of their compensation for loyal service to the revolution. Some of these military leaders were disgusted by the way in which Calles handled the religious question as well as presidential successions and felt that they might be able to do a better job of running the country than Calles had done. The assassination of president-elect Obregón exacerbated tensions between the antireelectionists, the obregonistas/anticallistas, and the callistas who supported the interim presidency of Emilio Portes Gil, adding fuel to a fire that had already compromised the security of the northern border garrisons—specifically in Chihuahua and Sonora, two of the most historically important military command zones on the border. All these factors created a situation in which counterrevolutionary exiles could make very important connections with the disgruntled military leaders just across the international line. These connections would help them, for the first and the last time, move toward securing the key border towns they would need to bring their conspiracies—hatched in hotel rooms, cafés, and private residences—to fruition in Mexican national territory.

# CONCLUSION

On 20 June 1929, the Mexican government came to an understanding with the hierarchy in Mexico over the religious question. Pres. Emilio Portes Gil; the US ambassador to Mexico, Dwight Morrow; and the bishop of Oaxaca, Leopoldo Ruiz y Flores, as well as other delegates from the Vatican, facilitated the *arreglos,* as the negotiations were called. Much to the chagrin of Cristeros still in arms in various regions of the republic, the *arreglos* effectively removed the impetus for further violence in defense of the church and religious freedom. The final agreement provided full amnesty for the bishops, priests, and the faithful who had taken up arms against the government. It restored church property, bishops' homes, and seminaries, and it provided for open relations between the Vatican and the Mexican church, meaning that a permanent apostolic delegate would remain in residence.[1] But it also removed the foundation upon which the Catholic contingent in exile had placed so many of their hopes for change in Mexico. Moreover, the Escobar Rebellion had been quashed easily enough, and while the escobaristas might have fanned the flames of Catholic rebellion in the center west, its failure marked the rapid decline of Cristero hostilities—at least until the second Cristiada of the mid-1930s.[2]

The agreements reached between Morrow and the Mexican episcopate ended the most violent outbursts of rebellion after 1929. As part of the terms of the final agreement, the Cristeros remaining in the field were offered complete and unconditional amnesty; their officers were allowed to keep their firearms and horses, and the rank and file were provided travel expenses and safe passage from wherever they were at the time to their homes.[3] In similar fashion, the exile rebels along the border, who had with such great hope and care plotted the overthrow of the Calles government, received the final blow with the agreement between the Mexican government and the church. With the end of the Escobar Rebellion as well, there would be scant possibility for a resurrection of their counterrevolutionary designs. Moreover, Calles, the man who had caused the faithful in Mexico such consternation, ceded power to provisional president Emilio Portes Gil. While most agreed that Calles was still *el jefe máximo* behind the scenes, it was Portes Gil who undertook the task that Calles could not—negotiations with the Mexican clergy. With the end of the religious war, the military rebellion, and the termination of Calles's term as president, the impetus for cross-border conspiracy and the dangerous alliances that gave rise to those plots were simultaneously dashed.

The 1920s was a period of intense violence, rivaling the previous decade of fratricidal conflict that historians commonly refer to as the "violent phase" of the revolution. However, the decade that witnessed the de la Huerta, Cristero, and Escobar rebellions—not to mention the rebellions of Arnulfo Gómez and Francisco Serrano—has been seen as separate or distinct from the previous decade of violence. In a sense, the return to relative electoral normalcy after the 1920 rebellion of Agua Prieta as well as the concerted effort among the obregonista majority in the national congress and in the military to carry out the reconstruction of the nation in the wake of the war between the factions has led historians to draw a somewhat artificial distinction between the 1910–20 period and the 1920–29 period. Certainly, the 1920s saw the implementation of profoundly significant reforms, a strong start to land reform, cessation of the war among the factions that cost millions of lives in the 1910s, and after 1923, official US recognition. The revolutionary governments that emerged from the war among the factions, however, were weak and contested on all sides. The constitutionalist army, such a decisive force in winning the revolution for Obregón, was top-heavy with officers who understood their military rank as commensurate with local political authority. The Mexican clergy had been, at best, anxious about the course of the revolution and the anticlerical attitudes of a majority of its northern leadership and, at worst, openly militant in its stance after the codification of the anticlerical articles in the Constitution of 1917.

To say that the revolutionary state after 1920 was weak is only half of the argument. The forces that challenged the Calles administration's claims to constitutional legitimacy were formidable and made their challenge at a particular moment when the foundations of revolutionary state power were at their weakest. Most important for this study is that Calles's opposition attempted to chip away at his regime from both sides of the border—in effect, extending the violence of the previous decade across the border into the United States and thereby intensifying the various conflicts of the 1920s in Mexico. The Calles regime, much like others before, made a similar extension of its forces across the border into the United States in the form of spies charged with the task of gathering intelligence on all rebel exile activities in an attempt to quash border rebellions before they started and to gather invaluable intelligence regarding counterrevolutionary activities within Mexico by investigating the connections between the various exile groups and their counterparts throughout the republic. These confidential agents and the intelligence they gathered allowed the Calles regime to detect counterrevolutionary plots from without and make best preparations for the rebellions afoot within the territorial boundaries of the nation.

While the narrative presented here at times appears to have been ripped from the pages of dime-store serials of fictionalized "G-men" and international spies, the work that confidential agents engaged in was, without a doubt, very real and every bit as dangerous, as this study's opening vignette testifies. The job that Confidential Department agents were expected to perform was complicated by the multifaceted and transborder nature of the various alliances that constituted the counterrevolutionary opposition. The Confidential Department's early operations were complicated by administrative conflicts among the Ministry of the Interior, the Confidential Department leadership, and the Department of the Treasury over the terms of reasonable compensation for the very agents the Mexican government trusted to gather quality intelligence against the various threats it faced. Bureaucratic roadblocks aside, agents on the ground were engaged in a high-stakes game of espionage and counterespionage with seasoned spies from previous regimes who had been brushed aside by the broader political currents of the revolution. Exile groups in the United States operated within a larger network of financiers and arms dealers and a political and religious leadership that protected their operations, provided key funding opportunities, and most often facilitated the exportation of arms and ammunition from the United States, Central America, and Canada to Cristeros in the field.

The connections that the counterrevolutionary exiles fostered in the United States as well as those they already had established in Mexico made the daily task of intelligence gathering and reporting to the Ministry of the Interior, border consulates, the Confidential Department, and the Bureau of Investigation a daunting responsibility, especially when we consider that at the most, the Confidential Department never supported more than twenty-five agents along the border at any point during the 1920s. Confidential agents subcontracted intelligence networks to augment their own intelligence-gathering capabilities. This tactic, however, multiplied the potential for misinformation, intentional and unintentional, and presented an altogether unique set of difficulties in the gathering and processing of information, including the potential complication of the enemy's utilization of double agents, a danger to which even the best of Mexico's secret agents fell prey.

The broader strain of support for the religious rebels among the faithful in the United States—specifically, among the most outspoken and influential members of the American Catholic hierarchy and the Knights of Columbus—also afforded the most dangerous elements among the exile population tremendous succor, which sustained their activities for the larger part of the decade. In many cases, these networks extended beyond religious circles and into the realm of local political networks that held much sway along the border. Confidential agents and consular officials constantly lamented the fact that exile populations plotting to overthrow the Mexican government were protected and, in many cases, openly supported by local law enforcement and elected officials suspected of sharing the same political or religious affiliations. Most commonly, local officials were suspect because of alleged membership in the Knights of Columbus, but it was also the case that local-level support for rebel exile activities was born of long-standing political enmity toward the Sonoran victors of the revolution or familial, political, or economic ties held just on the other side of the international boundary. The specific case of DA John Valls, a common source of consternation for the agents of the Mexican state, illustrates the strength and prominence of political grudges in the motivations of local law enforcement's support of various exile groups.

The initiation of the Cristero Rebellion in 1926 heightened rebel exile activities and allowed for the cultivation of new alliances based on Catholic loyalties and a shared perception that the Sonoran victors of the revolution were bent on implementing constitutional reforms that did not benefit the majority of the population in Mexico. When elite members of the Liga and exile prelates began to flood into places like El Paso and San Antonio, they found fertile ground for their anticallista propaganda and more than enough supporters, both within the exile community already existing on the border and within the American Catholic community. The point at which the shift in exile alliances became clear was in the case of Enrique Estrada's failed expedition of August 1926. While the expedition failed, it in part resulted in the arrival of many more of the Cristero Rebellion's exiles to San Antonio and El Paso who would then lend support to other counterrevolutionary plots and intrigues throughout the remainder of the decade. The failure of Estrada's rebellion thus marked a turning point in the fortunes of many of Mexico's enemies in the United States and began a new period of counterrevolutionary activity focused principally on the Catholic contingent in exile. Prior to the summer of 1926, law enforcement agencies in the United States, consular officials, and the agents of the Confidential Department had approached the prevention of counterrevolutionary plots with a certain confidence that exiles such as de la Huerta, Estrada, Díaz, and López de Lara, among others, lacked the resources necessary to constitute a legitimate threat. The Cristero Rebellion forced a reassessment of those threats and a concentrated focus on the activities of Catholics in exile.

Had the Catholic contingent in exile focused their energy solely on fostering relationships with political, financial, and religious backers in the United

States, perhaps they may not have been such a threat. However, they reached out to the military leaders of key border garrisons, playing on the discontent that old generals—such as José Gonzálo Escobar, Francisco Manzo, Roberto Cruz, and Marcelo Caraveo—were feeling toward the persistence of the religious question, the dominance of Calles on the political landscape, and the recent execution of Gens. Arnulfo Gómez and Francisco Serrano. Even into the late 1920s, there were serious deficiencies in the professionalization of the officer corps, and it is clear that their fidelity was never sufficiently guaranteed. Moreover, the reorganization of the military undertaken by Calles led to increased levels of discontent in the northern regions under the control of military chiefs who were least likely to accept challenges to their own local authority. In the case of other military conflicts in the course of the revolution, the generals who rebelled against the state were almost always driven by personal ambition and a desire to defend against any encroachment upon their own local power. The same was true for the Escobar Rebellion of March 1929. The Confidential Department was able to uncover the networks involving Catholic conspirators, such as Luz de Perches, José Gándara, and Guillermo Rosas Jr., and disgruntled military leaders on the border, giving the Calles and Portes Gil administrations opportunities to prepare for the worst in the event of a significant military uprising. In the case of the Escobar Rebellion, the intelligence provided allowed Calles to put an end to the conflict in the space of a mere two months.

Calles's triumph over the remaining recalcitrant sectors of the military, all in the border garrisons, also paved the way for the eventual professionalization of the military, a project already begun during Obregón's presidency. Following the defeat of the escobaristas and the calming of hostilities between the church and the state in the wake of the *arreglos*, no longer would major military rebellions of the sort so common in the 1920s plague the Mexican state. Moreover, the *arreglos* removed the wind from the sails of armed popular religious rebellions, although discontent over cardenista educational reforms would spark major protests in the 1930s. More important, the disappearance of the twin threats of Catholic rebellion and counterrevolutionary exile plots, as well as the fact that Pres. Lázaro Cárdenas reconciled with many of Obregón's and Calles's old foes in exile and allowed them to return in the mid-1930s, meant that the border would no longer be utilized as a springboard for counterrevolutionary conspiracies.

It is important to remember that exile, for most of the groups discussed in this study, was never a permanent state. While some returned in the first years of the 1930s, most of the leaders of the various conspiracies were allowed to return during the presidency of Lázaro Cárdenas. However, exile was certainly a political tool, and Calles was not the only president to utilize it as such. While under the Cárdenas administration, Adolfo de la Huerta, Enrique Estrada, José María Maytorena, Francisco Manzo, and Marcelo Caraveo, among many others considered dangerous exiles and enemies of the Mexican government during the previous decade were allowed to return to Mexico, the relationship between Calles and the new president was failing fast. Cárdenas's reliance on the ability to arbitrate conflicts between capital and labor and the alliances he made between national labor unions—such as Vicente Lombardo Toledano's Confederación de Trabajadores Mexicanos (Confederation of Mexican Workers; CTM)—infuriated Calles. He made numerous comments in the Mexico City press, denouncing what he considered an ill-advised labor policy, comments that won him the ire of Cárdenas's supporters.[4] In the blink of an eye, Calles had gone from being *el jefe máximo* of the revolution to a political pariah and an enemy of the new cardenista state. In a profound twist of irony, President Cárdenas, in part fearing the influence that Calles still held among certain sectors of the military and in part under pressure to distance himself from his old mentor, sent the old *jefe máximo* into exile on 9 April 1936.[5] Calles would not return to Mexico until May 1941, at which point he had ceased to be a force in Mexican politics.

Many exiles who had been involved in the various plots against Calles's government, and many more who played only minor supporting roles in counterrevolutionary activities, took the opportunity afforded by the conclusion of the military and religious rebellions of the latter half of the decade to petition the Ministry of the Interior to be allowed back into their country of birth. Some submitted successful petitions, but their compatriots in the Mexican government were wary of some of the more dangerous exiles as well as those who had not so readily yielded to the changed political climate in the patria. Even in the case of successful petitions, the road to reconciliation, for many, was fraught with bureaucratic pitfalls, and the stain of a decade of conspiracy against the Mexican government prevented the worst from returning until the mid-1930s.

Ex-colonel Carlos López, a former associate of Gen. Enrique Estrada in Los Angeles, was one of the many exiles who petitioned the Ministry of the Interior for their return. López had paid the same price that Estrada and his high-ranking officials paid at the termination of their trial in early 1927—a prison sentence and a not-so-insignificant fine. At the time of his petition in January 1928, he had renounced his role in the Estrada expedition and had begun to work in the film industry as an extra. He even offered the Ministry of the Interior intelligence on Cristero activities in the United States and in Mexico if allowed to return. The ministry declined his offer but put his petition through the meticulous process of review under the Confidential Department.[6] After years of miscommunications and bureaucratic wrangling, he was cleared to return to Mexico on 3 November 1930, nearly a full three years after his original petition.[7] Ex-general Cornelio Sánchez, an old delahuertista, had been living in exile in Eagle Pass since the end of the de la Huerta Rebellion in March 1924. He was allowed to return to Piedras Negras after a short exile and returned to life as normal in June 1925. Then in 1927, he was accused of having participated in the rebellion of Arnulfo Gómez and Francisco Serrano and was exiled once again.[8] Although there was no concrete evidence that he had actually participated or otherwise lent support to that rebellion, the Ministry of the Interior denied petition after petition for reentry for the remainder of the decade. His file ends with a response from the immigration office at Piedras Negras from October 1928, denying his most recent petition.[9]

There seemed to be no consistent method for determining whether a petitioner was worthy for consideration of repatriation, but the files held on petitioners in the Confidential Department were used exclusively in this final determination. Ismael Palafox, Adolfo de la Huerta's key financial agent in the United States, for instance, petitioned for repatriation on 16 August

1929. The governor of Veracruz, Manuel Padilla, who submitted the petition on Palafox's behalf, referred to him as an old revolutionary from an honorable lineage that had found himself in exile for having "indirectly" participated in the de la Huerta Rebellion.[10] Palafox's fundraising activities for the delahuertistas in exile must have fallen below the radar of the Confidential Department. Because the department had no formal file on Palafox, his petition was accepted and granted by 12 September 1929, less than a month after its original submission.[11]

René Capistran Garza, for his part, made no apologies for his involvement in fostering cross-border rebellions from exile in the 1920s. Nor did he ever file a petition for repatriation in the years following that decade. He remained informed, however, on consular appointments along the border and the foreign policy of subsequent administrations. Rather than claiming he played only a minor role in the various plots and arms shipments to Mexico between 1926 and 1930 or apologizing for his participation, vowing that it would never happen again, as many petitioners did, he lauded the recently appointed consul general of Mexico, Eduardo Hernández Cházaro, for not treating the nation's exiles in the United States in the same fashion that all of his predecessors had done. The exile community in San Antonio assumed that with the appointment of Hernández, they would again be subjected to the same level of hostility that had accompanied earlier appointments to the position. They were positively delighted to learn that the consul general had committed to open his doors to all of his compatriots "with no other consideration than their nationality and their needs."[12] It was because of the good faith that the consul demonstrated to Capistran Garza that he felt that he could make a request that under any other administration he would never have thought possible. Capistran Garza had earned a certain reputation and status in San Antonio, and although he had not become a wealthy man in exile, he was relatively content in his station. For this reason, according to his statement, he was not overwhelmed with a desire to return to Mexico. He went on to point out, however, that he did "feel, vehemently, a great desire . . . not to be an outlaw in [his] country, nor to be considered an enemy . . . of the [Pasqual] Ortiz Rubio government."[13] Rather than petitioning for reentry,

Capistran Garza merely wished to verify that should he make the choice to do so, he would not be prevented from petitioning his return to Mexico at some unspecified moment in the future. In reference to his counterrevolutionary past, he assured the consul that it had been three full years since he had participated in any plot, associated with the clerical element, or had otherwise been involved in public or political matters and that it was his wish, as he moved forward with his life, to leave all those activities behind him. In June 1933, he was reported to maintain a residence in San Antonio, traveling between that city and New Orleans with frequency, and rumored to be planning political activities in Mexico.[14]

Adolfo de la Huerta spent his remaining years in exile providing vocal lessons for the Los Angeles elite. He was known to have a profound love for music of all kinds and a wonderful singing voice, and he established his own studio in Los Angeles, in which he gave classes to a number of internationally renowned opera singers.[15] As much as he longed for the country of his birth, he would not be allowed to return to Mexico until President Cárdenas's general amnesty of 1935. De la Huerta took advantage of the opportunity and returned to his home on 28 November of that year.[16] Of his return to his beloved patria, don Adolfo commented, "Regarding the gloomy period of my exile, filled with enough bitterness and anguish to settle whatever wrong that I have involuntarily committed, I have been able to cast a veil of forgetting and serenity, allowing me . . . to moderate my energies and struggle, here or in any other part of the world, for . . . the cause of the proletariat."[17] De la Huerta would not have admitted to any of the more unsavory activities that he had directed and in which he had otherwise participated in the various plots to overthrow his old friend in the previous decade. Thus he made vague reference to "wrongs that [he had] involuntarily committed," and in an attempt to ingratiate himself with the new revolutionary regime, with all the support it enjoyed from the workers and *campesinos*, don Adolfo saw fit to give a nod to the proletariat.

It was the weakness of the state that made the condition of exile a necessity but also always only a temporary state. Individuals or groups involved in potentially seditious activities in Mexico could be relatively easily rooted out with the use of local police, military, and intelligence-gathering bodies. Exile, whether forced (as in the case of the clergy) or voluntary (as in the case of almost all the political and Catholic elite who found their way across the border over the course of the decade), was necessary to carry out further counterrevolutionary plots. As I have argued on several occasions, the border between the United States and Mexico served as a place of refuge, of political and spiritual succor for those opposed to the Mexican government and the anticlericalism it engendered. The perceived instability of the Mexican government meant, for these exiles, that in the not-so-distant future, the Calles regime would fall, and they would be welcomed back to their homeland with open arms by the succeeding regime. What they could not have foreseen, however, and what constituted a much more insidious form of governmental instability that had plagued various regimes throughout the revolution, was the power struggle between Cárdenas and Calles in the early 1930s. Though their efforts to topple Calles failed miserably, it was ultimately Cárdenas's struggle to free his administration from the political legacy left by the *jefe máximo* and forge his own bonds with *campesino* organizations and urban labor unions that allowed them to return to their homes. The particular stage of postrevolutionary development in which the Mexican government found itself in the 1920s made the condition of exile for the "losers" of the revolution distinct from the exile experience that the Cold War would generate in the climate of anticommunism in Central America and the Southern Cone later in the twentieth century, in which the support of the US government played such a prominent role in prolonging and intensifying state violence and repression.

The only other case of an exile population actively seeking support to topple a revolutionary and socially progressive regime from the safety of the United States in the twentieth century is that of revolutionary Cuba. Indeed, there are some similarities between the cases of Mexico and Cuba to consider. Mexican intellectuals sought refuge in the United States in an attempt to generate support for the ouster of Porfirio Díaz in the years before the revolution, just as exiles such as José Martí, Miguel Tolón, and Gaspar Betancourt Cisneros, to name only a few, did prior to Cuba's independence movement of the late nineteenth century. The experience of exile for Cuban activists and intellectuals was just as varied and vibrant as that of Mexican exiles prior to the revolution. Again, in the wake of the Cuban Revolution of 1958–59 that brought Fidel Castro to power, Fidel was forced to defend the revolution from its perceived enemies, who sought refuge in South Florida, in much the same way as the Mexican government had to protect its weak and embattled position against threats from its citizens in exile along the border in the 1920s. This is, however, where the similarities end. While the US government welcomed Cuban exiles fleeing Castro's communist regime and actively supported (and orchestrated, in the case of the infamous Bay of Pigs invasion) exile attempts to unseat him, Mexican exiles in the 1920s were unable to procure the same level of support from Washington.

Mexican exiles sought support from private business sectors, the American Catholic hierarchy, and occasionally senators and congressmen who shared their sentiments regarding land reform, oil laws, and the religious persecution. The key differences in the two cases, of course, were the heightened fears of the spread of communism and the global politics of the Cold War that accompanied the post–World War II social and political order. Outside the context of the Cold War, the case of Mexico in the 1920s presents us with the only Latin American example of a large and active exile population that utilized a border region to attempt to stunt the growth of a progressive state in formation by counterrevolutionary means. Unlike the left-wing exile political activists that fled the right-wing and military regimes in El Salvador, Guatemala, Chile, Argentina, Brazil, and others, the Mexican Revolution's "losers" made every attempt to turn back the tide of revolution in their homeland in the 1920s.

The Confidential Department of the 1920s can be said to have been quite distinct from its predecessors as well as the incarnations that followed it in the 1930s and through the 1950s. The security services in the postrevolutionary period lacked the professionalization that the intelligence organizations in the post–World War II period would possess. Moreover, the military leadership that marked its organizational structure would be eliminated by the 1940s. Aaron Navarro asserts that in the post–World War II era, the Mexican intelligence services became a political tool for the dominant party, the Partido Revolucionario Institucional (Institutional Revolutionary Party, PRI). They returned to the domestic intelligence operations that agents had performed in the years directly following the de la Huerta Rebellion and focused their energies on compiling dossiers on any and all potential political rivals to the PRI. While agents of the highest order would continue to carry out missions in the United States, those missions were limited in scope and lacked the consistent levels of funding that would be required for their completion.[18] The investigations carried out by agents of the Confidential Department in the 1920s were the most extensive and sustained operations outside of Mexican national territory in the postrevolutionary period. It was no coincidence that the confluence of the termination of both the Cristero Rebellion and border rebellions, such as that of Gen. José Gonzálo Escobar, also marked the end of major espionage operations along the border. The impetus for posting secret agents along the border had dissipated along with the threats posed by militant exile groups residing there.

Navarro notes that the intelligence services in the post–World War II period were exclusively at the command of the PRI, but in the 1920s, it was not always clearly the case that the Confidential Department's mandate relied purely on the executive in power. Certainly the Ministry of the Interior and the Confidential Department worked to protect the Mexican government and the chief executive of the particular administration in power. Rather than party loyalty, however, agents of the Confidential Department seemed to be motivated more by a directive to protect the government and nation from its external and internal threats, regardless of the particular executive in power, which further distinguished the early Confidential Department from later incarnations. This may have had something to do with the more-or-less independent leadership of the department as well as Francisco Delgado's recruitment, as Navarro points out, of at least 50 percent of its ranks from the educated and business classes. Delgado was a lawyer from Guadalajara whose "success as head of the agency was due in part to his selection of 'at least fifty percent of the agents from the ranks of former doctors, licenciados, professors, businessmen [and] women.'"[19] He also approached his leadership role as one in which he treated his agents with respect, as fellow collaborators in the gathering and processing of intelligence, rather than his subordinates.[20] With the institutionalization of the revolution following the administration of Lázaro Cárdenas, subsequent PRI administrations saw fit to reorganize the Mexican intelligence services in order to use the agency as a tool for quelling internal dissent and to gather intelligence on political rivals as a means of incorporating opposition elements in the PRI political platform, ensuring the PRI's continued electoral dominance.[21]

In the popular imaginary, the US-Mexico border has been a place of chronic violence and lawlessness. US media outlets perpetuate the myth that contemporary borderlands violence inevitably spills across the international line into major urban centers in the United States. This myth, in turn, has consistently (mis)informed our public discourse on the issue of immigration. Throughout this book, I have sought to illustrate the various instances in which Mexican secret agents operated on a level playing field with US border agents in the early twentieth century. Confidential Department operatives often expressed and exercised distinct but analogous notions of authority to those of their counterparts in the United States. Much as is the case today, the prevalence of violence, however, was in no way distributed evenly across the border. Exiles operated in a space in which the violence of the revolution was held just on the other side of the border. The fruits of their labors—arms smuggling, military recruiting, and alliance building—never resulted in acts of violence or military clashes in major cities on the US side of the border. In Mexico, the Cristiada and sundry military rebellions over the course of the period under examination here took tens of thousands of lives in a nation that had just emerged from fratricidal warfare that claimed between one and two million soldiers and civilians.[22] In this sense, the border has historically created and continues to create fundamental inequalities in residents' daily experiences with violence. In the last fifteen years, and certainly since the time of this writing, the Mexican side of the border has witnessed unspeakable violence as warfare between rival drug cartels and the Mexican military has spilled over into the civilian population. The violence associated with the underbelly of border cities like Ciudad Juárez, Nuevo

Laredo, and Matamoros is not new, and we must strive to historicize its longer legacy along the border resulting from periodic political instability and shifting power relations along the international line. The questions of sovereignty and control of national boundaries that I have discussed here are not temporally limited to the immediate postrevolutionary period. Mexico's ongoing war against its most vicious drug cartels and arms traffickers has compromised its territorial sovereignty in ways perhaps unforeseen by policy makers on both sides of the border. This compromise can be illustrated no better than through the case of the Bureau of Alcohol, Tobacco, Firearms and Explosives's (ATF) infamous 2009 Operation Fast and Furious.

In the fall of 2009, special agent in charge of the Phoenix division of the ATF, William Newell, devised a strategy for dealing with the problem of arms trafficking along the border whereby a network of cooperating Federal Firearms Licensees (FFL) would knowingly sell large quantities of arms and ammunition to suspected "straw purchasers."[23] These "straw purchasers" are individuals who purchase arms ostensibly for personal use but actually for sale to cartels in Northern Mexico. The plan, as envisioned by Newell, was that the arms and ammunition obtained by straw purchasers would be allowed to "walk" across the border, where they would then be handed off to the buyers. When those weapons resurfaced in Mexico, the ATF would be able to prosecute an international case, implicating not only the arms traffickers but the cartel leadership as well. ATF headquarters only approved the operation to incriminate the straw purchasers and to stop the guns before they crossed the border. The Phoenix division allowed the unauthorized "gun-walking" scheme to move forward without the knowledge of their superiors in Washington or the Mexican government. The resulting operation spiraled out of control, as weapons linked to Operation Fast and Furious were found at the scenes of intercartel shootouts as well as the murders of Mario González, son of attorney general of Chihuahua Patricia González, and US Border Patrol agent Brian Terry.[24]

The ATF's use of straw purchasers of arms and ammunition to prosecute a bigger cross-border case and the operation's failure illustrates the unpredictability of borderlands violence and the increased complications with enforcing territorial sovereignty along the international line. We might ask what the Phoenix division's reasonable expectations might have been when they allowed all of the nearly two thousand guns to "walk" across the border. The whistle-blower in the Operation Fast and Furious case, Agent John Dodson, testified to a conversation he had with the operation's case agent, Hope MacAllister, in which he pointedly asked MacAllister if she would be prepared to attend a US Border Patrol agent's funeral or that of a Cochise County deputy. "The sentiment that was given back to me by both her [and] the group supervisor," Dodson stated, "was that if you're going to make an omelet, you need to scramble some eggs."[25] That Newell and Agent MacAllister showed no concern regarding the possibility that the weapons might be used in violent crimes suggests a level of callous misunderstanding of the nature of borderlands violence that had previously affected the region in the early twentieth century. Moreover, the implementation of the operation indicated a profound lack of understanding of the strain that the Mexican war against the cartels had put on the exercise of Mexico's territorial sovereignty. Newell was confident that the ATF would be able to quickly trace the flow of the arms to the cartels, but in reality, they had absolutely no control over the weapons once they crossed the border. This lack of control had been illustrated all too well in the failure of Operation Fast and Furious's precursor, Operation Wide Receiver, in 2007, when a total of twenty-nine guns that were allowed to cross the border were lost because Mexican border officials "missed the handoff" with the buyers.[26] Perhaps due to a profound arrogance tainted with an equally profound ignorance of the nature of the border in periods of tremendous violence and crisis, the ATF lost control of 80 percent of the nearly two thousand weapons it allowed to flow across the border.

The failure of Operation Fast and Furious also demonstrates that federal officers working along the border can still (to a certain extent) operate on their own authority and with an understanding of the border as a lawless sort of place where any investigative strategy that gets the job done can be justified, regardless of the casualties. Newell was putting into place an operation that had not been entirely authorized as it was implemented and was keeping its details hidden from his superiors in Washington—at least until the murder of Agent Terry revealed Operation Fast and Furious weapons at the scene. The congressional investigation found that from the day that Newell became special agent in charge of the Phoenix office, he "consistently pushed the envelope of permissible investigative techniques. He had been reprimanded . . . before for crossing the line, but under a new administration and new Attorney General he reverted back to the use of risky gunwalking tactics."[27] In this sense, Newell operated in a way that was very similar to that of Texas district attorney John Valls in his obstructions of the work of various Mexican Confidential Department agents over the course of the 1920s.

Military discontent, popular reaction to the church-state conflict and anticlerical laws, and the crisis generated by exile groups working to topple Calles from the relative safety of the US-Mexico borderlands gave longevity to the rebellions of the 1920s in a way that would not be possible in succeeding years. In this sense, the violence that erupted along the border in March 1929 was distinguishable from the previous decade of factional warfare by its distinctively counterrevolutionary character and the support that the movement boasted from Catholic exiles and the North American clergy. Although the violence presently associated with the US-Mexico border is not new, it is historically contingent, and this book has sought to historicize the longer legacy of violence along the border and complicate the notion of innate and timeless borderlands violence. The violence that scarred the 1920s was not episodic and disconnected but entwined with movements that traversed the border. The movements were nurtured by translocal groupings of exiles, Anglo contraband smugglers, North American Catholics, migrant populations, and established Mexican American communities with familial, economic, and political ties on both sides of the border. These communities made use of the still-fluid nature of the international boundary to transport arms, ammunition, and capital to support the Cristero cause, and they did so at a moment when the border between the two nations was in the process of being transformed into the hardened political boundary we know today.

# APPENDIX

# LIST OF EXILE FACTIONS AND INDIVIDUALS

## DELAHUERTISTAS

The delahuertistas entertained alliances with the estradistas and the felicistas. However, for the better part of the 1924–26 period, they operated as an independent faction with little or no meaning full alliances made with the felicistas or estradistas. While the group was quite large, the individuals included here are those who most often appear in the larger narrative.

- Adolfo de la Huerta: ex-interim president of Mexico, minister of finance under President Obregón, and leader of the delahuertista faction in exile
- Alfonso de la Huerta: bother of Adolfo, financial and military advisor to the same
- Alfonso Gómez Morentín: arms purchaser and fundraiser for the delahuertista faction
- Cutberto Hidalgo: arms purchasing agent for the delahuertista faction
- Luis Gayou: advisor and arms purchaser for Adolfo de la Huerta

- Gen. Cesar Lopez de Lara: revolutionary general, served in the armies of Gen. Francisco Villa; only loosely affiliated with the delahuertistas, Lopez de Lara also entertained alliances with the Catholics and the felicistas

## FELICISTAS

The felicistas allied most significantly with the Catholic contingent in exile—mainly Luz Franco de Perches. They also maintained ties with the old porfirian intellectuals in exile in the United States, specifically newspaper owners and journalists contributing to the Spanish-language press in the United States.

- Félix Díaz: nephew of Porfirio Díaz; lent his support to the coup that ousted Francisco Madero and concluded with Madero and Vice Pres. Pino Suárez's assassination in 1913
- Guillermo Rosas Jr.: private secretary and advisor to Félix Díaz; was often the behind-the-scenes negotiator for many of the felicistas' dealings with the Catholic contingent in exile
- Francisco Lopez Carvajal: Porfirio Díaz's minister of foreign relations; served Félix Díaz in the capacity of intelligence broker, financial advisor, and arms purchaser

## ESTRADISTAS

The estradistas' tenure in the United States was quite short, and the group was also very small. Prior to their failed rebellion into Baja California in August 1926, they entertained alliances primarily with the delahuertistas. However, when it came to planning the rebellion, they relied on their own people and the immigrant community in Los Angeles for fundraising and arms purchases. The exception was their use of individual delahuertista agents, such as Cutberto Hidalgo, for contacts in the arms-smuggling community.

- Enrique Estrada: revolutionary general, ex-secretary of war and marine in Obregón's cabinet; military commander of the states of Jalisco, Colima, Nayarit, and Zacatecas; and the leader of the failed center-west regional component of the de la Huerta Rebellion of 1923–24
- Nicolás Rodriguez: recruiter and arms purchaser for Enrique Estrada
- Juan Pardo: recruiter, arms purchaser, and safe house operator on Los Angeles for the estradista faction

## CATHOLIC CONTINGENT

The Catholic contingent in exile was quite large. Only the most frequently mentioned individuals are included here.

- Luz Franco de Perches: high-ranking member of the Liga Nacional Defensora de la Libertad Religiosa (LNDLR), propagandist, and intelligence broker for the Catholic contingent
- Rene Capistran Garza: president of the Liga Defensora Religiosa (LDR) in the United States and former high-ranking member of the LNDLR in Mexico
- José Gándara: military chief for the LDR in the United States
- Supreme Knight James A. Flaherty: head of the Knights of Columbus; facilitated arms purchases for shipment to Cristero in Mexico
- Chandler P. Anderson: Washington, DC, attorney and American commissioner of the Mixed Claims Commission dealing with the case of the German sinking of the Lusitania; managed the logistics and the financial details of the arms network for Supreme Knight James A. Flaherty
- George Merrill: veteran contraband smuggler employed by Chandler P. Anderson and James A. Flaherty to facilitate the smuggling of arms to Mexico for use in the religious conflict

# NOTES

## INTRODUCTION

1 "More Showers in Store for San Antonio," *San Antonio Light*, 7 December 1926, 2.

2 Archivo General de la Nación, Dirección General de Investigaciones Políticas y Sociales (hereafter AGN, DGIPS), vol. 2053A, exp. 5 (no f.), Estanislao Mazuka to Consul Emiliano Támez, 10 December 1926. "Elementos fogueados como usted son los que necesitamos, pues no queremos inocentes en nuestras filas, y queda usted nombrado desde luego Coronel y a las inmediatas ordenes de General Cisneros."

3 Ibid. "Le suplico informar a nuestro Gobierno del papel que yo desempeño por que no se me vaya a confundir con los demás y no corra riesgo de mi vida. Pude observar que estos hombres no tienen desconfianza a unos y otros . . . y todos andan armados y tienen el instinto de bandidos . . . solo hablan de volar trenes y de robar dinero."

4 This was a very real possibility considering that just a year earlier, the bishop of San Antonio had publically proclaimed that neither he nor his parishioners would support Adolfo de la Huerta or anyone else who had a hand in producing the Constitution of 1917. See chapter 2.

5 See, for example, Rachel St. John, *Line in the Sand: A History of the Western U.S.-Mexico Border* (Princeton: Princeton University Press, 2011); Samuel Truett, *Fugitive Landscapes: The Forgotten History of the U.S.-Mexico Borderlands* (New Haven: Yale University Press, 2006).

6 Mario Sznajder and Luis Roniger, "Political Exile in Latin America," in *Exile and the Politics of Exclusion in the Americas*, ed. Luis Roniger, James N. Green, and Pablo Yankelevich (Portland: Sussex Academic Press, 2012); Yossi Shain, *The Frontier of Loyalty: Political Exiles in the Age of the Nation State* (Middletown, CT: Wesleyan University Press, 1989); Elliott Young, *Catarino Garza's Revolution on the Texas-Mexico Border* (Durham: Duke University Press, 2004); Julia Young, "The Calles Government and Catholic Dissidents: Mexico's Transnational Projects of Repression, 1926–1929," *The Americas* 70:1 (July 2013): 63–91.

7 Kelly Lytle Hernández, *Migra! A History of the U.S. Border Patrol* (Berkeley: University of California Press, 2010); Mae Ngai, *Impossible Subjects: Illegal Aliens and the Making of Modern America* (Princeton: Princeton University Press, 2004), 58.

8 George T. Díaz, *Border Contraband: A History of Smuggling across the Rio Grande* (Austin: University of Texas Press, 2015).

9 St. John, *Line in the Sand*, 4.

10 Mary Kay Vaughan, *Cultural Politics in Revolution: Teachers, Peasants, and Schools in Mexico, 1930–1940* (Tucson: University of Arizona Press, 1997); Stephen E. Lewis, *The Ambivalent Revolution: Forging State and Nation in Chiapas, 1910–1945* (Albuquerque: University of New Mexico Press, 2005); Ben Fallow, *Cárdenas Compromised: The Failure of Reform in Postrevolutionary Yucatán* (Durham: Duke University Press, 2001); Katherine Elaine Bliss, *Compromised Positions: Prostitution, Public Health, and Gender Politics in Revolutionary Mexico City* (University Park: Pennsylvania State University Press, 2001); Patience A. Schell, "Nationalizing Children through Schools and Hygiene: Porfirian and Revolutionary Mexico City," *The Americas* 60:4 (April 2004): 559–87; Andrae M. Marak, *From Many, One: Indians, Peasant, Borders, and Education in Callista Mexico, 1924–1935* (Calgary: University of Calgary Press, 2009).

11 Jennie Purnell, *Popular Movements and State Formation in Revolutionary Mexico: The Agraristas and Cristeros of Michoacán* (Durham: Duke University Press, 1999), 5.

12 Jürgen Buchenau, *Plutarco Elías Calles and the Mexican Revolution* (Lanham, MD: Rowman & Littlefield, 2007); Linda B. Hall, *Oil, Banks, and Politics: The United States and Postrevolutionary Mexico, 1917–1924* (Austin: University of Texas Press, 1995); Enrique Plasencia de la Parra, *Personajes y escenarios de la Rebelión Delahuertista 1923–1924* (México, DF: Instituto de Investigaciones Históricas, 1998); Enrique Plasencia de la Parra, *Historia y organización de la fuerzas armadas en México, 1917–1937* (México, DF: Universidad Autónoma de México, 2010); Pedro Castro Martínez, *Adolfo de la Huerta y la Revolución Mexicana* (México, DF: Instituto Nacional de Estudios Históricos de la Revolución Mexicana, 1992); Jean A. Meyer, *The Cristero Rebellion: The Mexican People between Church and State, 1926–1929* (Cambridge: Cambridge University Press, 1976); Purnell, *Popular Movements and State Formation*; Fidelina G. Llerenas and Jaime Tamayo, *El levantamiento delahuertista: cuatro rebeliones y cuatro jefes militares* (Guadalajara: Universidad de Guadalajara, 1995); Robert E. Quirk, *The Mexican Revolution and the Catholic Church 1910–1929* (Indiana: Indiana University Press, 1973); David C. Bailey, *¡Viva Cristo Rey! The Cristero Rebellion and the Church State Conflict in Mexico* (Austin: University of Texas Press, 1974); Matthew Butler, *Popular Piety and Political Identity in Mexico's Cristero Rebellion: Michoacán, 1927–29* (New York: Oxford University Press, 2004); Agustín Vaca, *Los silencios de la historia: las Cristeras* (Zapopan: Colegio de Jalisco, 1998); Alicia Olivera Sedano, *Aspectos del conflicto religioso de 1926 a 1929: sus antecedentes y consecuencias* (México, DF: Instituto Nacional de Antropología e Historia, 1966); Fernando M. González, *Matar y morir por Cristo Rey: aspectos de la Cristiada* (México, DF: Instituto de Investigaciones Sociales, Universidad Nacional Autónoma de México, 2001).

13 The articles of the 1917 Constitution that the Mexican clergy found most offensive were 3, 5, 27, and 130. Article 3 dictates that education should be provided exclusively by the state. Article 5 forbade the establishment of monastic orders. Article 27 claimed the ownership of land and subsoil within the national boundaries for the Mexican nation and subsequently denied religious institutions the right to hold land. Finally, Article 130

placed the church under the direct supervision of the state. It made marriage a purely civil act requiring only the recognition of secular authorities, subjected priests to civil law, and required any priest practicing in Mexico to be Mexican by birth.

14 Buchenau, *Plutarco Elías Calles*, 140.

15 James C. Scott, foreword to *Everyday Forms of State Formation: Revolution and the Negotiation of Rule in Modern Mexico*, ed. Gilbert Joseph and Daniel Nugent (Durham: Duke University Press, 1994), ix, emphasis in original. See also Joel S. Migdal, *Strong Societies and Weak States: State-Society Relations and State Capabilities in the Third World* (Princeton: Princeton University Press, 1988).

16 The postrevolutionary state, with its institutions and goals for the creation of a unified national consciousness, was well defined in institutions, such as the Secretaría de Educación Pública (SEP; Ministry of Public Education) and the Departamento de Salubridad Federal (Federal Department of Public Health), among others.

17 Gilbert M. Joseph and Daniel Nugent, eds., *Everyday Forms of State Formation: Revolution and the Negotiation of Rule in Modern Mexico* (Durham: Duke University Press, 1994); Vaughan, *Cultural Politics in Revolution*; Lewis, *Ambivalent Revolution*; Fallow, *Cárdenas Compromised*; Bliss, *Compromised Positions*; Schell, "Nationalizing Children"; Marak, *From Many, One*.

18 Michel Foucault, *"Society Must Be Defended": Lectures at the Collège de France*, ed. Mauro Bertani and Alessandro Fontana, trans. David Macey (New York: Picador, 2003); Giorgio Agamben, *Homo Sacer: Sovereign Power and Bare Life* (Stanford: Stanford University Press, 1998); John Agnew, "Sovereignty Regimes: Territoriality and State Authority in Contemporary World Politics," *Annals of the Association of American Geographers* 95:2 (June 2005): 437–61; Peter Sahlins, *Boundaries: The Making of France and Spain in the Pyrenees* (Berkeley: University of California Press, 1989).

19 Sahlins, *Boundaries*, 2.

20 Ibid., 7.

21 We can see examples of this in the extralegal deportations of Abelardo Hinojosa and Demitrio Torres, a.k.a. "Chaparreras," with the help of friendly immigration inspectors like Capt. W. M. Hanson. See chapter 2.

22 Agnew, "Sovereignty Regimes."

23 Ibid., 437.

24 Ibid.

25 Victoria Lerner Sigal, "Los exiliados de la Revolución Mexicana en Estados Unidos, 1910–1940," in *La comunidad Mexicana en Estados Unidos: aspectos de su historia*, ed. Fernando Sául Alanis Enciso (San Luis Potosí: Colegio de San Luis, 2004), 71. "Todos los sujetos son hombres con poder—mayor o menor—, que tuvieron que exiliarse 'vencidos' por otras fuerzas políticas que detentaron mayor poder político, militar, de convocatoria, etcétera."

26 Young, *Catarino Garza's Revolution*.

27 For an elaboration of these exile groups, see Lerner Sigal, "Exiliados de la Revolución Mexicana," 75–80.

28 Ibid., 81. "Los exiliados que llegaron entre 1920 y 1940 se unieron a quienes habían sido forzados a salir entre 1910 y 1920, y que no habían podido regresar. Por ejemplo, en

1921, los recién llegados carrancistas (gente como Lucio Blanco y Francisco Murguía) y Estaban Cantú se unieron con varios huertistas (Nemesio García Naranjo, Jorge Vera Estañol, etc.), con el felicista Pedro de Villar—representante de Félix Díaz—, y con Francisco Vázquez Gómez para luchar contra el gobierno obregonista."

29 Ibid., 84.

30 David A. Badillo, "Between Alienation and Ethnicity: The Evolution of Mexican-American Catholicism in San Antonio, 1910–1940," *Journal of American Ethnic History* 16:4 (Summer 1997): 62–83.

31 Alexandra Minna Stern, *Eugenic Nation: Faults and Frontiers of Better Breeding in Modern America* (Berkeley: University of California Press, 2005), 57–81.

32 Mae Ngai, "The Strange Career of the Illegal Alien: Immigration Restriction and Deportation Policy in the United States, 1921–1965," *Law and History Review* 21:1 (Spring 2003): 70.

33 Michiel Baud and Willem Van Schendel, "Toward a Comparative History of Borderlands," *Journal of World History* 8:2 (1997): 211.

34 Raymond B. Craib, *Cartographic Mexico: A History of State Fixations and Fugitive Landscapes* (Durham: Duke University Press, 2004).

35 Baud and Schendel, "Toward a Comparative History," 217.

36 Buchenau, *Plutarco Elías Calles*, xxvi–xxvii. See also Young, "Calles Government and Catholic Dissidents."

37 Baud and Schendel, "Toward a Comparative History," 218.

38 Truett, *Fugitive Landscapes*; Ngai, *Impossible Subjects*; St. John, *Line in the Sand*.

39 Charles H. Harris III and Louis R. Sadler, *The Border and the Revolution*, introduction by Michael C. Meyer (Las Cruces: Center for Latin American Studies / Joint Border Research Institute, New Mexico State University, 1988), 3.

40 W. Dirk Raat, *Revoltosos: Mexico's Rebels in the United States, 1903–1923* (College Station: Texas A&M University Press, 1981); Douglas Richmond, "Intentos externos para derocar al régimen de Carranza (1915–1920)," *Historia Mexicana* 32:1 (July–September 1982): 106–32; Harris and Sadler, *Border and the Revolution*; Victoria Lerner Sigal, "Espionaje y Revolución Mexicana," *Historia Mexicana* 44:4 (April–June 1995): 617–43; Michael M. Smith, "The Mexican Secret Service in the United States, 1910–1920," *The Americas* 59:1 (July 2002): 65–85; Aaron W. Navarro, *Political Intelligence and the Creation of Modern Mexico, 1938–1954* (University Park: Pennsylvania State University Press, 2010).

41 Only one such individual appears in this study. His name was Estanislao Mazuka. He had been contracted by Agent Fernando de la Garza to infiltrate a rebel cell in South Texas under the command of Gen. Cesar López de Lara. His cover was so complete that General López de Lara commissioned him with the rank of colonel in the rebel army. AGN, DGIPS, vol. 2053A, exp. 5 (no f.), Consul Emiliano Támez to Francisco Delgado, 10 December 1926.

42 Michael C. Meyer, introduction to Harris and Sadler, *Border and the Revolution*, 3.

## CHAPTER 1

1 W. Dirk Raat, *Revoltosos: Mexico's Rebels in the United States, 1903–1923* (College Station: Texas A&M University Press, 1981); Douglas Richmond, "Intentos externos para derocar al régimen de Carranza (1915–1920)," *Historia Mexicana* 32:1 (July–September 1982): 106–32; Charles H. Harris III and Louis R. Sadler, *The Border and the Revolution*, introduction by Michael C. Meyer (Las Cruces: Center for Latin American Studies / Joint Border Research Institute, New Mexico State University, 1988); Victoria Lerner Sigal, "Espionaje y Revolución Mexicana," *Historia Mexicana* 44:4 (April–June 1995): 617–43; Michael M. Smith, "The Mexican Secret Service in the United States, 1910–1920," *The Americas* 59:1 (July 2002): 65–85; Aaron W. Navarro, *Political Intelligence and the Creation of Modern Mexico, 1938–1954* (University Park: Pennsylvania State University Press, 2010).

2 Harris and Sadler, *Border and the Revolution*, 27.

3 Raat, *Revoltosos*, 178–81.

4 Harris and Sadler, *Border and the Revolution*, 33.

5 Smith, "Mexican Secret Service," 66.

6 Raat, *Revoltosos*, 151.

7 Ibid., 151–53.

8 Ibid., 229.

9 Harris and Sadler, *Border and the Revolution*, 31.

10 Raat, *Revoltosos*, 231.

11 Ibid., 243.

12 Smith, "Mexican Secret Service," 69.

13 Navarro, *Political Intelligence*, 52.

14 For example, Andrés García, who would later become a delahuertista agent in Tucson, was among the most effective of those carrancista consuls purged by Obregón. See Michael M. Smith, "Andrés G. García: Venustiano Carranza's Eyes, Ears and Voice on the Border," *Mexican Studies / Estudios Mexicanos* 23:2 (Summer 2007): 355–86.

15 Archivo General de la Nación, Dirección General de Investigaciones Políticas y Sociales (hereafter AGN, DGIPS), vol. 15, exp. 30, ff. 1–6, "Conferencias. Temas sutentados por los Agentes en la serie que ha organizado el Departamento," 16 March 1925.

16 Ibid. "Desgraciadamente en la actualidad entendemos por política a la revuelta de partidos, a la división de pareceres (opinions), al choque de intereses opuestos y no siempre legítimos, a la ambición del poder."

17 Ibid. "Puede decirse que su situación política es buena."

18 Ibid., ff. 7–11, "Tema Sustentados por el Agente de Primera Gaspar Trousselle, para Ser Discutido en la Academia que se Verificara en el Departamento Confidencial de la Secretaria de Gobernación," 23 March 1925. "Aguzar nuestra raquítica intelligencia, buscando los medios que nos ilustren para hacernos artistas."

19 Ibid., ff. 12–16, Agent Carlos I. Flores, 27 March 1925. "Discreción absoluta, amplias relaciones sociales, instrucción sólida sobre diversas materiales, filiación gobiernistas a toda prueba."

20 Ibid. "Y a quien puede encomendársele una misión delicada, con la seguridad de que sabrá desempeñarla."

21 Ibid. "Pero jamas para infundir temor, ni para abrirse credito en el comercio, ni para obtener servicios de ninguna naturaleza sis la debida retribucion."

22 Ibid., vol. 43, exp. 30, f. 43.

23 Ibid., vol. 54, exp. 9, f. 171, Fernando de la Garza to the Confidential Department, 10 June 1926.

24 Ibid., vol. 43, exp. 30, ff. 111–14, memorandum from Francisco Delgado to Gobernación, 14 December 1925. "Alentados por el ambiente de oposición . . . en la Unión Americana en contra de las Leyes de Extranjería y del Petroleo, los elementos mexicanos enemigos de la actual Administración, que allá se han refugiado, han desplgado también actividades . . . traer a nuestro país una nueva revuelta."

25 Ibid. "Servicio especial—dependiente del mismo [Departamento Confidencial], que se establezca en la frontera en en conexión con los Inspectores de Migración y Jefes de Operaciones Militares, por sólo el tiempo que dure este estado de cosas."

26 Ibid., f. 134, 22 January 1926. The agents would be distributed in the following manner: one in Mexicali; one in Nogales, Sonora; one in Naco, Sonora; one in Agua Prieta, Sonora; three in Ciudad Juárez; one in Ojinaga; three in Piedras Negras, Coahila; four in Nuevo Laredo; four in Matamoros; and one in Veracruz.

27 Ibid. The calculation for the peso-to-dollar exchange was derived using the $1.00/$0.50 exchange rate as found in the *New York Times*, 24 March 1925.

28 Ibid., f. 136.

29 Ibid., f. 140, 15 February 1926. "Se comprenderá dicha falta como no justificada, haciéndose efectivo el descuento de un día de sueldo al empleaeo [*sic*] que se encuentre en el caso anterior."

30 Ibid., vol. 48, exp. 2, ff. 27–30, December 1926. "Vandoleros [*sic*] que por lo menos pueden crearle al Gobierno, problemas de órden moral, económico e Internacionales." "Quedandonos solo el ambre [*sic*] y la miceria [*sic*] para los nacionales y la desesperación en los hogares."

31 Ibid. "No es ni siquiera suficiente para su propia manutención y mucho menos ahora que la plata Mexicana se cotiza aquí a treinta y cinco centavos oro y la vida es a base de dollars, es materialmente imposible que se pueda vivir, mucho menos distraer algo de esto para hacer algunos gastos extraordinarios que a cada momento se presentan para poder descubrir las maniobras del enemigo."

32 Records of the Department of State Relating to the Internal Affairs of Mexico, 1910–1929, RG 59, 812.00/28415, report from Special Agent in Charge (SAC) Gus T. Jones in San Antonio to the director of the Bureau of Investigation, 7 May 1927.

33 Ibid.

34 Ibid.

35 Ibid., 812.00/28703, report from SAC Jones in San Antonio, re: contraband arms shipments in violation of the arms embargo, 24 August 1927.

36 Ibid., 812.00/28415, report from SAC Jones in San Antonio to the director of the Bureau of Investigation, 7 May 1927. While there was always the remote possibility that agents such as Gus T. Jones might have been bribed to overlook certain indiscretions

(smuggling) along the border, there is no evidence in this case to support a claim of corruption. Indeed, Charles H. Harris III and Louis R. Sadler have noted that Jones had an exemplary record of service with the Texas Rangers as an immigration inspector in San Diego, California, in 1912 and as special agent in charge for the Bureau of Investigation in San Antonio from 1922 to 1944, during which time he served as a liaison officer to the British intelligence services in the West Indies (1943). For more information on Gus T. Jones, see Harris and Sadler, *The Texas Rangers and the Mexican Revolution: The Bloodiest Decade, 1910–1920* (Albuquerque: University of New Mexico Press, 2004), 582n43.

37 Archivo Histórico Genaro Estrada, Acervo Histórico Diplomático, Secretaría de Relaciones Exteriores (hereafter SRE), LE 852-117-R-6, f. 91, report from Consul A. P. Carrillo, 4 May 1927.

38 Ibid., 97.

39 Ibid., LE 1540 I, f. 355, letter from Consul Gen. Enrique Santibáñez to Mayor C. M. Chambers, 22 March 1929.

40 Ibid., 357.

41 Ibid., 358. "La Resistencia del Sr. Mayor C. M. Chambers para no cancelar el permiso concedido al secerdote español Camilo Torrente, para que se represente en el Auditorio la pieza teatral 'Los Martires de León,' se debe a mi juicio a compromiso politicos."

42 Ibid., 360.

43 Smith, "Andrés G. García," 355–86.

44 Ibid., 364.

45 De la Huerta was happy to take advantage of the experience that a man like García had acquired in his service to the Carranza regime. We know that García was working as a delahuertista agent and that Ignacio Lozano's San Antonio periodical, *La Prensa*, was very kind to the delahuertistas. It is reasonable to assert that García would have employed all his talents in the service of the delahuertista faction in the United States.

46 AGN, DGIPS, vol. 54, exp. 9, ff. 256–63, report from Fernando de la Garza to Francisco Delgado, 27 October 1926. "No se repita el ascandalo que hicieron los rebeldes cuando el caso de Prieto Laurens y los demas sediciosos encausados . . . dijeron, como se recordara, que el servicio Americano habia cohechado por el suscrito, etc. etc."

47 Ibid., f. 290, report from Fernando de la Garza to Francisco Delgado, 2 November 1926. "Cuentan con un servicio bien organizado de información secreta, que es proporcionada por personas al servicio de nuestro Gobierno en las diferentes Secretarias o Departamentos, y con especialidad por el elemento femenino que trabaja en las diferentes oficinas, quienes, tal vez algunas, inocentemente, son aprovechadas por personas expertas y mal intencionadas, para adquirir de ellas . . . información, que después es explotada por los enemigos."

48 Ibid. "Una Señora de apellido Perches, para adquirir información para el Clero."

49 While de la Garza trusted his intelligence linking these two government employees to at least one leak and reported it to his superiors, the documentation regarding action taken against the women is absent in this file.

## CHAPTER 2

1 Jürgen Buchenau, *Plutarco Elías Calles and the Mexican Revolution* (Lanham, MD: Rowman & Littlefield, 2007), 106–7; Fidelina G. Llerenas and Jaime Tamayo, *El levantamiento delahuertista: cuatro rebeliones y cuatro jefes militares* (Guadalajara: Universidad de Guadalajara, 1995); Enrique Plasencia de la Parra, *Personajes y escenarios de la Rebelión Delahuertista 1923–1924* (México, DF: Instituto de Investigaciones Históricas, 1998), 16–17.

2 Linda B. Hall, *Oil, Banks, and Politics: The United States and Postrevolutionary Mexico, 1917–1924* (Austin: University of Texas Press, 1995), 155–57.

3 Ibid.

4 US Department of State, RG 59, 812.002-812.011/25.

5 Adolfo de la Huerta, *Memorias de Don Adolfo de la Huerta, según su propio dictado*, ed. Roberto Guzman Esparza (México, DF: Ediciones Guzman, 1957), 252. "¡Vamos adelante! Y conste que es un mal paso que se da, pues es prematuro, pero para que vean que no es por falta de pantalones, ¡vamos adelante!, aunque tengo la convicción de que esto es demasiado precipitado."

6 Hall, *Oil, Banks, and Politics*, 157.

7 Archivo General de la Nación, Dirección General de Investigaciones Políticas y Sociales (hereafter AGN, DGIPS), vol. 250, exp. 2 (no f.), Vernon J. Rose to Arthur C. Rath, 31 May 1924.

8 The exact identity and position of Vernon J. Rose is still unknown. While more research is necessary, it is confirmed that the information that Rose provided to a Mr. Arthur C. Rath was obtained by agents of the Confidential Department in Mexico. Rose may have been a private investigator or perhaps an agent for the US Department of State. He noted in his letters to Rath on two occasions that he was disgusted by the attempts of some oil companies operating in Mexico to interfere in the internal politics of that nation. It seems unlikely that he would have been in the employ of any of the major Mexican oil producers.

9 AGN, DGIPS, vol. 250, exp. 2 (no f.), Vernon J. Rose to Arthur C. Rath, 31 May 1924.

10 Ibid. Rose had verified this information with a gentleman simply referred to as Johnson, who had lived in Mexico City for around twenty years and who held an official post with the Mexico City Power and Light Company. Johnson had been told by a government acquaintance that something really big was brewing for the summer and that he would not be safe in the city—or the country, for that matter.

11 Ibid., Vernon J. Rose to Arthur C. Rath, 7 June 1924.

12 Ibid., confidential report, Agent 3 to Col. Martín Bárcenas, 14 October 1924. "Por otro lado persigue el embarque de material de Guerra que ya tiene comprados en Inglaterra, este material será enviado a las costas de Tuxpam en barcos petroleros, de allí se envian al sur, en los barcos aceiteros de Aguila." It is reasonable to assume that the last remnants of the de la Huerta Rebellion in the south were being fueled by arms shipments arranged by de la Huerta via the Pearson interests in England. Another real possibility, given the proliferation of old WWI armaments floating around the globe, was that at least some of these arms shipments were destined for rebel movements in the Central American republics.

13 Fideicomiso Archivos Plutarco Elías Calles y Fernando Torreblanca (hereafter FAPECFT), Colección Documental Embajada de Estados Unidos en México, 1918–28, serie 1924, exp. 090102, inv. 32, leg. 6/6. Agregado Militar de Estados Unidos: Informes, f. 83, report from J. A. Moss, 5 November 1924.

14 Ibid.

15 Ibid., Colección Documental del Archivo Adolfo de la Huerta: Exilio, Actividades Conspirativas, 1924–28, not cataloged. File: Alfonso de la Huerta Marcor, Adolfo de la Huerta to Alfonso de la Huerta, 6 October 1925. "Tú te has figurado que aquí en New York se recoge el dinero con palas o que yo poséo una varita mágica para abrir las cajas de los banqueros, y estás en un error. Estos hombres son 'Business Men' que para soltar un peso necesitan conocer las probabilidades de éxito que tengan, todo hasta el último detalle y estudiar el asunto bajo bases firmes. Tú estás creyendo que estos hombres son fáciles de engañar y estás en un error . . . por eso a veces me vienen momentos de desesperación contigo."

16 Ibid. File: Alvarez del Castillo, Juan Manuel, Juan Manuel Alvarez del Castillo to Adolfo de la Huerta, 27 February 1925.

17 Ibid. File: Reynaldo Esparza Martínez, letter from Reynaldo Esparza Martínez to Adolfo de la Huerta, 25 September 1925. Esparza Martínez made specific reference to a man named Mr. Hegewisch (sometimes Hegewish), who was already associated with de la Huerta in an arms-dealing capacity. "Están más capacitados que nosotros para dar una cuota regular."

18 Ibid. File: Almeida, M. C., letter from M. C. Almeida to Mr. J. Case (alias for Adolfo de la Huerta), 7 January 1925. "Debido a la poca atingencia del Lic. Palafox, quien tuvo la peregrina idea de depositar los fondos que se le confiaron en un Banco de crédito dudoso, influenciado segun tuve informes, por coyotes interezados [*sic*] en malos negocios."

19 Ibid. File: Ismael Palafox, Ismael Palafox to Adolfo de la Huerta, 22 July 1925:

> Empeñado doblemente en el arreglo de la cuestion económica, tanto por las recommendaciones que ud. me hace, cuanto por que veo la necesidad que hay de conseguir fondos para muy diversos y aprediantes usos; no he dejado de buscar los medios de arbitrármelos, y en perspectiva tengo hacerlo por alguno de los siguentes: I,—Abrirme un crédito por dos mil dollars, en el American Trust and Saving Bank [*sic*], para lo cual doy como guarantia el próximo abono del City National Bank, y como quisieren alguna más amplia, les dije que pidiesen informes de mi solvencia a México. II,—Si esto no diese resultado o demorase aun, entonces me valdré del Doctor, abonándole un rédito mayor que el legal, pero no exajerado. III,-Si tampoco con esto se obtuviesen fondos, caeré en manos del judio, quien aunque aun no resuelve y por lo mismo no detalla, pero si, insinúa, habria que darle no menos del ocho por ciento.—Y por último, si ningunos de estos medios diesen resultado, disminuia el importe del prestamo, a reserva de extenderlo despues mas.

20 AGN, DGIPS, vol. 264, exp. 18, f. 49, report from Agente de Primera 47, 11 March 1926. "Franca y abiertamente, que aunque ellos están trabajando activamente y trabajarán por el derrocamiento del actual Gobierno de nuestro país, no unirán sus esfuerzos con

de la Huerta, ni con ningun lider que haya defendido, ni defienda la Constitución de 1917."

21 Ibid. (no exp., no f.), Demetrio Torres (a) Chaparreras, Manuel Sorola to Juan N. Martínez (jefe del Servicio Confidencial de los Ferrocarriles), 26 October 1925.

22 Ibid., Agent 47, Fernando de la Garza to the Secretaría de Gobernación, 27 October 1925.

23 Ibid., Secretary of Foreign Relations Aaron Saenz to Gobernación, 29 October 1925.

24 Ibid., vol. 62, exp. 7, f. 13.

25 Ibid., vol. 264 (no exp., no f.), Demetrio Torres (a) Chaparreras, Fernando de la Garza to the Secretaría de Gobernación, 11 January 1926. "Para no dar motivo a que se haga escándalo por la prensa como sucedió con el caso de Abelardo Hinojosa."

26 Ibid.

27 Ibid., Jorge Prieto Laurens et al. to the US Secretary of Labor, 16 November 1925. "Rogamos se resuelva a la mayor brevidad la libertad del ciudadano mexicano Demetrio Torres preso en esta ciudad por violaciones involuntarias a las leyes de inmigracion como refugiado politico cuya honorabilidad podemos atestiguar quien cruzo la frontera huyendo de la persecuciones de sus enemigos politicos para salvar su vida."

28 Ibid., Fernando de la Garza to the Secretaría de Gobernación, 17 November 1925.

29 Fernando de la Garza was the Confidential Department's best and most prolific agent in San Antonio.

30 AGN, DGIPS, vol. 264 (no exp., no f.), Demetrio Torres (a) Chaparreras, Fernando de la Garza to the Secretaría de Gobernación, 11 January 1926.

31 Ibid., Fernando de la Garza to the Secretaría de Gobernación, 13 January 1926.

32 *El Universal*, 31 January 1926.

33 Ibid., 15 March 1926. "Agente W. N. Hanson, de San Antonio [A. P. Carrillo], como uno de los hombres de confianza del ex-secretario del Interior Albert Fall, diciendo que ese sujeto colocó personalmente a Torres en un automóvil y lo condujo a la frontera para entregarlo al comandante militar de la guarnición de Nuevo Laredo."

34 AGN, DGIPS, vol. 264 (no exp., no f.), Demetrio Torres (a) Chaparreras, Fernando de la Garza to Francisco Delgado, 30 April 1926.

35 Evelyn Hu-DeHart, *Yaqui Resistance and Survival: The Struggle for Land and Autonomy, 1821–1910* (Madison: University of Wisconsin Press, 1984), 94–154; Jürgen Buchenau, *The Last Caudillo: Alvaro Obregón and the Mexican Revolution* (Malden, MA: Wiley-Blackwell, 2011), 28.

36 Buchenau, *Plutarco Elías Calles*, 66.

37 Ibid., 68.

38 Linda B. Hall, *Álvaro Obregón: Power and Revolution in Mexico, 1911–1920* (College Station: Texas A&M University Press, 1981), 199. Moreover, Carranza made the mistake of attempting to use the military occupation of Sonora to incite a fresh Yaqui rebellion by installing Gen. Manuel Diéguez as military chief in the state. Diéguez was one of the Yaquis' most contemptible foes. Carranza's gamble did not pay off. Instead, it only generated more support for the obregonistas. See also John W. F. Dulles, *Yesterday in Mexico: A Chronicle of the Revolution, 1919–1936* (Austin: University of Texas Press, 1961), 23.

39 Ibid., 18–19.

40 Buchenau, *Last Caudillo*, 121.
41 Ibid., 151.
42 Dulles, *Yesterday in Mexico*, 311–12.
43 AGN, DGIPS, vol. 246, exp. 17, f. 3, manifesto attributed to Luis Matuz, general en jefe de las Tribuas Yaqui y Mayo, 7 September 1926. There are two variations on the spelling of Matus's name: Matus and Matuz. For the sake of consistency, I have chosen the most common of the two, Matus. "Don Adolfo de la Huerta . . . es el único en la actualidad que podrá cumplir con los intereses de la patria, llevandola por el buen sendero del progreso y de la paz."
44 Ibid. "Indignos dictadores, despotas y tiranos." "Es tiempo de que se acaben las dictaduras que siempre nos desvian del progreso y de la paz."
45 Ibid. "Al manifestar estas palabras al pueblo en general, no nos guía ninguna pasión, por que somos enemigos de todo acto reprobable. Los Ocho Gobernadores y los Ocho pueblos protestamos enérgicamente ante las arbitrariedades de un ejecutivo que se ha salido del carril de la democracia." "Los principios de la libertad de pensamiento." "Cuando tengamos un Gobierno que sepa respetar los derechos de cada ciudadano, ese gobierno tambien será respetado."
46 Ibid., f. 9, letter from Agent 21 in Piedras Negras to the Departamento Confidencial, 23 September 1926. "Yo presumo que los causantes de esta labor en lo que respecta a este rumbo son los señores Rafael Muzquiz y ex-Coronel Ramon Muzquiz, reconocidos elementos de la huertistas que radican en Eagle Pass, Tex. Individuos que frequentan con sus correligionarios de El Paso y San Antonio."
47 Ibid., f. 11, manifesto attributed to Luis Matus, 4 September 1926.
48 Ibid., f. 32; "Operaciones en el Yaqui," *El Universal*, 27 October 1926.
49 AGN, DGIPS, vol. 246, exp. 17, f. 49; "La activa campaña contra los Yaquis rebeldes esta comenzando en el Bacatete," *Excélsior*, 2 December 1926.
50 AGN, DGIPS, vol. 246, exp. 17, f. 38, report from Agent 9 to the Secretaría de Gobernación, 30 October 1926. "Aportaban fondos para la Iglesia, en diferentes cantidades, de acuerdo con las cuotas de cada asociación, así como el número de sus miembros; los fondos de estas asociaciones se destinaban para el sostenimiento del culto, mejoras en las Iglesias etc." "Cuando sucedió el levantamiento, al Obispo se le oyó decir que los Yaquis tenían razón de pelear por que se les habían cortado todas su libertades, entre ellas la de conciencia que era lo mas sagrado."
51 Ibid.
52 Ibid., 39. "Por intrigas del Presidente Municipal . . . y el Notario Público . . . por ser muy católicos y ser el Pueblo donde llegaba siempre el Obispo, los voluntarios se desistieron de prestar sus servicios."
53 Ibid.
54 Ibid., f. 76, report from Agent 2 to the Secretaría de Gobernación, Oficina Confidencial, 8 December 1926.
55 Ibid. The rest of the report is sprinkled with remarks denigrating the shoddy treatment that the Department of Justice was giving the surveillance of exiles, such as de la Huerta, and also what he perceived as the halfhearted response of Washington in guarding against neutrality law violations.

56 Ibid. "Algunos cabecillas Yaquis, quienes según informes obtenidos sobre el particular, se encontraban a corta distancia de la frontera con dicho lugar con una escolta de doscientos hombres, para conducir a Don Adolfo al Cuartel General de los Indios rebeldes por instrucciones del Jefe Matus."
57 Ibid. "Pero que les aseguraba que no estaba lejano el día en que se pusiera al frente de ellos para asumir toda la responsabilidad de su actitud hostil ante el Gobierno, para lo cual tambien solo esperaba que cualquiera de los grupos armados capturaran un Pueblo de la frontera, para pasar a territorio Nacional por la puerta sin violar las leyes de neutralidad de Estados Unidos."
58 Ibid., f. 66; "Los Yaquis se quejan de un engaño del Sr. De la Huerta," *Excélsior*, 8 January 1927.
59 Archivo Histórico Genaro Estrada, Acervo Histórico Diplomático, Secretaría de Relaciones Exteriores (hereafter SRE), LE 710, f. 576, letter from Consul J. E. Anchondo to the consul general in El Paso, Texas, 15 September 1927. "Para cuyo efecto se les proporcionaron armas, municiones y equipos diversos."
60 Ibid., f. 558, letter from A. T. Spence to J. E. Anchondo at Nogales, Arizona, 29 August 1927.
61 Ibid., LE 822, R-103-8, ff. 212–15, E. B. Elfers to the consul in El Paso, Texas, 11 May 1927.
62 Ibid.
63 Ibid., LE 852, f. 134, confidential report no. 103 (n.d.). The report was forwarded to the SRE by Consul A. P. Carrillo on 13 May 1927.
64 Ibid.
65 FAPECFT, Colección Documental del Archivo Adolfo de la Huerta: Exilio, Actividades Conspirativas, 1924–28, not cataloged. File: Luis Gayou, statement recorded by the Department of Justice (n.d.). Original text in English.
66 Ibid.
67 Ibid.

## CHAPTER 3

1 US Department of Justice, headquarters file 64-306, Gen. Enrique Estrada, "Report made by J. G. Findlay," 24 August 1926.
2 Ibid., "Report made by A. A. Hopkins, Re. Parker Hardware Co.," 5 August 1926.
3 Ibid., 2.
4 Ibid., 2–3.
5 Ibid., "Report made by Edwin N Atherton," 18 September 1926.
6 Fidelina G. Llerenas and Jaime Tamayo, *El levantamiento delahuertista: cuatro rebeliones y cuatro jefes militares* (Guadalajara: Universidad de Guadalajara, 1995), 73.
7 Ibid.
8 Ibid., 75. "Los militares se sentían afectados por medidas como las de reducir el radio de acción de cada caudillo al aumentar el número de las jefaturas de operaciones militares."

9 Jürgen Buchenau, *Plutarco Elías Calles and the Mexican Revolution* (Lanham, MD: Rowman & Littlefield, 2007), 113.
10 US Department of Justice, headquarters file 64-306, Gen. Enrique Estrada, "Report made by Emilio Kosterlitzki," 7 January 1926.
11 Mae Ngai, *Impossible Subjects: Illegal Aliens and the Making of Modern America* (Princeton: Princeton University Press, 2004).
12 Ibid., 3.
13 Ibid., 23.
14 Linda B. Hall, "Creating a Schizophrenic Border: Migration and Perception, 1920–1925," in *The Mexican Revolution: Conflict and Consolidation, 1910–1940*, ed. Douglas Richmond and Sam W. Haynes (College Station: Texas A&M University Press, 2013), 91. See also Linda B. Hall and Don Coerver, *Revolution on the Border: The United States and Mexico, 1910–1920* (Albuquerque: University of New Mexico Press, 1988).
15 Ngai, *Impossible Subjects*, 53–57.
16 Kelly Lytle Hernández, *Migra! A History of the U.S. Border Patrol* (Berkeley: University of California Press, 2010), 5.
17 Ibid., 74.
18 Commissioner general of immigration, *Annual Report of the Commissioner General of Immigration to the Secretary of Labor* (Washington, DC: Government Printing Office, 1923), 1. Hereafter cited CGI with publication year and page number.
19 Ibid., 17.
20 Ibid., 19.
21 Ibid.
22 Ibid.
23 Ibid., 19–20.
24 Ibid., 1925, 17.
25 Ibid.
26 Rhodri Jeffreys-Jones, *The FBI: A History* (New Haven: Yale University Press, 2007).
27 Kenneth D. Ackerman, *Young J. Edgar: Hoover, the Red Scare, and the Assault on Civil Liberties* (New York: Carroll and Graf, 2007).
28 Hall and Coerver, *Revolution on the Border*, 150.
29 US Department of Justice, headquarters file 64-306, Gen. Enrique Estrada, "Memorandum for Mr. Tolson," 1 November 1936.
30 Ibid., "Report made by A. A. Hopkins," 1 December 1926, 3.
31 Ibid.
32 Ibid., 4.
33 Ibid., 6.
34 Ricardo Romo, *East Los Angeles: History of a Barrio* (Austin: University of Texas Press, 1983), 54–55.
35 Ibid., 55. Romo drew his statistics from the work of Paul S. Taylor, *A Spanish-Mexican Peasant Community* (Berkeley: University of California Press, 1933), 39.
36 Parole reports in the Department of Justice file state the date and status of entry for those accused of violation of US neutrality laws. All the leaders entered the United

States between 1921 and 1925. See US Department of Justice, headquarters file 64-306, Gen. Enrique Estrada.

37 Pedro G. Castillo, "The Making of a Mexican Barrio: Los Angeles, 1890–1920" (PhD diss., University of California, Santa Barbara, 1979), 72.

38 It must be noted that out of fifty-seven testimonies, approximately half of those accompanied a statement of place of residence. It is not clear whether the other half had no place of residence or the designation "Los Angeles" was considered sufficient data for the Department of Justice. The conclusions here are based on a limited data set, but it can be assumed that Estrada's recruiters most likely established firm relationships among the residents of these communities and probably recruited to a much greater extent that what can be seen in the visual representation.

39 Castillo, "Making of a Mexican Barrio," 105–13.

40 Ben Fallaw, "Varieties of Mexican Revolutionary Anticlericalism: Radicalism, Iconoclasm, and Otherwise, 1914–1935," *The Americas* 65:4 (April 2009): 482.

41 US Department of Justice, headquarters file 64-306, Gen. Enrique Estrada, "Report made by E. Kosterlitzky," 26 March 1926. Reference was made to a similar statement in a previous chapter, in which Estrada referred to the government in Mexico as "a religious Government up side down." Miguel Comodurán was quoted as having told one of the recruits, Angel Novar, that they were going to attack the Mexican government "because it was not a liberal government." Ibid., "Report made by A. A. Hopkins," 1 December 1926.

42 Fideicomiso Archivos Plutarco Elías Calles y Fernando Torreblanca (hereafter FAPECFT), Archivo Plutarco Elías Calles (PEC), serie 43, exp. 35, inv. 2900, leg. 3/6, "Informes Confidenciales," ff. 123–24 (n.d.). "En la ciudad de Los Angeles, y ciudades circunvecinas hay dos facciones que trabajan por destruir al Gobierno de nuestra República, la primera esta integrada de los revolucionarios de la Huertistas y residuos del Carrancismo." The *Christian Science Monitor* reported that information from the Foreign Office suggested that there were "religious elements" in Southern California that were funding Estrada's movement. "Mexico Moves Quickly to End Uprising Plots," *Christian Science Monitor*, 18 August 1926.

43 FAPECFT, PEC, serie 43, exp. 35, inv. 2900, leg. 3/6, "Informes Confidenciales," ff. 123–24 (n.d.). "Actualmente estan esperando dinero del Arzobispo de Guadalajara Dr. Francisco Jimenez Orozco, quien en carta reciente le ha ofrecido al Gral Estrada, facilitar una fuerte suma, la que sera mandada por conducto de un banquero de dicha ciudad de Guadalajara que responde al nombre de Salvador Ugarte."

44 Ibid. "Tiene una poderosa ayuda del Arzobispo de Guadalajara, Orozco Jimenes [*sic*] que es un elemento de gran valia entre el Clero Mexicano."

45 "Catholic Women Linked to Foiled Revolt Plot," *Los Angeles Times*, 18 August 1926.

46 Ibid.

47 Ibid.

48 "Se descubrio en Mexico un complot para derrocar el actual gobierno," *El Informador*, 17 August 1926.

49 Centro de Estudios de História de México, Grupo CARSO (hereafter CEHM), fondo 621, Félix Díaz 1926–27, carpeta 13/18, leg. 1290, letter from Sra. Luz de Perches to

Guillermo Rosas Jr., 27 October 1926. For a more detailed discussion of Perches' activities in exile, see chapters 4 and 5.

50 US Department of Justice, headquarters file 64-306, Gen. Enrique Estrada, "Report made by E. Kosterlitzky," 26 March 1926.

51 For a more detailed account of Díaz's activities during the revolution, see Peter V. N. Henderson, *Félix Díaz, the Porfirians, and the Mexican Revolution* (Lincoln: University of Nebraska Press, 1981), 98.

52 Victoriano Huerta died in El Paso in January 1916 while under house arrest, under the guard of the US military.

53 Henderson, *Félix Díaz*, 125–28.

54 CEHM, fondo 621, Félix Díaz 1924–25, carpeta 11/18, leg. 1051, letter from J. D. Ibarra, MD, to Guillermo Rosas Jr., 24 September 1924. "Terminar con las ismos y con las istas, y formar un gran Partido que se ocupara unicamente de la reconstrucción Nacional."

55 Ibid., Félix Díaz 1923–24, carpeta 10/18, leg. 1026, letter from J. Espinosa Ibarra to Richard Williams, 2 June 1924. "Y el resultado de esta, sera, tal vev, el triunfo de nuestra causa." The idea, it seems, was that the contenders advocated such radical policies that they themselves would elicit a violent reaction from the opposition.

56 Ibid., leg. 971, letter from E. to Guillermo Rosas Jr., 7 December 1923. "Momento supremo para el Jefe dada la disolución del Gobierno y el estado de revolución del pais, sin contar con otras poderosas que reclaman la actitude definida de la Casa Blanca."

57 Ibid., leg. 937, letter from Brigido Caro to Félix Díaz, 30 September 1923. "La ruptura del triángulo de Agua Prieta nos ofrecerá en muy pocos dias la mejor oportunidad de llevar acabo nuestros patrióticos proyectos."

58 Ibid., leg. 999, letter from Federico Garcia y Alva to Guillermo Rosas Jr., 27 January 1923. "El movimiento delahuertista no solo es la Patria, sino que es uno facción del mismo nucléo que la ha desgarrado, por sus ambiciones personales y bastardas."

59 Ibid., Félix Díaz 1925–26, carpeta 12/18, leg. 1185, letter from J. Uríburu to Guillermo Rosas Jr., 17 November 1925. "No está de acuerdo con ellos [estradistas] ni creé que podrán hacer nada." It must be noted that the relationship among Uríburu, Rosas Jr., and Estrada was incredibly complex. While he was serving as an informant for Agent Emilio Kosterlitzky, he was also feeding information to Félix Díaz while possibly attempting to ensnare Estrada. It is not entirely clear if his intent in the Estrada case was to thwart or facilitate the rebellion. What is clear is that he was informing a number of important people about the activities of all the others.

60 Ibid., leg. 1194, letter from Uríburu to Rosas Jr., 5 December 1925.

61 The meetings took place in January 1926, but it is not clear exactly when the meetings were held. Bureau agents only reported on the matter in early August. US Department of Justice, headquarters file 64-306, Gen. Enrique Estrada, "Report made by A. A. Hopkins," 1 August 1926.

62 CEHM, fondo 621, Félix Díaz 1925–26, carpeta 12/18, leg. 1217, letter from Enrique Estrada to Félix Díaz, 9 February 1926.

63 Ibid., carpeta 13/18, leg. 1258, letter from Pedro de León to Mariano Viesca Arzipe, 9 February 1926.

64 "Calles Forces Heartened," *New York Times*, 18 August 1926.

65 "U.S. Neutrality Pleases Mexico," *Excélsior*, 18 August 1926, English section.
66 "Amaro Proceeds to US Border," *Excélsior*, 18 August 1926, English section.
67 US Department of Justice, headquarters file 64-306, Gen. Enrique Estrada, "Report made by A. A. Hopkins," 11 March 1927.

## CHAPTER 4

1 *El Universal*, 4 February 1926, quoted in David C. Bailey, *¡Viva Cristo Rey! The Cristero Rebellion and the Church State Conflict in Mexico* (Austin: University of Texas Press, 1974), 62.
2 For more detail on the causes and outcomes of the Cristero Rebellion, see Robert E. Quirk, *The Mexican Revolution and the Catholic Church 1910–1929* (Indiana: Indiana University Press, 1973); Bailey, *¡Viva Cristo Rey!*; Jean A. Meyer, *The Cristero Rebellion: The Mexican People between Church and State, 1926–1929* (Cambridge: Cambridge University Press, 1976); Jennie Purnell, *Popular Movements and State Formation in Revolutionary Mexico: The Agraristas and Cristeros of Michoacán* (Durham: Duke University Press, 1999); Matthew Butler, *Popular Piety and Political Identity in Mexico's Cristero Rebellion: Michoacán, 1927–29* (New York: Oxford University Press, 2004); Agustín Vaca, *Los silencios de la historia: las Cristeras* (Zapopan: Colegio de Jalisco, 1998); Alicia Olivera Sedano, *Aspectos del conflicto religioso de 1926 a 1929: sus antecedentes y consecuencias* (México, DF: Instituto Nacional de Antropología e Historia, 1966); Francisco Barbosa Guzmán, *Jalisco desde la revolución*, vol. 6, *La iglesia y el gobierno civil* (Guadalajara: Universidad de Guadalajara, 1988); Fernando M. González, *Matar y morir por Cristo Rey: aspectos de la Cristiada* (México, DF: Instituto de Investigaciones Sociales, Universidad Nacional Autónoma de México, 2001).
3 Alan Knight, *The Mexican Revolution*, vol. 1, *Porfirians, Liberals and Peasants* (Lincoln: University of Nebraska Press, 1986), 302.
4 Patience A. Schell, "Of the Sublime Mission of Mothers of Families: The Union of Mexican Catholic Ladies in Revolutionary Mexico," in *The Women's Revolution in Mexico, 1910–1953*, ed. Stephanie Mitchell and Patience A. Schell (New York: Rowman & Littlefield, 2007), 100–101.
5 Ibid., 101.
6 Centro de Estudios de História de México, Grupo CARSO (hereafter CEHM), fondo 621, Félix Díaz 1926–27, carpeta 13/18, leg. 1302, letter from Sra. Luz de Perches to Guillermo Rosas Jr., 25 November 1926.
7 Ibid., leg. 1307, letter from Sra. Luz de Perches to Guillermo Rosas Jr., 4 December 1926.
8 Ibid. "Yo le hice algunas pertinentes observaciones sobre la persona de Capistran, no le pongo yo defectos personales, es un buen muchacho, muy honrado, muy valiente, muy de fácil palabra para levanter las multitudes, magnifico para orador de salon, magnifico para lider pacifico, y un buen catolico ferviente ductilpara que las altas personalidades Catolicas tengan quien les obedesca ciegamente."
9 Ibid., carpeta 14/18, leg. 1337, letter from Sra. Luz de Perches to Félix Díaz, 27 January 1927. "Muy disgustados con Capistran, que todos aquí en El Paso quieren convencerlo

de que deben ponerse en contacto con Ud. Y asi continuar para llegar al éxito deseado, que al no conseguirlo tal vez le quiten el mando a Cap."

10 US Department of State, RG 59, 812.00/28132, letter from José Gándara to Secretary of State Frank Kellogg, 17 December 1927.

11 Julia Grace Darling Young, "Mexican Emigration during the Cristero War, 1926–1929" (PhD diss., University of Chicago, 2009), 125–28.

12 Ibid., 129.

13 Ibid., 132. Young provides a very detailed account of Gándara's plan to rebel against the Mexican government. See also US Department of State, *Records of the State Department Relating to the Internal Affairs of Mexico 1910–1929* (Washington, DC: National Archives, 1985), reel 85, for brief accounts of the arrest and trial of José Gándara.

14 Archivo General de la Nación, Dirección General de Investigaciones Políticas y Sociales (hereafter AGN, DGIPS), vol. 266, exp. 7/011.3(73) 4 (no f.), report from Confidential Agent (CA; alias) José García to the Secretaría de Gobernación, 6 February 1926. Valls accused him of having been one of the agents involved in the assassination of Lucio Blanco in the summer of 1922.

15 Ibid. "Su Consul vale una chingada, aqui no más yo mando."

16 "Extradition for Slaying Suspect Being Discussed," *Los Angeles Times*, 17 February 1926. The deputy in question was a J. T. Holloway of San Antonio, Texas.

17 AGN, DGIPS, vol. 266, exp. 7/011.3(73) 4 (no f.), report from CA (alias) José García to the Secretaría de Gobernación, 6 February 1926. "Por indiscreciones de la Policía Americana."

18 Ibid.

19 AGN, DGIPS, vol. 266, exp. 7/011.3(73) 4 (no f.), report from Consul Alfredo C. Vásquez at Brownsville, 14 April 1927. "Segun informes fidedignos llegados a esta ofna. de mi cargo, Felix Diaz en su reciente visita a Laredo, Tex., el Fiscal de Distrito en dicha ciudad John A. Valls, en conferencia que celebro con Diaz le prometio, en caso de que se resolviera a encabezar un movimiento armado contra el Gobierno del Gral. Calles, ayudarlo con su influencia politica y Oficial para que por la jurisdiccion de Laredo se pasaran las armas y parque que se encesitara [*sic*] para revolucionar."

20 Ibid. See also the report from CA Fernando de la Garza, 6 May 1927.

21 AGN, DGIPS, vol. 266, exp. 7/011.3(73) 4 (no f.), report from Consul Alfredo C. Vásquez at Brownsville, 14 April 1927. "Habiendo dicho don Félix Díaz a varios de sus amigos que lo despedian en la estación de Laredo, que 'un grupo de hombres como Valls, era suficiente para cambiar el gobierno de México.'"

22 Ibid., report from CA Fernando de la Garza, 6 May 1927.

23 Ibid. "Rangers, Policia etc, lejos de perjudicarlo, le cuidaria la espalda, y prestarian toda la ayuda necesaria para que la rebelion cundiera en el Norte de Mexico, etc."

24 Ibid.

25 Ibid., report from CA Fernando de la Garza, 1 September 1928. "Al cual pertenecen los alto funcionarios Federales, inclusive el Presidente Collidge, para empujar todo lo posible en contra del expresado Fiscal Valls, tanto para que sea castigado por la falta de respeto y los insultos que acaba de lanzar en contra de la Secretaría de Estado, como para que no logre su intento de re-elegirse para el cargo que desempeña en Laredo, Texas."

26 Archivo Histórico Genaro Estrada, Acervo Histórico Diplomático, Secretaría de Relaciones Exteriores (hereafter SRE), LE 815-100-R-24, f. 50, report from Rafael de la Colina to the SRE, 2 April 1929. "No hay duda de que se halla colocado en una situación difícil a este respecto, toda vez que por razones políticas de mucho peso no puede malquistarse con quienes dominan políticamente desde hace muchos años en el Condado de Webb, los que, encabezados por el licenciado Juan A. Valls, han hostilizado siempre directa o indirectamente a nuestro Gobierno y a sus funcionarios."

27 "John Valls Regresa a su Puesto," *La Prensa*, 27 September 1929.

28 See chapter 2; AGN, DGIPS, vol. 264, exp. 18, f. 49, report from Agente de Primera 47, 11 March 1926.

29 Matthew Redinger, *American Catholics and the Mexican Revolution, 1924–1936* (Notre Dame: University of Notre Dame Press, 2005).

30 SRE, LE 1540, pt. 1, f. 9, report from A. P. Carrillo to the Secretaría de Relaciones Exteriores, 4 March 1926.

31 Ibid.

32 Ibid., ff. 15–16, report from A. P. Carrillo to the Secretaría de Relaciones Exteriores, 8 March 1926. "Llego a suponer que este trabajo está influenciado por el elemento Católico y como desgraciadamente hay algunos periódicos que concuerdan con sus ideas, no tienen empacho en poner lo que les acomoda, imprimiendo noticias tan absurdas como las de que hemos tenido policía secreta y guardias en este Consulado General."

33 Arthur Drossaerts, foreword to *No God Next Door: Red Rule in Mexico and Our Responsibility*, by Michael S. J. Kenny (New York: William J. Hirten, 1935), iv. See also Redinger, *American Catholics*, 58.

34 Kenny, *No God Next Door*, 1.

35 Redinger, *American Catholics*, 59.

36 Ibid., 120–21.

37 Ibid., 117–18.

38 "Flaherty Confers with President," *Atlanta Constitution*, 1 September 1926.

39 Redinger, *American Catholics*, 119.

40 "K. of C. Denies It Is Fomenting Mexico Revolt: Launches $1,000,000 War of Propaganda," *Chicago Daily Tribune*, 6 November 1926.

41 Fideicomiso Archivos Plutarco Elías Calles y Fernando Torreblanca (hereafter FAPECFT), Fondo Plutarco Elías Calles, gaveta 89, exp. 1, leg. 1, inv. 1391, actividades desarrolladas en EEUU por los Caballeros de Colón, letter from Mr. Chalmers to Aaron Saenz, September 1926.

42 "Los Angeles Bank Gets German Claim: Total of $217,337.14 Paid to Fifteen Californians in Awards," *Los Angeles Times*, 7 December 1925.

43 AGN, DGIPS, vol. 225, exp. 10, f. 9, report from Fernando de la Garza, Agente de Primero, to Francisco Delgado, 6 January 1927.

44 Ibid., f. 15, report from Fernando de la Garza, Agente de Primero, to Francisco Delgado, 28 December 1926.

45 Ibid.

46 It is possible that these men were also involved in the acquisition of arms for Estrada's rebellion, but the documentation regarding their activities only verifies that they began smuggling arms for the Knights of Columbus in mid- to late 1926.

47 FAPECFT, Fondo Plutarco Elías Calles, gaveta 89, exp. 1, leg. 1, inv. 1391, actividades desarrolladas en EEUU por los Caballeros de Colón, f. 30, letter from George Merrill to Chandler P. Anderson, 4 November 1926.

48 Ibid.

49 Ibid., f. 47, list of expenditures submitted by Chandler P. Anderson to James A. Flaherty, 1 October 1926.

50 Fernando de la Garza was held to be one of the best and most experienced agents in the service of the Confidential Department. He was highly regarded by the head of the department, Col. Francisco Delgado.

51 AGN, DGIPS, vol. 225, exp. 10, f. 2, report from Fernando de la Garza to Francisco Delgado, 7 December 1926.

52 Ibid. "Manejarse con un escrupuloso cuidado."

53 Ibid., f. 9, report from Fernando de la Garza to Francisco Delgado, 6 January 1927.

54 Ibid., f. 15, report from Fernando de la Garza to Francisco Delgado, 28 December 1926.

## CHAPTER 5

1 See Robert Carriedo, "The Man Who Tamed Mexico's Tiger: General Joaquin Amaro and the Professionalization of Mexico's Revolutionary Army" (PhD diss., University of New Mexico, 2005); Enrique Plasencia de la Parra, *Historia y organización de la fuerzas armadas en México, 1917–1937* (México, DF: Universidad Autónoma de México, 2010); Edwin Lieuwen, *Mexican Militarism: The Political Rise and Fall of the Revolutionary Army, 1910–1940* (Albuquerque: University of New Mexico Press, 1968).

2 Carriedo, "Man Who Tamed Mexico's Tiger," 98.

3 Obregón famously boasted that no Mexican general could resist a $25,000- or $50,000-peso cannon shot. The story has been related using both figures.

4 Carriedo, "Man Who Tamed Mexico's Tiger," 103.

5 Ibid., 104–5.

6 Ibid., 107. See also Ernest Gruening, *Mexico and Its Heritage* (New York: Century, 1928), 320.

7 Archivo General de la Nación, Dirección General de Investigaciones Políticas y Sociales (hereafter AGN, DGIPS), vol. 228, exp. 15, f. 9, report from the jefe de la guarnición, Piedras Negras, Coahila, Jesús Fuentes Dávila, 26 April 1927.

8 Ibid. "Como gran numero de sus feligreses mexicanos proceden de la Ciudad de Piedras Negras, siendo a quienes se dirige exitandoles para que se declaren en rebelión . . . me permito sugerir . . . se dicten las ordenes conducentes para que la oficina de Migración en Piedras Negras, prohiba que nuestros conacionales de ambos sexos residentes en aquella ciudad vengan a los servicios dominicales a la iglesia catolica de Eagle Pass."

9 Ibid., f. 11, el oficial mayor del secretario de guerra y marina to el jefe de operaciones militares, Piedras Negras, 16 May 1927. "Ya se giraron órdenes al Delegado de Migración de ese lugar a fin de que impida el paso a Territorio Nacional a todas aquellas personas que frecuenten al citado Centurioni."

10 Plasencia de la Parra, *Historia y organización*, 327.

11 Ibid., 329. "Militares . . . tenían por costumbre intervenir en cuestiones políticas en todos los lugares a donde eran enviados. No siempre seguían una línea política que les mandara la presidencia o la Secretaría de Guerra sino que se guiaban por motivaciones personales."

12 María Teresa Fernández-Aceves, "José Guadalupe Zuno Hernández and the Revolutionary Process in Jalisco," in *State Governors in the Mexican Revolution, 1910–1952: Portraits in Conflict, Courage, and Corruption*, ed. Jürgen Buchenau and William H. Beezley (Lanham, MD: Rowman & Littlefield, 2009), 98.

13 Ibid., 102.

14 The files in the Joaquín Amaro Archive at the Fideicomismo Archivos Plutarco Elías y Fernando Torreblanca are replete with telegrams from municipal and state representatives to the secretary of war accusing their political enemies of being old delahuertistas. Most of these claims were ignored.

15 The speech appears in its entirety in Froylán C. Manjarrez, *La jornada institucional*, vol. 1, *La crisis de la política* (México, DF: Talleres Gráficos Editorial y Diario Oficial, 1930), 25–40.

16 Plasencia de la Parra, *Historia y organización*, 339.

17 Manjarrez, *Jornada institucional*, 44. "El Ejército debe conservar la respetabilidad que se ha creado guardando una perfecta unificación, porque si esa unificación se quebranta, nada consigueremos . . . desunido el Ejército, vendría como consecuencia ineludible la desunión de toda la familia revolucionaria, porque una parte de esa familia se iría con un grupo y otra con otro grupo, y entonces, si un Gobierno llegara a contituirse en semejantes condiciones, no sería un Gobierno nacional, sería Gobierno de facción."

18 Ibid., 59. "Contestar al señor Presidente con toda lealtad, con toda honradez, y creo que todos los divisionarios tienen la obligación de hacer lo mismo."

19 Ibid., 60. "Los cuartelazos, las asonadas, etc., ya pasaron a la historia; que esa palabras ya no deben de sonar entre nosotros, porque considero que el Ejército ha quedado definitivamente purgado de los elementos sin vergüenza, y porque todos los componentes del Ejército ya han dado una prueba bien clara, bien amplia, de lealtad, de disciplina, de subordinación y de honradez. Ya no debemos de admitir la palabra 'cuartelazo,' debe ser proscrita absolutamente."

20 AGN, DGIPS, vol. 2022B, exp. 39, report from "R" to the Secretaría de Gobernación, 21 September 1927.

21 Jürgen Buchenau, *Plutarco Elías Calles and the Mexican Revolution* (Lanham, MD: Rowman & Littlefield, 2007), 140.

22 Ibid.

23 Archivo Histórico Genaro Estrada, Acervo Histórico Diplomático, Secretaría de Relaciones Exteriores (hereafter SRE), LE 822 R-103-8, f. 16, confidential report no. 7 (n.d.).

"La muerte del General Francisco Serrano causó profundo descontento entre los militares de Chihuahua y principalmente en el General Caraveo, quien no trató de ocultar su cólera por lo que él llamó asesinato. Sin embargo, dijo el mismo General Caravo que ya (eso) estaba hecho y que por tanto no había nada que hacer."

24 Centro de Estudios de História de México, Grupo CARSO (hereafter CEHM), fondo 621, Félix Díaz 1926–27, carpeta 13/18, leg. 1290, letter from Sra. Luz de Perches to Félix Díaz, 27 October 1926.

25 Ibid. "Que era casi imposible que Caraveo diera color mientras Calles tubiera [*sic*] dominio, que ademas Caraveo era Obregonista y le gustaba militar en aquellas filas por las manos libres que dejaban."

26 Historian Francisco R. Almada traces Caraveo's trajectory after 1914 to somewhere in the United States, ignoring his route through Havana. See Almada, *Gobernadores del estado de Chihuahua* (Chihuahua: Centro Librero la Prensa, 1980), 568.

27 Ibid., 569.

28 Ibid.

29 Fideicomiso Archivos Plutarco Elías Calles y Fernando Torreblanca (hereafter FAPECFT), Fondo Plutarco Elías Calles, gaveta 91, exp. 4, inv. 1566, leg. 1, f. 3, "Caraveo, Marcelo (Gral.)," letter from Marcelo Caraveo to Diputado Nicolás Pérez, 29 January 1927. "Después hacen alusión a mi persona asegurando que estoy de acuerdo con los rebeldes y que por conducto de mi señora he estado tratando con los felicistas, sirviendo de intermediaria la Sra Perches, a quien supongo la representante de esa facción."

30 Ibid. "Tu ya acordarás que la Sra Perches tuvo un papel muy activo en los asuntos religiosos en esa Capital y hasta estuvo presa por tales motivos."

31 Ibid.

32 CEHM, fondo 621, Félix Díaz 1926–27, carpeta 13/18, leg. 1296, letter from Sra. Luz de Perches to Félix Díaz, 14 November 1926. "En el futuro podia presentársele a su marido otra oportunidad de las que no se presenten dos veces."

33 AGN, DGIPS, vol. 2022B, exp. 39 (no f.), report from Agent 2, 5 November 1927.

34 Ibid. *Antireelecionismo* was a key tenet of the revolution of 1910, referring to the perpetually "re-elected" president Porfirio Díaz, whom the revolution ousted. Chihuahuan antireelectionistas in this context were opposed to the reelection bid of Obregón, which required a constitutional amendment to allow said reelection.

35 CEHM, fondo 621, Félix Díaz 1926–27, carpeta 13/18, leg. 1302, letter from Sra. Luz de Perches to Guillermo Rosas Jr., 25 November 1926.

36 Ibid.

37 Almada, *Gobernadores del estado de Chihuahua*, 560–61.

38 FAPECFT, Fondo Plutarco Elías Calles, gaveta 91, exp. 4, inv. 1566, leg. 1, f. 3, "Caraveo, Marcelo (Gral.)," letter from Marcelo Caraveo to Juan Andrew Almazan, 1 May 1927. "Puedo asegurarte que el elemento militar no tuvo la participación que se atribuye y que los hace aparecer como partícipes en estos acontecimientos."

39 Ibid. "Tal vez el Sr. Presidente tiene ya conocimiento de la impopularidad de todo este grupo dirigido por Luis Esther Estrada; pero lo que indudablement ignora, esla [*sic*] perfidia con que se han conducido estos señores, abusando de la magnanimidad con que he venido obrando, precisamente, para no provocar un conflicto."

40 Ibid. "Ahora tenga la confianza absoluta en el Estado de Chihuahua, que confié en que todos como un solo hombre estaremos con él [Calles] para castigar a los falsos revolucionarios en el momento que se ha [*sic*] necesario."

41 CEHM, fondo 621, Félix Díaz 1926–27, carpeta 13/18, leg. 1232, letter from López Carvajal to Guillermo Rosas Jr., 3 June 1926.

42 Ibid.

43 Ibid.

44 Ibid., leg. 1251, letter from Guillermo Rosas Jr. to Gen. Marcelo Caraveo, 31 July 1926.

45 Ibid.

46 AGN, DGIPS, vol. 264, exp. 19, "Informe Numero Uno," report from Agent 47, Fernando de la Garza, 2 January 1928.

47 FAPECFT, Fondo Plutarco Elías Calles, MFN:622, serie 8, gaveta 89, exp. 1, leg. 1, inv. 1391, actividades desarrolladas en EEUU por los Caballeros de Colon, f. 50, report from Sr. Roy Bowie to Manuel Tellez, Mexican ambassador in Washington, regarding the activities of the Knights of Columbus (n.d.). "Que el movimiento se estaba llevando a cabo de acuerdo con los señores General Obregón, Manzo, Cruz (Inspector General de Policía de la Ciudad de México) y otro general radicado en esta misma Capital."

48 AGN, DGIPS, vol. 233, exp. 29, f. 2, report from Gilberto Ramírez, 18 June 1928:

> Se sabe que la Secretaría de Guerra ha girado por tres veces la órden de que el General Manzo se presente á esta Capital y en ninguna de las tres veces ha sido obedecido esta órden. En vista de esto se mando una persona que fuera á relevarlo y se negó á entregar el mando de la zona que tiene a su cargo, y notifico al que lo iba á relevar de que deba retirarse á lo haría desaparecer; esto obliga al Sr. General Amaro, Secretario de Guerra a salir personalmente con una columna de diez o doce mil hombres para atacar a Manzo si este se muestra revelde a acatar las ordenes que se le den. La Prensa dice que el Sr. General Amaro sale a visitar varias Jefaturas de Operaciones para hacerse cargo de como se encuentran las fuerzas que guarnecen dichas Jefaturas, pero en realidad su viaje obedece a lo expuesto antes en este parte. Este rumor es de persona que se dice bien informada de cuanto ocurre en la Secretaría de Guerra.

49 Ibid., f. 1. "Se sigue rumorando que el General Manzo, en el Estado de Sonora, guarda una actitud revelde, negándose á entregar el mando de las fuerzas que tiene en la Zona que es á su cargo manifestando que el, solo obedese órdenes del General Obregón, siendo esta su contestación categorica. Parece que la Secretaría de Guerra ha dipuesto reconcentración de fuerzas en San Luis Potosí para de alli ir reforsando á su paso para Sonora, el contingente de elementos de guerra para atacar á Manzo, si insiste en su actitud."

50 Plasencia de la Parra, *Historia y organización*, 334.

51 Buchenau, *Plutarco Elías Calles*, 148.

52 "Sonora Settles Differences in Mexican Dispute," *Douglas Daily Dispatch*, 20 February 1929.

53 John W. F. Dulles, *Yesterday in Mexico: A Chronicle of the Revolution, 1919–1936* (Austin: University of Texas Press, 1961), 415. As Gonzálo Santos recounted, Valenzuela resigned his post as the minister of the interior over a disagreement regarding

presidential involvement in deciding the 1925 gubernatorial race between Carlos Riva Palacios and David Montes de Oca in the state of Mexico. Montes de Oca obtained the electoral majority—a dubious majority, as Santos related—and when Calles ordered Valenzuela to recognize Riva Palacios as the winner of the election, Valenzuela refused and resigned his post. See Gonzalo N. Santos, *Memorias* (México, DF: Editorial Grijalbo, 1986), 334–35.

54 Roberto Cruz, *Roberto Cruz en la Revolución Mexicana* (México, DF: Editorial Diana, 1976), 106. Cruz recounted in his memoir that he was happy to perform this duty for Calles but that the moment Portes Gil was sworn in as provisional president, he immediately began to treat Cruz as part of the hired help. When Cruz spoke at a meeting of the CROM against the policies of the Portes Gil administration regarding the rights of organized labor, Portes Gil confronted him, demanding that he make a public apology for the speech he had made. Cruz refused and resigned his post in the military. Portes Gil then met with Calles, according to Cruz, to ruin his reputation with his old friend. The ultimate result of the conflict was a rupture between Calles and Cruz as well as the latter's complete separation from the army.

55 "Mexico Quiet Again as Sonora Demonstrates Strength of Men Backing Demand for Fair Deal," *Douglas Daily Dispatch*, 21 February 1929.

56 Ibid.

57 Ibid.

58 "Manzo Denies Any Intent of Inciting Revolt in Mexico," *San Antonio Express*, 20 February 1929.

59 "No hay rebellion en Sonora y Sinaloa," *La Prensa*, 20 February 1929. "Son enteramente inexactas las noticias que han circulado respecto a que haya estallado un movimiento revolucionario en el Estado de Sonora. Dicho Estado se halla en calma y mantiene buenas relaciones con el gobierno federal."

60 Buchenau, *Plutarco Elías Calles*, 152.

61 AGN, DGIPS, vol. 235, exp. 28, f. 124, "¡Alerta Corazón Católico!," anonymous Catholic circular. "Él [the military] te ha visto sufrir y ha sufrido también en lo recóndito del corazón, la privación amarga de sus más nobles y justificados derechos, y te ha compadecido. . . . Ayúdale en el terreno en que te lo pida. . . . Tu cooperación será lícita, porque tendrá un triple motivo: el amor a la Patria que se hunde; el amor a las libertades, a los derechos y al honor de un pueblo; y el amor a tu Dios ta ultrajado por espíritus ateos."

62 "Bombing of Torreon Assailed by Montero," *New York Times*, 19 March 1929.

63 SRE, LE 817, f. 312. "El gobierno emanado del Movimiento Renovador defenderá las dotaciones y restituciones de ejidos concedidas anteriormente; fomentara la colonización en las regiones en que la colonia agricola sea preferible al ejido por las circunstancias del lugar o por voluntad libremente expresada por los propios campesinos, y fomentara igualmente la cooperación y el crédito agricola."

64 Ibid., f. 314. "Por eso la Revolución en su programa de renovación, en sus propósitos de hacer gobierno nacional en vez de gobierno sectarista, gobierno liberal en vez de gobierno intolerante, proclama la urgencia de terminar la guerra fratricida provocada por la cuestión religiosa."

65 Ibid., LE 815 100-R-27, f. 15.
66 Ibid., f. 21.
67 Ibid., f. 28, José M. Tapía to Enrique Liekens, 18 March 1929. "Para formular un convenio a fin de que cece el derrammamiento de sangre en la republica." "Que el Gobierno de la Republica nada tiene que tratar con los infidentes que desconociendo sus deberes y pasando por todo principio de lealtad han provocado un movimiento armado que los pone no solamente fuera del decoro que alegan, sino tambien fuera de toda ley."
68 Cruz, *Roberto Cruz,* 118. Cruz claims to have moved north with a small group of loyal soldiers to eventually join Caraveo in Chihuahua, but upon his arrival, he received news that Caraveo had retreated across the border to El Paso.
69 "Manzo Quits Rebels; New Clash at Naco. Deposed Western Commander and Staff Seek Safety across Frontier in Nogales," *New York Times,* 13 April 1929; "Francisco Manzo, Once Mexican Rebel General, a Leader in Uprising against Portes Gil, Dies," *New York Times,* 3 February 1940.

## CONCLUSION

1 David C. Bailey, *¡Viva Cristo Rey! The Cristero Rebellion and the Church State Conflict in Mexico* (Austin: University of Texas Press, 1974), 278–79.
2 Much less widespread and less violent than its predecessor, the second Cristiada was a reaction the radical cardenista state education program if the mid-1930s. See Marjorie Becker, *Setting the Virgin on Fire: Lázaro Cárdenas, Michoacán Peasants, and the Redemption of the Mexican Revolution* (Berkeley: University of California Press, 1995).
3 Bailey, *¡Viva Cristo Rey!,* 282.
4 Jürgen Buchenau, *Plutarco Elías Calles and the Mexican Revolution* (Lanham, MD: Rowman & Littlefield, 2007), 179–83.
5 Ibid., 183.
6 Archivo General de la Nación, Dirección General de Investigaciones Políticas y Sociales (hereafter AGN, DGIPS), vol. 232, exp. 30, ff. 4–5.
7 Ibid., f. 27, Gobernación to the Confidential Department, 3 November 1930.
8 Ibid., vol. 228, exp. 21, f. 7, Lic. J. García Villarreal to Lic. Emilio Portes Gil (Gobernación), 28 September 1928.
9 Ibid., f. 17, Gobernación to Lic. J. García Villarreal, 10 October 1928.
10 Ibid., vol. 241, exp. 31 (no f.), Manuel Padilla to Gobernación, 16 August 1929.
11 Ibid. (no f.), Francisco Delgado to Manuel Padilla, 12 September 1929.
12 Ibid., vol. 252, exp. 9, f. 157, letter from Rene Capistran Garza to Consul Gen. of Mexico Eduardo Hernández Cházaro, 3 September 1931. "Sin atender a otra razón que a su nacionalidad y a sus necesidades."
13 Ibid. "Sí siento, y con gran calor y vehemencia, el deseo muy grande de, aún viviendo en el extranjero, no ser un proscrito de mi país, ni ser considerado como un enemigo u ultranza del gobierno del señor ingeniero Ortiz Rubio."
14 Ibid., f. 153, J. M. Puig Casauranc to the Secretaría de Gobernación, 17 July 1933. "Entrar en actividades política [*sic*] en nuestro país."

15 Pedro Castro Martínez, *Adolfo de la Huerta y la Revolución Mexicana* (México, DF: Instituto Nacional de Estudios Históricos de la Revolución Mexicana, 1992), 130.

16 Ibid., 132.

17 *Excélsior*, 29 November 1935, quoted in Castro Martínez, *Adolfo de la Huerta*, 132. "Como sobre el paréntesis sombrío de mi destierro, lleno de amarguras y de angustias suficientes para saldar cualquier error que involuntariamente haya cometido, he podido echar un velo de olvido y serenidad, sirviéndome, en cambio, para templar mis energías y luchar, aquí o en cualquier parte del mundo, por . . . la causa del proletariado."

18 Aaron W. Navarro, *Political Intelligence and the Creation of Modern Mexico, 1938–1954* (University Park: Pennsylvania State University Press, 2010), 175.

19 Ibid., 159.

20 Ibid.

21 Navarro adeptly argues that for the post-WWII period, the security services were a fundamental tool in ensuring that the PRI had the information it needed to crush opposition candidates and secure electoral victories.

22 Estimates of the revolution's death toll vary widely. See Robert McCaa, "The Missing Millions: The Demographic Costs of the Mexican Revolution," *Mexican Studies / Estudios Mexicanos* 19:2 (Summer 2003): 367–400.

23 In fact, Fast and Furious was not the first operation of its kind. Special Agent in Charge William Newell was involved in an earlier failed attempt to pass weapons that the ATF could trace across the border into Mexico in the fall of 2007 called Operation Wide Receiver. See House Committee on Oversight and Government Reform and Senate Committee on the Judiciary, Joint Staff Report, *Fast and Furious: The Anatomy of a Failed Operation*, pt. 1/3, 112th Cong., 2012, 139, http://oversight.house.gov, accessed 7 August 2014, http://oversight.house.gov/wp-content/uploads/2012/07/7-31-12-FF-Part-I-FINAL-REPORT.pdf.

24 Ibid., 127.

25 "Dodson Transcript" (exhibit 93), quoted in ibid., 98.

26 Ibid., 141–42.

27 Ibid., 139. The new administration mentioned was that of Pres. Barack Obama, and the new attorney general for the district of Arizona was Dennis Burke.

# BIBLIOGRAPHY

## ARCHIVAL SOURCES

Archivo General de la Nación, Mexico City.
Dirección General de Investigaciones Políticas y Sociales.
Archivo Histórico Genaro Estrada, Acervo Histórico Diplomático, Secretaría de Relaciones Exteriores, Mexico City.
Biblioteca Nacional de Antropología e Historia, Mexico City.
Programa de Historia Oral.
Centro de Estudios de História de México, Grupo CARSO, Mexico City.
Fideicomiso Archivos Plutarco Elías Calles y Fernando Torreblanca, Mexico City.
Instituto Libre de Filosofía y Ciencias, Guadalajara, Jalisco.
Fondo Cristero.
Instituto Nacional de Antropología e Historia, Guadalajara, Jalisco.
Programa de Historia Oral.
United States Department of Justice, headquarters file 64-306.

## PUBLISHED PRIMARY SOURCES

De la Huerta, Adolfo. *Memorias de Don Adolfo de la Huerta, según su propio dictado*. Edited by Roberto Guzmán Esparza. México, DF: Ediciones Guzmán, 1957.
Elías Calles, Plutarco. *Correspondencia personal 1919–1945*. Edited by Carlos Macías. México, DF: Fondo de Cultura Económica, 1991.
García Naranjo, Nemesio. *Memorias de Nemesio García Naranjo*. Vol. 9. Monterrey, Nuevo León: Talleres de "El Porvenir," n.d.
Murray, Robert Hammond. *Mexico before the World: Public Documents and Addresses of Plutarco Elías Calles*. Translated by Murray Robert Hammond. New York: Academy Press, 1927.
Santos, Gonzálo N. *Memorias*. México, DF: Grijalbo, 1986.

Secretaría de Hacienda y Crédito Público. *La Controversia Pani-de la Huerta: documentos para la historia de la última Asonada Militar*. México, DF: Publicaciones de la Secretaría de Hacienda y Crédito Público, 1924.
United States Department of Labor. *Annual Report of the Commissioner General of Immigration to the Secretary of Labor*. Washington, DC: Government Printing Office, 1923.
United States Department of State. *Records of the Department of State Relating to Internal Affairs of Mexico, 1930–39*. Washington, DC: National Archives, 1985.

## NEWSPAPERS

*Christian Science Monitor*
*Douglas Daily Dispatch*
*Excélsior*
*El Informador*
*New York Times*
*La Opinión*
*La Prensa*
*San Antonio Light*
*El Universal*

## SECONDARY SOURCES

Agamben, Goirgio. *Homo Sacer: Sovereign Power and Bare Life*. Stanford: Stanford University Press, 1998.
Agnew, John. "Sovereignty Regimes: Territoriality and State Authority in Contemporary World Politics." *Annals of the Association of American Geographers* 95:2 (June 2005): 437–61.
Aguayo, Sergio Quezada. *La Charola: una historia de los servicios de inteligencia en México*. México, DF: Editorial Grijalbo, 2001.
Alarcón Menchaca, Laura. *José María Maytorena: una biografía política*. México, DF: El Colegio de Jalisco, El Colegio de Sonora, and Universidad Iberoamericana, 2008.
Alessio Robles, Miguel. *Historia política de la revolución*. México, DF: Ediciones Botas, 1946.
Alessio Robles, Vito. *Desfile sangriento*. México, DF: Del Bosque, 1936.
Almada, Francisco R. *Gobernadores del estado de Chihuahua*. Chihuahua: Centro Librero la Prensa, 1980.
Anderson, Benedict. *Imagined Communities: Reflections on the Origin and Spread of Nationalism*. London: Verso, 1991.
Andreas, Peter. *Border Games: Policing the US-Mexico Divide*. Ithaca: Cornell University Press, 2000.
———. *Smuggler Nation: How Illicit Trade Made America*. New York: Oxford University Press, 2013.

Badillo, David A. "Between Alienation and Ethnicity: The Evolution of Mexican-American Catholicism in San Antonio, 1910–1940." *Journal of American Ethnic History* 16:4 (Summer 1997): 62–83.

Bailey, David C. *¡Viva Cristo Rey! The Cristero Rebellion and the Church State Conflict in Mexico*. Austin: University of Texas Press, 1974.

Bantjes, Adrian A. "Saints, Sinners, and State Formation: Local Religion and Cultural Revolution in Mexico." In *The Eagle and the Virgin: Nation and Cultural Revolution in Mexico 1920–1940*, edited by Mary Kay Vaughan and Stephen E. Lewis, 137–56. Durham: Duke University Press, 2006.

Barbosa Guzmán, Francisco. *Jalisco desde la revolución*. Vol. 6, *La iglesia y el gobierno civil*. Guadalajara: Universidad de Guadalajara, 1988.

Barkan, Elazar, and Marie-Denise Shelton, eds. *Borders, Exiles, Diasporas*. Stanford: Stanford University Press, 1998.

Baud, Michiel, and Willem Van Schendel. "Toward a Comparative History of Borderlands." *Journal of World History* 8:2 (1997): 211–42.

Becker, Marjorie. *Setting the Virgin on Fire: Lázaro Cárdenas, Michoacán Peasants, and the Redemption of the Mexican Revolution*. Berkeley: University of California Press, 1995.

Benjamin, Thomas. *La Revolución: Mexico's Great Revolution as Memory, Myth, and History*. Austin: University of Texas Press, 2000.

Berbusse, Edward J. "The Unofficial Intervention of the United States in Mexico's Religious Crisis, 1926–1930." *The Americas* 23:1 (July 1966): 28–62.

Bliss, Katherine Elaine. *Compromised Positions: Prostitution, Public Health, and Gender Politics in Revolutionary Mexico City*. University Park: Pennsylvania State University Press, 2001.

Boylan, Kristina A. "Gendering the Faith and Altering the Nation: Mexican Catholic Women's Activism, 1917–1940." In *Sex and Revolution: Gender Politics, and Power in Modern Mexico*, edited by Jocelyn Olcott, Mary Kay Vaughan, and Gabriela Cano, 199–222. Durham: Duke University Press, 2006.

Brading, David A., ed. *Caudillo and Peasant in the Mexican Revolution*. New York: Cambridge University Press, 1980.

Brown, Jonathan C. *Oil and Revolution in Mexico*. Berkeley: University of California Press, 1993.

Brunk, Samuel. *Emiliano Zapata: Revolution and Betrayal in Mexico*. Albuquerque: University of New Mexico Press, 1995.

Brush, David Allen. "The De la Huerta Rebellion in Mexico, 1923–1924." PhD diss., Syracuse University, 1975.

Buchenau, Jürgen. *The Last Caudillo: Alvaro Obregón and the Mexican Revolution*. Malden, MA: Wiley-Blackwell, 2011.

———. *Plutarco Elías Calles and the Mexican Revolution*. Lanham, MD: Rowman & Littlefield, 2007.

———. *Tools of Progress: A German Merchant Family in Mexico City, 1865–Present*. Albuquerque: University of New Mexico Press, 2004.

Buchenau, Jürgen, and William H. Beezley, eds. *State Governors in the Mexican Revolution, 1910–1952: Portraits in Conflict, Courage, and Corruption*. Lanham, MD: Rowman & Littlefield, 2009.

Butler, Matthew. "The 'Liberal' Cristero: Ladislao Molina and the Cristero Rebellion in Michoacán, 1927–9." *Journal of Latin American Studies* 31 (October 1999): 645–71.

———. *Popular Piety and Political Identity in Mexico's Cristero Rebellion: Michoacán, 1927–29.* New York: Oxford University Press, 2004.

Carriedo, Robert. "The Man Who Tamed Mexico's Tiger: General Joaquin Amaro and the Professionalization of Mexico's Revolutionary Army." PhD diss., University of New Mexico, 2005.

Castillo, Pedro G. "The Making of a Mexican Barrio: Los Angeles, 1890–1920." PhD diss., University of California, Santa Barbara, 1979.

Castro Martínez, Pedro. *Adolfo de la Huerta y la Revolución Mexicana.* México, DF: Instituto Nacional de Estudios Históricos de la Revolución Mexicana, 1992.

Cockcroft, James D. *Intellectual Precursors of the Mexican Revolution, 1900–1913.* Austin: University of Texas Press, 1976.

Cortés, Carlos E., ed. *Cuban Exiles in the United States.* New York: Arno Press, 1980.

Cox, Patrick L. "'An Enemy Closer to Us Than Any European Power': The Impact of Mexico on Texan Public Opinion before World War I." *Southwestern Historical Quarterly* 105:1 (July 2001): 40–80.

Craib, Raymond B. *Cartographic Mexico: A History of State Fixations and Fugitive Landscapes.* Durham: Duke University Press, 2004.

Cruz, Roberto. *Roberto Cruz en la Revolución Mexicana.* México, DF: Editorial Diana, 1976.

Cumberland, Charles C. *Mexican Revolution: Genesis under Madero.* Austin: University of Texas Press, 1952.

———. *Mexican Revolution: The Constitutionalist Years.* Austin: University of Texas Press, 1974.

Curly, Robert. "Anticlericalism and Public Space in Revolutionary Jalisco." *The Americas* 65:4 (April 2009): 511–33.

DeLay, Brian. "How Not to Arm a State: American Guns and the Crisis of Governance in Mexico, Nineteenth and Twenty-First Centuries." *Southern California Quarterly* 95:1 (Spring 2013): 5–23.

Díaz, George T. *Border Contraband: A History of Smuggling across the Rio Grande.* Austin: University of Texas Press, 2015.

Dolan, Jay P., and Gilberto Hinojosa, eds. *Mexican Americans and the Catholic Church, 1900–1965.* Notre Dame: University of Notre Dame Press, 1994.

Dulles, John W. F. *Yesterday in Mexico: A Chronicle of the Revolution, 1919–1936.* Austin: University of Texas Press, 1961.

Dulles, Allen. *The Craft of Intelligence.* New York: Harper & Row, 1963.

Espinosa, David. "'Restoring Christian Social Order': The Mexican Catholic Youth Association, 1913–1932." *The Americas* 59:4 (April 2003): 451–74.

———. "Student Politics, National Politics: Mexico's National Student Union, 1926–1943." *The Americas* 62:4 (April 2006): 533–62.

Ettinger, Patrick. "'We Sometimes Wonder What They Will Spring on Us Next': Immigrants and Border Enforcement in the American West, 1882–1930." *Western Historical Quarterly* 37:2 (Summer 2006): 159–81.

Evans, Peter S., Dietrich Rueshemeyer, and Theda Skocpol. *Bringing the State Back In.* Cambridge: Cambridge University Press, 1985.

Fallow, Ben. *Cárdenas Compromised: The Failure of Reform in Postrevolutionary Yucatán*. Durham: Duke University Press, 2001.

———. "Varieties of Mexican Revolutionary Anticlericalism: Radicalism, Iconoclasm, and Otherwise, 1914–1935." *The Americas* 65:4 (April 2009): 481–509.

Fallaw, Ben, and Terry Rugeley, eds. *Forced Marches: Soldiers and Military Caciques in Modern Mexico*. Tucson: University of Arizona Press, 2012.

Fernández-Aceves, María Teresa. "Guadalajaran Women and the Construction of National Identity." In *The Eagle and the Virgin: Nation and Cultural Revolution in Mexico 1920–1940*, edited by Mary Kay Vaughan and Stephen E. Lewis, 297–313. Durham: Duke University Press, 2006.

———. "José Guadalupe Zuno Hernández and the Revolutionary Process in Jalisco." In *State Governors in the Mexican Revolution, 1910–1952: Portraits in Conflict, Courage, and Corruption*, edited by Jürgen Buchenau and William H. Beezley, 95–108. Lanham, MD: Rowman & Littlefield, 2009.

———. "The Political Mobilization of Women in Revolutionary Guadalajara, 1910–1940." PhD diss., University of Illinois at Chicago, 2000.

Foucault, Michel. *"Society Must Be Defended": Lectures at the Collège de France, 1975–76*. Edited by Mauro Bertani and Alessandro Fontana. Translated by David Macey. New York: Picador, 2003.

Gilly, Adolfo. *The Mexican Revolution*. Foreword by Friedrich Katz. Translated by Patrick Camiller. New York: New Press, 2005.

González, Fernando M. *Matar y morir por Cristo Rey: aspectos de la Cristiada*. México, DF: Instituto de Investigaciones Sociales, Universidad Nacional Autónoma de México, 2001.

González Ruiz, Édgar. *Los otros Cristeros y su presencia en Puebla*. Puebla: Gobierno del Estado de Puebla, 2004.

Gould, Lewis L. "Progressives and Prohibitionists: Texas Democratic Politics, 1911–1921." *Southwestern Historical Quarterly* 75:1 (July 1971): 5–18.

Gruening, Ernest. *Mexico and Its Heritage*. New York: Century, 1928.

Hall, Linda B. *Álvaro Obregón: Power and Revolution in Mexico, 1911–1920*. College Station: Texas A&M University Press, 1981.

———. "Creating a Schizophrenic Border: Migration and Perception, 1920–1925." In *The Mexican Revolution: Conflict and Consolidation, 1910–1940*, edited by Douglas W. Richmond and Sam W. Haynes, 89–116. College Station: Texas A&M University Press, 2013.

———. *Oil, Banks, and Politics: The United States and Postrevolutionary Mexico, 1917–1924*. Austin: University of Texas Press, 1995.

Hall, Linda B., and Don M. Coerver. *Revolution on the Border: The United States and Mexico, 1910–1920*. Albuquerque: University of New Mexico Press, 1988.

Harris, Charles H., III, and Louis R. Sadler. *The Border and the Revolution*. Introduction by Michael C. Meyer. Las Cruces: Center for Latin American Studies / Joint Border Research Institute, New Mexico State University, 1988.

———. *The Secret War in El Paso: Mexican Revolutionary Intrigue, 1906–1920*. Albuquerque: University of New Mexico Press, 2009.

———. *The Texas Rangers and the Mexican Revolution: The Bloodiest Decade, 1910–1920*. Albuquerque: University of New Mexico Press, 2004.

Hart, John Mason. *Revolutionary Mexico: The Coming and Process of the Mexican Revolution.* Berkeley: University of California Press, 1987.

Hatfield, Shelly Bowen. *Chasing Shadows: Indians along the United States-Mexico Border, 1876–1911.* Albuquerque: University of New Mexico Press, 1997.

Hechter, Michael. *Containing Nationalism.* New York: Oxford University Press, 2001.

Henderson, Peter V. N. *Félix Díaz, the Porfirians, and the Mexican Revolution.* Lincoln: University of Nebraska Press, 1981.

Hu-DeHart, Evelyn. *Yaqui Resistance and Survival: The Struggle for Land and Autonomy, 1821–1910.* Madison: University of Wisconsin Press, 1984.

Hudson, James J. "California National Guard and the Mexican Border." *California Historical Society Quarterly* 34:2 (June 1955): 157–71.

Hutchinson, John, and Anthony D. Smith, eds. *Nationalism.* New York: Oxford University Press, 1994.

Joseph, Gilbert M., ed. *Reclaiming the Political in Latin American History: Essays from the North.* Durham: Duke University Press, 2001.

Joseph, Gilbert M., and Daniel Nugent, eds. *Everyday Forms of State Formation: Revolution and the Negotiation of Rule in Modern Mexico.* Durham: Duke University Press, 1994.

Kenny, Michael S. J. *No God Next Door: Red Rule in Mexico and Our Responsibility.* New York: William J. Hirten, 1935.

Knight, Alan. *The Mexican Revolution.* Vol. 1, *Porfirians, Liberals and Peasants.* Cambridge: Cambridge University Press, 1986.

———. *The Mexican Revolution.* Vol. 2, *Counter-revolution and Reconstruction.* Cambridge: Cambridge University Press, 1986.

———. "Popular Culture and the Revolutionary State in Mexico." *Hispanic American Historical Review* 74 (August 1994): 393–444.

Knightly, Phillip. *The Second Oldest Profession: Spies and Spying in the Twentieth Century.* New York: Norton, 1986.

Kunz, Egon F. "Exile and Resettlement: Refugee Theory." *International Migration Review* 15:1/2 (Spring–Summer 1981): 42–51.

Lazo, Rodrigo. *Writing to Cuba: Filibustering and Cuban Exiles in the United States.* Chapel Hill: University of North Carolina Press, 2005.

León, Luis D. *La Llorona's Children: Religion, Life, and Death in the U.S.-Mexican Borderlands.* Berkeley: University of California Press, 2004.

León de Palacios, Ana María. *Plutarco Elías Calles: creador de instituciones.* México, DF: Instituto Nacional de Administración Pública, 1975.

Lerner Sigal, Victoria. "Espionaje y Revolución Mexicana." *Historia Mexicana* 44:4 (April–June 1995): 617–43.

———. "Los exiliados de la Revolución Mexicana en Estados Unidos, 1910–1940." In *La comunidad Mexicana en Estados Unidos: aspectos de su historia,* edited by Fernando Saúl Alanis Enciso, 71–126. San Luis Potosí: Colegio de San Luis, 2004.

Lewis, Stephen E. *The Ambivalent Revolution: Forging State and Nation in Chiapas, 1910–1945.* Albuquerque: University of New Mexico Press, 2005.

Lieuwen, Edwin. *Mexican Militarism: The Political Rise and Fall of the Revolutionary Army, 1910–1940.* Albuquerque: University of New Mexico Press, 1968.

Llerenas, Fidelina G., and Jaime Tamayo. *El levantamiento delahuertista: cuatro rebeliones y cuatro jefes militares*. Guadalajara: Universidad de Guadalajara, Centro de Investigaciones Sobre los Movimientos Sociales, 1995.

Lomnitz, Claudio. *Deep Mexico, Silent Mexico: An Anthropology of Nationalism*. Minneapolis: University of Minnesota Press, 2001.

Loveman, Brian. *The Constitution of Tyranny: Regimes of Exception in Spanish America*. Pittsburgh: University of Pittsburgh Press, 1993.

Lytle Hernández, Kelly. *Migra! A History of the U.S. Border Patrol*. Berkeley: University of California Press, 2010.

Manjarrez, Froylán C. *La jornada institucional*. Vol. 1, *La crisis de la política*. México, DF: Talleres Gráficos Editorial y Diario Oficial, 1930.

Marak, Andrae M. *From Many, One: Indians, Peasant, Borders, and Education in Callista Mexico, 1924–1935*. Calgary: University of Calgary Press, 2009.

Maytorena, José María. *Algunas verdades sobre el General Álvaro Obregón*. Los Angeles: Impr. del Heraldo de México, 1919.

McCaa, Robert. "The Missing Millions: The Demographic Costs of the Mexican Revolution." *Mexican Studies / Estudios Mexicanos* 19:2 (Summer 2003): 367–400.

Meyer, Jean A. *The Cristero Rebellion: The Mexican People between Church and State 1926–1929*. Cambridge: Cambridge University Press, 1976.

———. "An Idea of Mexico: Catholics in the Revolution." In *The Eagle and the Virgin: Nation and Cultural Revolution in Mexico 1920–1940*, edited by Mary Kay Vaughan and Stephen E. Lewis, 281–96. Durham: Duke University Press, 2006.

Migdal, Joel S. *Strong Societies and Weak States: State-Society Relations and State Capabilities in the Third World*. Princeton: Princeton University Press, 1988.

Minna Stern, Alexandra. *Eugenic Nation: Faults and Frontiers of Better Breeding in Modern America*. Berkeley: University of California Press, 2005.

Monroy Durán, Luis. *El ultimo caudillo: apuntes para la historia de México, acerca del movimiento armado de 1923, en contra del gobierno constitutido*. Edited by Jose S. Rodríguez. México, DF: J.S. Rodríguez, 1924.

Navarro, Aaron W. *Political Intelligence and the Creation of Modern Mexico, 1938–1954*. University Park: Pennsylvania State University Press, 2010.

Ngai, Mae. *Impossible Subjects: Illegal Aliens and the Making of Modern America*. Princeton: Princeton University Press, 2004.

———. "The Strange Career of the Illegal Alien: Immigration Restriction and Deportation Policy in the United States, 1921–1965." *Law and History Review* 21:1 (Spring 2003): 69–107.

Olivera Sedano, Alicia. *Aspectos del conflicto religioso de 1926 a 1929: sus antecedentes y consecuencias*. México, DF: Instituto Nacional de Antropología e Historia, 1966.

Pani, Alberto J. *Las conferencias de Bucareli*. México, DF: Editorial Jus, 1953.

Patterson, Thomas G. "California Progressives and Foreign Policy." *California Historical Society Quarterly* 47:4 (December 1968): 329–42.

Plasencia de la Parra, Enrique. *Historia y organización de la fuerzas armadas en México, 1917–1937*. México, DF: Universidad Autónoma de México, 2010.

———. *Personajes y escenarios de la Rebelión Delahuertista, 1923–1924*. México, DF: Instituto de Investigaciones Históricas, 1998.

Proctor, Tammy M. *Female Intelligence: Women and Espionage in the First World War*. New York: New York University Press, 2003.

Purnell, Jennie. *Popular Movements and State Formation in Revolutionary Mexico: The Agraristas and Cristeros of Michoacán*. Durham: Duke University Press, 1999.

Quirk, Robert E. *The Mexican Revolution and the Catholic Church 1910–1929*. Bloomington: Indiana University Press, 1973.

———. *The Mexican Revolution, 1914–1915: The Convention of Aguascalientes*. New York: W. W. Norton, 1960.

Raat, Dirk W. *Revoltosos: Mexico's Rebels in the United States, 1903–1923*. College Station: Texas A&M University Press, 1981.

Rath, Thomas. *Myths of Demilitarization in Postrevolutionary Mexico, 1920–1960*. Chapel Hill: University of North Carolina Press, 2013.

Redinger, Matthew A. *American Catholics and the Mexican Revolution, 1924–1936*. Notre Dame: University of Notre Dame Press, 2005.

Reguer, Consuelo. *Dios y mi derecho*. Vol. 1, *Los inicios 1923–1926*. México, DF: Editorial Jus, 1997.

Richmond, Douglas. "Intentos externos para derocar al régimen de Carranza (1915–1920)." *Historia Mexicana* 32:1 (July–September 1982): 106–32.

Romo, Ricardo. *East Los Angeles: History of a Barrio*. Austin: University of Texas Press, 1983.

Roniger, Luis, James N. Green, and Pablo Yankelevich, eds. *Exile and the Politics of Exclusion in the Americas*. Portland: Sussex Academic Press, 2012.

Rubenstein, Anne. *Bad Language, Naked Ladies, and Other Threats to the Nation: A Political History of Comic Books in Mexico*. Durham: Duke University Press, 1998.

Sack, Robert D. "Human Territoriality: A Theory." *Annals of the Association of American Geographers* 73:1 (March 1983): 55–74.

Sahlins, Peter. *Boundaries: The Making of France and Spain in the Pyrenees*. Berkeley: University of California Press, 1989.

Salibury, Richard V. "Mexico, the United States, and the 1926–1927 Nicaraguan Crisis." *Hispanic American Historical Review* 66:2 (May 1986): 319–39.

Santos, Gonzalo N. *Memorias*. México, DF: Editorial Grijalbo, 1986.

Schell, Patience A. "Nationalizing Children through Schools and Hygiene: Porfirian and Revolutionary Mexico City." *The Americas* 60:4 (April 2004): 559–87.

———. "Of the Sublime Mission of Mothers of Families: The Union of Mexican Catholic Ladies in Revolutionary Mexico." In *The Women's Revolution in Mexico, 1910–1953*, edited by Stephanie Mitchell and Patience Schell, 99–123. Lanham, MD: Rowman & Littlefield, 2007.

Scott, James C. *Seeing like a State: How Certain Schemes to Improve the Human Condition Have Failed*. New Haven: Yale University Press, 1998.

Shain, Yossi. *The Frontier of Loyalty: Political Exiles in the Age of the Nation State*. Middletown, CT: Wesleyan University Press, 1989.

Sheridan, Thomas E. *Los Tucsonenses: The Mexican Community in Tucson, 1854–1941*. Tucson: University of Arizona Press, 1986.

Smith, Benjamin T. *The Roots of Conservatism in Mexico: Catholicism, Society, and Politics in the Mixteca Baja, 1750–1962*. Albuquerque: University of New Mexico Press, 2012.

Smith, Michael M. "Andrés G. García: Venustiano Carranza's Eyes, Ears and Voice on the Border." *Mexican Studies / Estudios Mexicanos* 23:2 (Summer 2007): 355–86.

———. "The Mexican Secret Service in the United States, 1910–1920." *The Americas* 59:1 (July 2002): 65–85.

St. John, Rachel. *Line in the Sand: A History of the Western U.S.-Mexico Border*. Princeton: Princeton University Press, 2011.

Stout, Joseph A., Jr. *Spies, Politics, and Power: El Departamento Confidencial en México, 1922–1946*. Fort Worth: Texas Christian University Press, 2012.

Sznajder, Mario, and Luis Roniger. "Political Exile in Latin America." In *Exile and the Politics of Exclusion in the Americas*, edited by Luis Roniger, James N. Green, and Pablo Yankelevich, 13–34. Portland: Sussex Academic Press, 2012.

———. *The Politics of Exile in Latin America*. Cambridge: Cambridge University Press, 2009.

Tamayo, Jaime. *La conformación del estado moderno y los conflictos políticos 1917–1929*. Guadalajara: Universidad de Guadalajara, 1988.

Tannenbaum, Frank. *Mexico: The Struggle for Peace and Bread*. New York: Knopf, 1950.

Taylor, Paul S. *A Spanish-Mexican Peasant Community*. Berkeley: University of California Press, 1933.

Truett, Samuel. *Fugitive Landscapes: The Forgotten History of the U.S.-Mexico Borderlands*. New Haven: Yale University Press, 2006.

Truett, Samuel, and Elliot Young, eds. *Continental Crossroads: Remapping U.S.-Mexico Borderlands History*. Durham: Duke University Press, 2004.

Tutino, John. *From Insurrection to Revolution in Mexico: Social Bases of Agrarian Violence, 1750–1940*. Princeton: Princeton University Press, 1986.

Unterman, Katherine. *Uncle Sam's Policemen: The Pursuit of Fugitives across Borders*. Cambridge: Harvard University Press, 2015.

Vaca, Agustín. *Los silencios de la historia: las Cristeras*. Zapopan: Colegio de Jalisco, 1998.

Vanderwood, Paul. *Disorder and Progress: Bandits, Police, and Mexican Development*. Lincoln: University of Nebraska Press, 1981.

———. *The Power of God against the Guns of Government: Religious Upheaval in Mexico at the Turn of the Nineteenth Century*. Stanford: Stanford University Press, 1998.

Vaughan, Mary Kay. *Cultural Politics in Revolution: Teachers, Peasants, and Schools in Mexico, 1930–1940*. Tucson: University of Arizona Press, 1997.

———. "Transnational Processes and the Rise and Fall of the Mexican Cultural State: Notes from the Past." In *Fragments of a Golden Age: The Politics of Culture in Mexico since 1940*, edited by Gilbert M. Joseph, Anne Rubenstein, and Eric Zolov, 471–87. Durham: Duke University Press, 2001.

Wasserman, Mark. "Strategies for Survival of the Porfirian Elite in Revolutionary Mexico: Chihuahua during the 1920s." *Hispanic American Historical Review* 67:1 (February 1987): 87–107.

Wilkie, James W., and Albert L. Michaels, eds. *Revolution in Mexico: Years of Upheaval, 1910–1940*. Tucson: University of Arizona Press, 1984.

Wright-Rios, Edward. *Revolutions in Mexican Catholicism: Reform and Revelation in Oaxaca, 1887–1934*. Durham: Duke University Press, 2009.

Young, Elliott. *Catarino Garza's Revolution on the Texas-Mexico Border*. Durham: Duke University Press, 2004.

Young, Julia Grace Darling. "The Calles Government and Catholic Dissidents: Mexico's Transnational Projects of Repression." *The Americas* 70:1 (July 2013): 63–91.

———. "Mexican Emigration during the Cristero War, 1926–1929." PhD diss., University of Chicago, 2009.

———. *Mexican Exodus: Emigrant, Exiles, and Refugees of the Cristero War*. Oxford: Oxford University Press, 2015.

# INDEX